# EFFECTIVE TEC TOOLS FOR SCHOOL LEADERSHIP

This book prepares educational leaders with the knowledge needed to critically evaluate, select, and use technological tools to be effective school leaders. Authors Jones and Kennedy explore the technology tools needed to support the full range of responsibilities of a school leader, including management and administration, personnel and evaluation, security and safety, instructional leadership, organizational culture and climate, external relationships, and action research. Each chapter unpacks advantages and pitfalls of various technological tools and includes case scenarios that contextualize these ideas for readers. Chapter content is also aligned with The Professional Standards for Educational Leaders (PSEL), the National Educational Leadership Preparation Standards (NELP), and the International Society of Technology Standard in Education (ISTE) standards. This timely and important book adds to the toolbox for educators preparing to become effective and cutting-edge school leaders.

**Leslie Jones** is Professor of Executive Leadership and Education at the University of Holy Cross, New Orleans, USA.

**Eugene Kennedy** is Professor of Education at Louisiana State University, Baton Rouge, USA.

# EFFECTIVE TECHNOLOGY TOOLS FOR SCHOOL LEADERSHIP

## Understanding Digital and Data-Driven Strategies

Leslie Jones and
Eugene Kennedy

Routledge
Taylor & Francis Group

NEW YORK AND LONDON

Cover image: © Getty Images

First published 2023
by Routledge
605 Third Avenue, New York, NY 10158

and by Routledge
4 Park Square, Milton Park, Abingdon, Oxon, OX14 4RN

*Routledge is an imprint of the Taylor & Francis Group, an informa business*

© 2023 Leslie Jones and Eugene Kennedy

*Library of Congress Cataloging-in-Publication Data*
Names: Jones, Leslie, 1970 October 5- author. | Kennedy, Eugene, 1955- author.
Title: Effective technology tools for school leadership: understanding
digital and data-driven strategies / Leslie Jones and Eugene Kennedy.
Description: New York, NY: Routledge, 2023. | Includes bibliographical
references and index.
Identifiers: LCCN 2022023068 (print) | LCCN 2022023069 (ebook) |
ISBN 9781032216706 (hardback) | ISBN 9781032216690 (paperback) |
ISBN 9781003269472 (ebook)
Subjects: LCSH: School management and organization–Technological
innovations. | Educational leadership–United States. | Educational
leadership–Standards–United States. | Education–Effect of
technological innovations on.
Classification: LCC LB2806.17 .J66 2023 (print) | LCC LB2806.17 (ebook) |
DDC 371.2–dc23/eng/20220707
LC record available at https://lccn.loc.gov/2022023068
LC ebook record available at https://lccn.loc.gov/2022023069

ISBN: 9781032216706 (hbk)
ISBN: 9781032216690 (pbk)
ISBN: 9781003269472 (ebk)

DOI: 10.4324/9781003269472

Typeset in Sabon
by Deanta Global Publishing Services, Chennai, India

# CONTENTS

# PREFACE

Media outlets are reporting the impact of COVID 19 on employers and the workforce. Early in the pandemic, entertainment entities, restaurants, and the in-person retail industry closed. Other businesses shifted employees to working remotely. Intuitions of higher learning and K-12 schools shifted to virtual learning. It is noteworthy that the medical profession and delivery workers do not have the option to work remotely. Many businesses have re-opened; some employers continue to have employees working remotely; and institutions of higher learning and K-12 schools alternate between in-person and remote working assignments. In many instances, school districts provide both options. The challenges for educators and specifically educational leaders provide the impetus for this publication as a resource to assist school leaders in their work.

The critical work for school leaders is documented in the literature; however, COVID 19, weather events, and other challenges including employee shortages have heightened the significance of the work of school leaders and educators. In this publication, we provide technology tools to assist school leaders in their work. Advances in technology have impacted every aspect of modern life, from the ways in which we communicate, socialize, and form relationships to the ways in which we conduct our work. This is certainly true in education as the technological tools available to students, teachers, and school leaders are greater than ever and continue to evolve. The use of technology tools does not replace the necessary skills, knowledge, and dispositions required of school leaders. Assistance and increased efficiency in the work of school leaders can be accomplished using technology tools.

The goal of the book is to provide K-12 school leaders with the knowledge needed to critically evaluate, select, and use technological advances in six areas of their work (1) management and administration, (2) personnel and evaluation, (3) security and safety, (4) teaching and learning, (5) organizational culture and climate, and (6) external relationships. The benefits of using specific tools are provided along with other pertinent information; many of the tools have multiple applications and are advantageous in several areas of work. This notion is noted throughout the publication. Case scenarios are also included in Chapters 2–7, and research examples are included in Chapter 8. The work of school leaders is also standards based. The Professional Standards for Educational Leaders (PSEL), the National Educational Leadership Preparation Standards (NELP), and the International Society of Technology Standard in Education (ISTE) are included in Chapter 1, and the most relevant standards are included in Chapters 2–7 as the specific roles of school leaders are addressed. A secondary goal of the book is to provide school leaders, aspiring school leaders, and other educators with resources.

# CHAPTER 1

## Introduction

**ABSTRACT**

In Chapter 1, an introduction to the book is presented. The importance of school leaders to the success of schools is discussed along with the various functions and roles of school leaders. The potential use of technology to accomplish these roles is described. The publication is not intended to minimize or replace the knowledge, skills, and dispositions needed for effective leadership; in fact, the leadership standards are included throughout the publication. The historical context of the leadership standards is also discussed, and the alignment of Professional Standards of Educational Leaders (PSEL), the National Educational Leadership Preparation Standards (NELP), and the International Society for Technology in Education (ISTE) standards related to leadership roles are included in each chapter. In addition to the Leadership Standards, the national goals are noted from the Office of Technology in the U.S. Department of Education in Chapter 1. We begin this chapter with a discussion on the *Critical Work of School Leaders* followed by the link of the work of school leaders to the standards. We then discuss *Technology and the Work of the School Principal*. Technological tools are discussed and their potential to increase and/or improve the efficiency of leaders is addressed. We note that there are many technology tools and Learning Management Platforms available to school leaders. Throughout this book we highlight selected technology tools and discuss how they can be used. The chapter ends with an overview of the publication.

## CRITICAL WORK OF SCHOOL LEADERS

With current demands for schools to be academically effective, the expectations of school principals have changed (Tan, 2018). In the past,

DOI: 10.4324/9781003269472-1

it was sufficient for principals to function mainly as managers, ensuring a functional, safe, and orderly environment. However, in the era of educational accountability, principals are increasingly held responsible for the teaching and learning that occurs in their schools (Mitani, 2018). In 1992, Murphy predicted that the roles of principals would be significantly different in this era. He noted that instructional and curricular leadership would be at the forefront, and school leaders would have to remain focused on teaching and learning. This shift is supported by research as there is significant evidence that effective schools require effective leaders (Leithwood et al., 2006; Leithwood et al., 2010). A large and growing body of literature has focused on factors that differentiate effective from ineffective principals (Branch et al., 2013). Frequently noted in this literature is the observation that effective principals are more likely to utilize data in their decision-making process (New Leaders, 2011). The importance of data-driven decision-making is reflected in national standards for the certification of school principals (Jones, 2017).

In *A Guide to Data-Driven Leadership in Modern Schools*, Jones and Kennedy (2015) included a comprehensive plan for data-driven leadership and decisions in schools. Data-driven decision-making requires that we have in place a process that recognizes the interconnected nature of educational processes; collects and analyzes relevant data; and presents it in such a way that it can inform decisions. A comprehensive plan requires the following:

1. Adopt a Systems View of Educational Data
   Distinguish between the different types of data and focus on their interrelationships. Researchers have divided data into a variety of types:
   (The following is one of the categorizations)
   - Assessment data includes: grades and GPA, state assessments.
   - Perceptive data includes: parent data, student data, teacher surveys, news articles, media coverage, school websites, and discipline incidents.
   - Demographic data includes: attendance, enrollment, ethnicity, gender, disability, economic status, grade level, and work habit, and program data – institution, culture placement.
2. Determination of the Current State of Affairs
   Understanding the types of data currently collected and how they are used is a key stage in the process of developing an effective data plan. We noted above that every school leader has a data plan, often a mixture of informal observations, counts, and the like. The same can be said of every teacher. What data are considered and how it is

used is a first step to being able to evaluate its adequacy. The failure of many "imported" data plans is that they are considered by the people who must use them to be inferior to the status quo.

3. Determine Areas of Need

   Identifying areas of need usually begins with a focus on outcomes, especially those that are not positive, and working back through a series of hypotheses as to why. This process will expose the "gaps" in available information (i.e., what is collected and when it is available) and help set priorities.

4. Develop a Data Plan

   Develop a plan to collect, process, and transform data into usable information. Some data will be useful for monitoring processes and others will have diagnostic utility. An important part of these analyses will involve understanding how different elements are related to one another.

5. Develop a Plan to Transform Data into Useable Knowledge

   This stage will involve developing the human resources necessary to interpret and make sense of available data.

Schools are complex organizations with, in some cases, thousands of children and adults interacting in a variety of contexts over seven- or eight-hour periods daily. It is not exaggerating to state that literally millions of pieces of data are generated in school settings daily. More so than in any previous period, technology has made it possible to capture much of this data in accessible and actionable formats. As pressures for educators to employ data-driven decision-making have increased, the amount of data available to educators has grown exponentially (Lachat et al., 2006).

One reason is that in the current era of educational accountability, national initiatives have led to an unprecedented expansion of standardized testing and its use for evaluating students, teachers, and school administrators (Faria et al., 2014). These testing programs can include end-of-year examinations as well as formative or benchmark examinations, the latter providing educators with data that can be used to inform educational decisions during an academic year. These developments have greatly expanded the data available to teachers and administrators as they make important instructional and administrative decisions. It is also the case that policy makers have promoted and even mandated that school principals utilize data to inform their administrative decisions (Marsh et al., 2017; Koyama, 2014). In a similar fashion, teachers are increasingly required to demonstrate that they are using data to inform their instructional decisions (Odom and Bell, 2017).

Technological developments have kept pace with the push toward data-driven decision-making in schools as tools have become available to school principals and teachers that allow them to collect more data than ever before and to do so in formats that permit analytics and visualizations that can guide decision-making (Wayman, 2005). As with many other areas of leadership, technology integration education relies heavily on the leadership of the school principal (Thannimalai and Raman, 2018). According to Davies (2010) the principal should model technology use in his/her work and support and facilitate teachers and even students doing the same.

Unlike the classroom teacher, the school principal will have access to data not for just one classroom, as is the case with a teacher, but for all classes in a school and from a myriad of other databases related to his/her other roles. Understanding the types of data available to school principals and how these data are used is essential for educational researchers, as administrative data can provide information on educational processes not accessible from other sources. The role of the school leader is therefore very critical.

## THE CRITICAL ROLE OF SCHOOL LEADERS WITH A STANDARDS-BASED APPROACH

For most of the 20th century, conventional wisdom was that education played a significant role in the social stratification of U.S. society (Greer, 1972). The congressionally funded Coleman report of the 1960s challenged this by demonstrating that schools accounted for little variation in student achievement once family background was controlled (Towers, 1992). While the report was largely ignored by policy makers, it did cast a shadow on the mythical narrative that education was the great equalizer in American society. This debate remained in force until the mid-1970s when researchers at Harvard University demonstrated that schools that served similar populations of low-income students experienced dramatically different achievement levels, largely, as a result of the policies and culture created by school administrators (Edmonds, 1979).

In *The Relevance of Instructional Leadership* (Cognella Academic Publishing, 2020), it is noted that Graham (1991) suggested that it was no longer acceptable for students to "slide" through weak curricula. It has been and is widely debatable in terms of where the responsibility for learning lies and/or who should be involved in the shared governance for educating students. However, there are heightening emphases on the roles of school leaders (principals) and teachers as linked to accountability. There are multiple studies that point to the significance of teachers and studies that point to the significance of leaders for impacting student learning. Schmoker (2011) and Siccone (2012) acknowledged that educators are aware of best practices for improving achievement. The challenge often lies with implementation. The implementation challenge for all professionals is also acknowledged in Pfeffer and Sutton's *The Knowing-Doing Gap: How Smart Companies Turn Knowledge into Action* (Harvard Business School Press, 2001). Pfeffer and Sutton (2000) noted across most professionals there are factors that impede the implementation of best practices. We can be very aware of best practices and not carry them through. There is evidence that the gap exists, and knowing what to do is not enough. Jones (2017) cited multiple sources that pinpoint the implementation challenges educators have.

The following are noted by Pfeffer and Sutton (2000) as reasons as to why individuals do not act:

- Talk substitutes for action.

  *Talk substitute for action when: No follow-up is done; people forget that making decisions does not change anything; planning, meeting, and report wiring is defined as "action is valuable in its own right; people believe that because they have said it and it is in the mission it is must be true; people are evaluated on how smart they sound rather than on what they do; talking a lot is mistaken for doing a lot; complex language, ideas, processes, and structures are thought to be better than simple ones; there is a belief that managers are people who talk and other do; internal status comes from talking a lot, interrupting, and being critical of others' ideas* making decisions as a substitute for action, making presentations as a substitute for action, using mission statement as a substitute for action;
- When memory is a substitute for thinking.
- Precedent in action.

  Role of precedent (trapped in their History)

  *The company has such a strong identity; there are pressures to be consistent with past decisions, to avoid admitting mistakes, and to show perseverance; people have strong needs for cognitive closure and avoiding ambiguity; decisions are made based on implicit, untested, and inaccurate models of behavior and performance; people carry expectations from the past about what is and isn't possible;*
- Fear prevents action.
- Measurement obstructs good judgment.

Effective schools have been described as those in which there is strong and active leadership from the school principal, high academic expectations for students, an orderly and safe environment, a focus on basic skills, and frequent monitoring of student progress (Teddlie and Stringfield, 1993). The effective schools movement, which started in the 1970s, has influenced school improvement efforts nationally and internationally for decades (Reynolds and Teddlie, 2000). This literature unambiguously pointed to the school principal as a key factor in creating an effective educational experience for students (Rai and Prakash, 2014).

A central question from this movement was the issue of how principals affect changes and improvement in schools (Dutta and Sahney, 2016). The basic model, supported by a large body of research, is that they do so with policies and practices that control who teaches at the school, provide teachers with the support and materials needed to be effective, monitor both teachers and students, ensure that progress is being made toward the school's mission, create a climate of collaboration, and establish an environment perceived to be safe and orderly (Liebowitz and Porter, 2019). Evidence in support of this characterization of effective principals is substantial and led to the development of the first national standards for principals, published in the 1990s (Dunlap et al., 2015).

The first set of leadership standards for educational leaders was published in 1996 by the Council of Chief State School Officers (Jones, 2017). Modest revisions were published in 2008 to the Interstate School Leaders Licensure Consortium (ISLLC) Standards based on pertinent research in 2008. The Educational Leadership Constituents Council (ELCC) Standards were an extension of the ISLLC Standards. The ELCC Standards transitioned to the National Educational Leadership Preparation (NELP) Standards (Jones, 2017).

ISLLC transitioned to the Professional Standards for Education Leaders (PSEL) in 2015 (Jones, 2017). These and similar standards have been embraced by most professional organizations of school administrators, including the American Association of Colleges of Teacher Education, American Association of School Administrators, Council for the Accreditation of Educator Preparation, Council of Chief State School Officers, National Association of Elementary School Principals, National Council of Professors of Educational Administration, National School Board Association, and the University Council for Educational Administration.

The PSEL standards are practitioner-based standards, and are used as a basis for certification and licensure examinations while the NELP standards are used to guide educational leadership preparation programs in the development of courses. NELP includes school-district level and school-building level standards. In the *Relevance of the Leadership Standards,* Jones (2017) presents a discussion of the commonalities and differences in ISLLC, PSEL, ELCC, and NELP standards. According to the National Policy Board for Educational Administration (https://www.npbea.org/nelp/), the NELP standards are aligned to PSEL. NELP is designed to identify performance expectations for school leaders, and PSEL provides a "broad" definition for educational leadership. The 10 PSEL standards are listed below (Jones, 2017):

- Standard 1: Mission, Vision, and Core Values
  Effective educational leaders develop, advocate, and enact a shared mission, vision, and core values of high-quality education and academic success and well-being of each student.
- Standard 2: Ethics and Professional Norms
  Effective educational leaders act ethically and according to professional norms to promote each student's academic success and well-being.
- Standard 3: Equity and Cultural Responsibility
  Effective educational leaders strive for equity of educational opportunity and culturally responsive practices to promote each student's academic success and well-being.
- Standard 4: Curriculum, Instruction, and Assessment
  Effective educational leaders develop and support intellectually rigorous and coherent systems of curriculum, instruction, and assessment to promote each student's academic success and well-being.
- Standard 5: Community of Care and Support for Students
  Effective educational leaders cultivate an inclusive, caring, and supportive school community that promotes the academic success and well-being of each student.
- Standard 6: Professional Capacity of School Personnel
  Effective educational leaders develop the professional capacity and practice of school personnel to promote each student's academic success and well-being.
- Standard 7: Professional Community for Teachers and Staff
  Effective educational leaders foster a professional community of teachers and other professional staff to promote each student's academic success and well-being.
- Standard 8: Meaningful Engagement of Families and Community
  Effective educational leaders engage families and the community in meaningful, reciprocal, and mutually beneficial ways to promote each student's academic success and well-being.
- Standard 9: Operations and Management
  Effective educational leaders manage school operations and resources to promote each student's academic success and well-being.
- Standard 10: School Improvement
  Effective educational leaders act as agents of continuous improvement to promote each student's academic success and well-being.
  **http://www.npbea.org/**

Jones (2017) noted in *The Relevance of the Leadership Standards* (Rowman and Littlefield Publishing) that PSEL 1, 2, 3, and 10 are referred to as the "drivers." The interrelationship and/or common elements of PSEL 1, 2, 3, and 10 are discussed. PSEL 4 and 5 are described as "the core." For example, it is important for school leaders and teachers to communicate and work with parents (PSEL 5) specifically in meeting learner needs linked to Curriculum, Instruction, and Assessments (PSEL 4). Competencies embedded in PSEL 6, 7, 8, and 9 are essential to support the roles of leaders and are referred to as "the supports."

As reflected in PSEL, the work of school principals can be classified into two broad categories, instructional leadership, and managerial leadership. A similar analogy can be made regarding the NELP Standards. Instructional leadership refers to the role of the principal in ensuring that the instruction provided to students is effective. A discussion of Instructional Leadership is noted in Chapter 5 of this book. Managerial leadership refers to leadership related to physical and material resources, personnel, and human resources. Additionally, the management role of the school principal encompasses managing internal and external relationships and school culture.

As mentioned above, the NELP Standards replaced ISLLC Standards and are used to guide preparation programs for educational administrators. Below are the NELP Standards:

NELP Standard 1: Mission, Vision, and Improvement
Component 1.1 Program completers understand and demonstrate the capacity to collaboratively evaluate, develop, and communicate a school mission and vision designed to reflect a core set of values and priorities that include data use, technology, equity, diversity, digital citizenship, and community.
Component 1.2 Program completers understand and demonstrate the capacity to lead improvement processes that include data use, design, implementation, and evaluation.
NELP Standard 2: Ethics and Professional Norms
Component 2.1 Program completers understand and demonstrate the capacity to reflect on, communicate about, cultivate, and model professional dispositions and norms (i.e., fairness, integrity, transparency, trust, digital citizenship, collaboration, perseverance, reflection, lifelong learning) that support the educational success and well-being of each student and adult.
Component 2.2 Program completers understand and demonstrate the capacity to evaluate, communicate about, and advocate for ethical and legal decisions.
Component 2.3 Program completers understand and demonstrate the capacity to model ethical behavior in their personal conduct and relationships and to cultivate ethical behavior in others.

NELP Standard 3: Equity, Inclusiveness, and Cultural Responsiveness

Component 3.1 Program completers understand and demonstrate the capacity to use data to evaluate, design, cultivate, and advocate for a supportive and inclusive school culture.

Component 3.2 Program completers understand and demonstrate the capacity to evaluate, cultivate, and advocate for equitable access to educational resources, technologies, and opportunities that support the educational success and well-being of each student.

Component 3.3 Program completers understand and demonstrate the capacity to evaluate, cultivate, and advocate for equitable, inclusive, and culturally responsive instruction and behavior support practices among teachers and staff.

NELP Standard 4: Learning and Instruction

Component 4.1 Program completers understand and can demonstrate the capacity to evaluate, develop, and implement high-quality technology-rich curricula programs and other supports for academic and non-academic student programs.

Component 4.2 Program completers understand and can demonstrate the capacity to evaluate, develop, and implement high-quality and equitable academic and non-academic instructional practices, resources, technologies, and services that support equity, digital literacy, and the academic and non-academic systems of the school.

Component 4.3 Program completers understand and can demonstrate the capacity to evaluate, develop, and implement formal and informal culturally responsive and accessible assessments that support data-informed instructional improvement and student learning and well-being.

Component 4.4 Program completers understand and demonstrate the capacity to collaboratively evaluate, develop, and implement the curriculum of the school, instruction, technology, data systems, and assessment practices in a coherent, equitable, and systematic manner.

NELP Standard 5: Community and External Leadership

Component 5.1 Program completers understand and demonstrate the capacity to collaboratively engage diverse families in strengthening student learning in and out of school.

Component 5.2 Program completers understand and demonstrate the capacity to collaboratively engage and cultivate relationships with diverse community members, partners, and other constituencies for the benefit of school improvement and student development.

Component 5.3 Program completers understand and demonstrate the capacity to communicate through oral, written, and digital means within the larger organizational, community, and political contexts when advocating for the needs of their school and community.

NELP Standard 6: Operations and Management

Component 6.1 Program completers understand and demonstrate the capacity to evaluate, develop, and implement management, communication, technology, school-level governance, and operating systems that support each student's learning needs and promote the mission and vision of the school.

Component 6.2 Program completers understand and demonstrate the capacity to evaluate, develop, and advocate for a data-informed and equitable resourcing plan that supports school improvement and student development.

Component 6.3 Program completers understand and demonstrate the capacity to reflectively evaluate, communicate about, and implement laws, rights, policies, and regulations to promote student and adult success and well-being.

NELP Standard 7: Building Professional Capacity

Component 7.1 Program completers understand and have the capacity to collaboratively develop the professional capacity of the school through engagement in recruiting, selecting, and hiring staff.

Component 7.2 Program completers understand and have the capacity to develop and engage staff in a collaborative professional culture designed to promote school improvement, teacher retention, and the success and well-being of each student and adult in the school.

Component 7.3 Program completers understand and have the capacity to personally engage in, as well as collaboratively engage school staff in, professional learning designed to promote reflection, cultural responsiveness, distributed leadership, digital literacy, school improvement, and student success.

Component 7.4 Program completers understand and have the capacity to evaluate, develop, and implement systems of supervision, support, and evaluation designed to promote school improvement and student success.

NELP Standard 8: Internship

Component 8.1 Candidates are provided a variety of coherent, authentic field, and/or clinical internship experiences within multiple school environments that afford opportunities to interact with stakeholders, synthesize and apply the content knowledge, and develop and refine the professional skills articulated in each of the components included in NELP building-level program standards 1 through 7.

Component 8.2 Candidates are provided a minimum of six months of concentrated (10 to 15 hours per week) internship or clinical experiences that include authentic leadership activities within a school setting.

Component 8.3 Candidates are provided a mentor who has demonstrated effectiveness as an educational leader within a building setting; is present for a significant portion of the internship; is selected collaboratively by the intern, a representative of the school and/or district, and program faculty; and has received training from the supervising institution.

As previously noted, NELP includes specific competencies for school and district-level leaders. The competency descriptions are available at https://www.npbea.org/nelp/. In the *Relevance of the Leadership Standards,* there is a crosswalk between PSEL, ISLLC, and ELCC. A discussion of the crosswalk is included below demonstrating the commonalities between PSEL and NELP.

Standards 1 through 4 for both PSEL 2015 and NELP 2015 center around the same or similar tenants. Standard1 in both leadership entities centers around mission and vision. In PSEL, core values are included with mission and vision, and school improvement is included with mission and vision for NELP. Ethics and norms are included for Standard 2 in both leadership entities. For Standard 3 in both leadership associations, equity is addressed. For PSEL, culturally responsiveness accompanies equity; while inclusiveness and culturally responsiveness accompanies equity in NELP. Standard 4 for PSEL and NELP centers around curriculum and instruction. Standard 4 for PSEL also includes assessment, and learning is included for NELP.

Standards 6 and 7 of PSEL, professional capacity of care and professional community for educators, align with Standard 7 of NELP. Standard 8 of PSEL and Standard 5 of NELP both address engaging the community; PSEL 8 has more of a focus on family engagement. Operation and management are addressed in PSEL 9 and NELP 6. PSEL includes a Standard 10, "school improvement," which is addressed primarily in Standard 4 of NELP. PSEL does not have a standard for internship; however, NELP Standard 8 is internship.

The application of the NELP Standards is the guidance of Principal/Leader Preparation Programs, and the application of PSEL is the day-to-day parameters for school and building-level leaders. The International Society for Technology in Education (ISTE) also has standards for Educational Leadership. According to ISTE's website (http://www.iste.org/standards/for-education-leaders) the standards "support the implementation of the ISTE Standards for Students and the ISTE Standards for Educators and provide a framework for guiding digital age learning. These standards target the knowledge and behaviors required for leaders to empower teachers and make student learning possible." The standards are Equity and Citizenship

Advocate, Visionary Planner, Empowering Leader, Systems Designer, and Connected Learner.

The focus of the Equity and Citizenship Advocate Standard is to increase equity, inclusion, and digital citizenship practices. The competencies are:

Ensure all students have skilled teachers who actively use technology to meet student learning needs.

Ensure all students have access to the technology and connectivity necessary to participate in authentic and engaging learning opportunities.

Model digital citizenship by critically evaluating online resources, engaging in civil discourse online, and using digital tools to contribute to positive social change.

Cultivate responsible online behavior, including the safe, ethical, and legal use of technology.

(http://www.iste.org/standards/for-education-leaders)

The core of the Visionary Planner Standard is to establish a vision, strategic plan, and ongoing evaluation cycle for transforming learning and technology. The competencies are:

Engage education stakeholders in developing and adopting a shared vision for using technology to improve student success, informed by the learning sciences.

Build on the shared vision by collaboratively creating a strategic plan that articulates how technology will be used to enhance learning.

Evaluate progress on the strategic plan, make course corrections, measure impact, and scale effective approaches for using technology to transform learning.

Communicate effectively with stakeholders to gather input on the plan, celebrate successes, and engage in a continuous improvement cycle.

Share lessons learned, best practices, challenges, and the impact of learning with technology with other education leaders who want to learn from this work.

(http://www.iste.org/standards/for-education-leaders)

The emphasis of the Empowering Leader Standard is to create a culture where teachers and learners are empowered to use technology in innovative ways to enrich teaching and learning. The competencies are:

Empower educators to exercise professional agency, build teacher leadership skills, and pursue personalized professional learning.

Build the confidence and competency of educators to put the ISTE Standards for Students and Educators into practice.

Inspire a culture of innovation and collaboration that allows the time and space to explore and experiment with digital tools.

Support educators in using technology to advance learning that meets the diverse learning, cultural, and social-emotional needs of individual students.

Develop learning assessments that provide a personalized, actionable view of student progress in real time.

(http://www.iste.org/standards/for-education-leaders)

The focus of the Systems Designer Standard is team building and system building to implement, sustain, and continually improve the use of technology to support learning. The competencies are:

Lead teams to collaboratively establish robust infrastructure and systems needed to implement the strategic plan.

Ensure that resources for supporting the effective use of technology for learning are sufficient and scalable to meet future demand.

Protect privacy and security by ensuring that students and staff observe effective privacy and data management policies.

Establish partnerships that support the strategic vision, achieve learning priorities, and improve operations.

(http://www.iste.org/standards/for-education-leaders)

The core of the Connected Learner Standard is to model and promote continuous professional learning for themselves and others. The competencies are:

Set goals to remain current on emerging technologies for learning, innovations in pedagogy, and advancements in the learning sciences.

Participate regularly in online professional learning networks to collaboratively learn with and mentor other professionals.

Use technology to regularly engage in reflective practices that support personal and professional growth.

Develop the skills needed to lead and navigate change, advance systems, and promote a mindset of continuous improvement for how technology can improve learning.

(http://www.iste.org/standards/for-education-leaders)

It should be noted that there are also ISTE Standards (http://www.iste .org/standards) for students, educators (in general), coaches, as well as educational leaders. The educational leadership standards are included above. ISTE also has a "Seal of Alignment." This is a program that recognizes educational technology products that align to the ISTE Standards. There are also essential conditions outlined by ISTE. The essential conditions are 14 critical elements to "effectively leverage technology for learning." The 14 critical elements are:

- Shared vision,
- Empowered leaders,
- Implementation planning,
- Consistent and adequate funding,
- Equitable access,
- Skilled personnel,
- Ongoing professional learning,
- Technical support,
- Curriculum framework,
- Student-centered learning,
- Assessment and evaluation,
- Engage communities,
- Support policies, and
- Supportive external context.

The additional area addressed by ISTE is computational thinking competencies. The goals of the computational thinking competencies are to assist educators in integrating students' computational thinking across all disciplines. Computational thinking is noted for the learner. For the leader, equity leadership competencies are outlined. For the collaborator, collaborating around computing is addressed. Creativity and design are outlined for the designer, and integrating computational thinking is outlined for the facilitator. In Chapter 5 of this book the principal as "instructional leader" is the focus. We present technological tools to assist principals in their roles as instructional leaders. Principals must also nurture cultures in learning environments to help teachers in creating learning experiences online. Online learning has become a viable alternative due to COVID 19, weather events, and other circumstances. According to ISTE, a variety of elements should be included to provide the best learning opportunities for students in a remote and digital environment.

The following are the elements:

- Learning environments that allow for rich educator and student collaboration and communication, that may also include collaboration with subject matter experts, instructional support personnel, and peers.

- Digital learning content and interactive learning experiences that engage students in reaching specific learning goals.
- The use of data and information to personalize learning and/or provide targeted instruction.
- A wide variety of computer-based formative and summative assessments.

Although PSEL, NELP, and ISTE Standards for Leaders were developed by different professional organizations for unique purposes for school leadership as previously noted, concepts like vision, academic learning, student engagement, and equity are addressed in PSEL, NELP, and ISTE Standards. These concepts are among the principles essential to the work of school leaders and areas like instructional leadership and accountability where there are heightened emphases.

Within the U.S. Department of Education, there is an Office of Educational Technology. The National Technology Plan includes sections on learning, teaching, leadership, assessment, and infrastructure. The leadership section of the plan addresses the roles of principals and other leaders in technology. The national goal for technology pertinent to leadership is to "embed an understanding of technology-enabled education within the roles and responsibilities of education leaders at all levels and set state, regional, and local visions for technology in learning." As previously noted we focus on technological tools to assist school leaders. There is an alignment of the national goal in the Office of Educational Technology to the goal of this book. In addition to using technology, school leaders should also facilitate professional development opportunities for teachers and other staff and nurture cultures to embrace technology (https://tech.ed.gov/netp/leadership/).

Nicole Kruger (2021, December) noted that there are so many technology tools available complemented with marking claims that educators must take on the roles of researchers, pedagogical experts, IT developers, and legal consultants when choosing appropriate tools for classrooms. Kruger describes the variety of technology tools available as a part of the technology ecosystem. Locating technological solutions may be time intensive and intimidating. The EdSurge Product Index (https://index.edsurge.com/) is a resource for technology users to search and compare technology products. As noted in the ISTE, NELP, PSEL Standards, and through the Office of Educational Technology in the U.S. Department of Education; school leaders must nurture the learning environments for teachers to research, explore, and use technology to enhance learning for students as well as for their own professional development. We will revisit the notion of the school leader as nurturing the environments for technology enhancements throughout the book.

It is suggested by the Office of Technology of the U.S. Department of Education that a shared vision must be created by leaders to take full advantage of technology to transform student learning. One of the technological challenges for K-12 schools is infrastructure. Many of the tools noted in the publication require adequate internet. As early as 2013, President Obama set national priorities linked to the infrastructure challenges called ConnectED. The four goals are:

Within five years, connect 99% of America's students through next-generation broadband and high-speed wireless in their schools and libraries.

Empower teachers with the best technology and training to help them keep pace with changing technological and professional demands.

Provide students with feature-rich educational devices that are price competitive with basic textbooks.

Empower students with digital-learning content and experiences aligned with college- and career-ready standards being adopted and implemented by states across America.

(https://tech.ed.gov/netp/leadership/)

The Office of Technology has also established *Future Ready Focus Areas* for technology. The four tenants of the *Future Ready Focus Areas* are collaborative leadership, personalized student learning, robust infrastructure, and professionalized professional learning. Each one of the tenets is described by the Office of Technology. Many of the concepts embedded in the Office of Technology's tenants are included in the NELP, PSEL, and ISTE Standards.

Collaborative leadership is described as:

Education leaders develop a shared vision for how technology can support learning and how to secure appropriate resources to sustain technology initiatives. Leaders seek input from a diverse team of stakeholders to adopt and communicate clear goals for teaching, leading, and learning that are facilitated by technology. They model tolerance for risk and experimentation and create a culture of trust and innovation.

Leaders communicate with all stakeholders by using appropriate media and technology tools and establish effective feedback loops. While implementing the vision through a collaboratively developed strategic plan, leaders use technology as a learning tool for both students and teachers. Leaders are creative and forward-thinking in securing sustainable streams of human and capital resources to support their efforts, including appropriate partnerships both within their institutions and beyond.

(https://tech.ed.gov/netp/leadership/)

Professional student learning is described as:

Technology enables personalized pathways for student learning through active and collaborative learning activities. Clearly defined sets of learning outcomes guide instruction. The outcomes, and the aligned curriculum, instruction, and assessment, reflect the multidisciplinary nature of knowledge; prepare students for our participatory culture through attention to digital literacy and citizenship; and attend to general skills and dispositions, such as reflection, critical thinking, persistence, and perseverance.

Leaders ensure that policies and resources equip teachers with the right tools and ongoing support to personalize learning in their classrooms.

Teachers collaborate to make instructional decisions based on a diverse data set, including student and teacher observations and reflections, student work, formative and summative assessment results, and data from analytics embedded within learning activities and software aided by real-time availability of data and visualizations, such as information dashboards. Leadership policy and teacher methods support student voice and choice in the design of learning activities and the means of demonstrating learning. Students frequently complete a series of self-directed, collaborative, multidisciplinary projects and inquiries that are assessed through a profile or portfolio. Technology is integral to most learning designs, used daily within and beyond the classroom for collaboration, inquiry, and composition, as well as for connecting with others around the world. In the classroom, teachers serve as educational designers, coaches, and facilitators, guiding students through their personalized learning experiences.

(https://tech.ed.gov/netp/leadership/)

Robust infrastructure is described as:

A robust technology infrastructure is essential to Future Ready learning environments, and leaders need to take ownership of infrastructure development and maintenance. The 2015 CoSN Annual E-rate and Infrastructure Survey found that affordability remains the primary obstacle for robust connectivity; network speed and capacity pose significant challenges for schools; and, finally, too many school systems report a lack of competition for broadband services in many parts of the United States, particularly in rural areas. Leaders are responsible for meeting these challenges and ensuring ubiquitous access among administrators, teachers, and students to connectivity and devices and for supporting personnel to ensure equipment is well maintained. Future Ready leaders take direct responsibility to ensure infrastructure remains up-to-date (both in terms of security and relevant software, apps, and tools) and open to appropriate Web content and social media tools to enable collaborative learning. Leaders also recognize the importance of building capacity among those responsible for creating and maintaining the technology infrastructure. Future Ready leaders support all of these efforts through careful planning and financial stewardship focused on long-term sustainability.

(https://tech.ed.gov/netp/leadership/)

Personalized professional learning is described as:

Leaders ensure the availability of ongoing, job-embedded, and relevant professional learning designed and led by teachers with support from other experts. Leaders develop clear outcomes for professional learning aligned with a vision for student learning.

In Future Ready schools, teachers and leaders engage in collaborative inquiry to build the capacity of both the participating staff and the school as a whole through face-to-face, online, and blended professional learning communities and networks. Leaders ensure that professional learning planning is participatory and ongoing. Leaders learn alongside teachers and staff members, ensuring that professional learning activities are supported by technology resources and tools, time for collaboration, and appropriate incentives.

(https://tech.ed.gov/netp/leadership/)

## TECHNOLOGY AND THE WORK OF THE SCHOOL PRINCIPAL

As previously noted, the digital age has given rise to an unprecedented array of technological tools school principals can utilize in their various roles. These include instructional support software and systems, administrative management software and systems, communications tools, and security systems (Ogle, 2002). The expansive array of mobile devices, video and image sensors, text and voice capturing tools, and analytic systems, to name a few, add to the data available to the school principal, which is greater than ever before (Håkansson-Lindqvist and Petterson, 2019). The ever-growing use of technology in the work of teaching and learning and social interactions among students and among teachers creates a potential cache of data and computing power not available to school principals in any previous era (Sorensen, 2019).

Principals and teachers can promote positive communication using digital media. Facebook, Instagram, Tumblr, Twitter, and LinkedIn are among the platforms available. In all of the roles of school leaders, effective communication is key. On Facebook, individuals and entities may create profiles and follow the profiles of others. Delack (2022, January) noted that there is an abundance of social media platforms available. There is a need to understand which channels to use and the purpose of each channel. Consideration should be given to what is safe, what is effective, and what is worth the time.

Delack (2022, January) suggested that four social media platforms should be used by school districts in 2022. They are: Facebook, Twitter, Instagram, and LinkedIn. Facebook is free and is the most widely used social media platform. In recent months, the developers of Facebook and Twitter have experienced media coverage surrounding negativity linked to the use of the tool. Delack (2022, January) suggests Facebook is a good platform to share information and engage parents. However, using Facebook to post crisis updates, COVID 19 protocol adjustments, or news that could begin the circulation of negativity should be avoided. Facebook posts should be positive and uplifting. Declack (2002, January) recommends that leaders should start small – one specific page when beginning to use Facebook and expand slowly. There is also an application that can be used that makes it easier to respond directly to posts; it is the Facebook business page manager application.

Instagram has features that are similar to Facebook in which the following of profiles is widely used. Users of Instagram share and upload pictures, videos, and images; users can also directly message and video call. According to Delack (2022, January), Instagram has an audience of the younger generation and is most popular with teens. Instagram is most effective with middle school and junior high school students. Stories, Highlights, and Reels are popular on Instagram. Stories tend to be short-lived posts that appear for 24 hours that allow for quick updates. The Highlights feature allows for stories to live permanently on the user's page. Reels are similar to TikTok; the videos of Reels are usually linked with music. Like Facebook, users of Instagram should start small and be consistent. It is important to have high-quality videos on a permanent feed while lower-quality videos should live on Stories. Later .com must be used to post videos to Instagram from laptops or desktops. In addition to uploading photos and videos, Tumblr allows users to post artwork, writing, and audio. Tumblr is a microblogging service in which real-time blogs are available. Information is available at http://www.tumblr.com.

On Twitter, users share short posts or tweets. There is a limit of 280 characters for Twitter users. Links, images, location data, keywords, and polls may be tweeted which are labeled by placing a hashtag prior to the keyword or phrase. Tweets are public even to individuals without a Twitter account. Twitter also has a direct messaging feature and additional information is available at http://www.twitter.com. Delack (2022, January) suggests that leaders should create a list of teachers and staff who use Twitter and follow them. This makes it easy to locate quality posts and retweet them. The same hashtag should be used consistently. Leaders should build up more frequent posting after posting once a day as when just beginning to tweet.

LinkedIn is a social media platform with a professional focus. Like Facebook, individuals may create profiles and follow the profiles of others. It is free; however, there is an option to acquire additional features at a cost. On LinkedIn's web page, it is marketed as a hiring, marketing, selling, and learning tool. Delack (2022, January) notes that LinkedIn is a good recruiting tool. There are also opportunities for educators to engage in many professional development initiatives. We also view it as a branding opportunity. School leaders may share the positive initiatives and announcements from their schools. Additional information is available at http://www.linkedin.com.

Major (2019b, November) presents the *Top 12 Social Media Mistakes Hurting Engagement*. These concepts are applicable to school leaders. They are:

- not posting enough,
- posting too much,
- not using stories,
- not using visuals,
- not using visual that are engaging,
- not using data to understand what the community wants to see,
- not engaging with your community,
- using multiple accounts instead of groups,
- using content all about you, not using a hashtag, and
- not promoting the social media account on the website.

Major (2019b, November) recommends that a post should be made to social media outlets once per day. Content for social media outlets may come from social media holidays; content should be scheduled in advance; and some content is recurring. Take advantage of posts related to student of the week, athlete of the week, etc.

While some leaders do not post enough, some post too much. Major (2019b, November) notes that for Facebook, posts should be made one to two times per day. Posts should be made to Twitter five to ten times per day; posts to Instagram should be made one to two times per day; and about one post per day should be made to LinkedIn. Stories should be used on Facebook and Instagram. As previously noted, the content in Stories disappears after 24 hours unless they are saved to highlights. However, the content of Stories is most ideal for engagement. To increase engagement using social media outlets, it is important to use visuals. Videos, live videos, and photo slides are favored formats for Twitter and Facebook. Of course, the visual options are the only post option for Instagram.

In addition to using visuals on social media platforms, it is equally important for visuals to be engaging. To optimize the engagement, the free tool Canva can be used to enhance the presentation of the design. Canva includes a library of fonts and images, and graphic design skills are not required. Videos should be used when possible, and at least one should be used weekly. Facebook and Instagram have tools like stickers, emojis, and GIFs that increase engagement levels when used. School leaders should experiment with such tools along with the editing tool. There are free applications like Lightroom CC that edit photos for the users.

Major (2019b, November) notes the importance of using data to determine what the community/followers want to see. Social media platforms include data on who is viewing, their location, the most popular content posted, and the most popular times of viewing. Knowing the demographics of followers on platforms helps leaders to focus on strategies to use for posting on different platforms, and posts with a higher number of viewers are the kinds of posts to continue most frequently. It is equally important to respond to posts. Major (2019b, November) reported that one of the most common mistakes of school leaders when using social media is not responding to comments. Not responding limits the engagement.

Having too many accounts may be another imposed challenge that impacts engagement negatively. Major (2019b, November) recommends the use of groups as opposed to multiple accounts. With the multiple accounts, school leaders are dividing the traffic and setting up "self-competition." Content that is shared in a Facebook group becomes favored in news feeds. Facebook defines groups as the "place for small group communication and for people to share their common interests and express their opinion. Groups allow people to come together around a common cause, issue or activity to organize, express objectives, discuss issues, post photos and share related content."

The school community can be expanded online using Facebook Groups to include parents, alumni, students, and others (Major, 2019a, October). Content posted in groups tends to get priority over other content because Facebook algorithms embrace human connections instead of brand engagement. Grade level-based groups; groups for interests, activities, and clubs; and alumni-specific groups are examples of the kinds of groups to form. The benefit of groups that are grade-level focused is that the content streams are free of clutter. Creating groups of interests, activities, and clubs on Facebook is a way to keep members of groups motivated and engaged with authentic communication. The increased engagement leads to the group expanding to other groups creating chain reactions. Such chain reactions can also be created through alumni groups. Keeping alumni groups engaged in school communities is a way to continue harvesting the pride among the graduates, and school leaders tap into a path of communication that would otherwise be closed.

Many of the resources available to school leaders through social media are free; however, Ads must be purchased. Major (2019a, October) provides advice on the Ads to increase engagement for school leaders. Major (2022, January) also suggests that social media should be treated like relationships (it must be two-way). All of a school's social media content should not be about the school. Several social media content strategies are proposed including the 4–1–1 rule and the 60–30–10 rule. Applying the 4–1–1 rule, one repost and one -self-serving post should be posted for every four posts focused on helpful or educational-related content. Using the 60–30–10 rule, 60% of the content should be content engaging people to reach, comment, and share; 30% should be content shared from other pages; and 10% should be content to promote the school and its events. The use of either rule indicates that content shared on social media should be a mix of content that promotes the school and engages the community.

One of the easiest ways to increase engagement in social media is to add a hashtag. Adding a hashtag provides a simple way to find content for the school to share. The followers of the school are also encouraged to share the school's brand on their personal pages. Another easy manner to increase engagement in social media is to add the school's social media accounts to the school's web page. This increases the possibility of the content being viewed. The social media information can also be emailed or included in the signature lines of employees (Major, 2022, January). In the discussion above on *12 Social Media Mistakes Hurting Engagement,* we noted that messages should be managed. COVID 19 has generated a shift in how communication occurs. Parents and other followers will post negative comments. School leaders must strategize to address such comments and all comments and messages.

Major and Doverspike (2020, October) noted that today's world expects immediacy. We previously cited that responses to social media should occur within 24 hours. Responding to comments helps to build trust and transparency with current and prospective families, opens up two-way conversations, and helps with organic reach. Major and Doverspike (2020, October) refer to a concept of *Social Media Etiquette 101*. It is recommended that responses are provided for positive and negative comments. Responses to positive comments can assist in general perception and organic reach. In responding to negative comments, there are parameters that guide the responses. It is important to determine if the negative commenter is a member of the school or district's community. Do the necessary research to determine if the information is true; it can also be very damaging to do automatic deletes; this may cause additional backlash. When there are inappropriate comments in violation of social media policy, they should be deleted.

A proactive strategy school leaders can develop is to set up templates. The templates may serve as reference points when responding to negative posts. Major and Doverspike (2020, October) provide this template as an example for a response to a parent commenting on a negative experience for their child. It is also important to personalize as illustrated in the template:

*Hi [First Name], We're so sorry to learn about [information about experience]. Here at [School Name], we strive to provide the best-possible experience for all students. [Head of School, Superintendent, or other faculty name] will be in contact with you shortly to hear more about this and to help find a solution.*

Although it may be uncomfortable, Major and Doverspike (2020, October) pinpoint responding to negative comments as key to building trust in the community. Transparency is also established. It is important to be personable when responding to negative comments while being as unspecific as possible. Depending on the issue to address, school leaders may respond to negative comments online, offline entirely, or both. The response demonstrates that the school leaders care (particularly if done online – everyone can see the care) and makes the concerned party aware of the desire to rectify the situation.

It is also important that the workload of social media accounts be managed by school leaders. It is important for school leaders to set boundaries and expectations individually and for team members who manage comments. Approximately 30 minutes each day should be dedicated to responding across all channels. School leaders may solicit additional help if 30 minutes is not enough time and seek expert advice when necessary. It is helpful for school leaders to include a FAQ page on the school's website addressing questions from social media. There is always the potential for challenges to develop that were not anticipated with the use of social media (Mangold).

Mangold also suggests that school leadership should create a social media policy. There are three things to consider:

- Develop guidelines to ensure that the social media presence cultivates the values of the missions of the school.
- Consider the value of a private or public presence.
- Use feeds to filter content on the school's site.

Social media is discussed in Chapter 7, as it relates to the school leader in leading external relationships. In addition to the social media platforms discussed here; others are introduced in Chapter 7. In Chapter 2, we refer to the social media platforms discussed in this chapter in the section: **Technological Tools Applicable to Many Administrative Tasks.** In Chapter 3, in the section: **Hiring of Non-Instructional and Instructional Personnel,** we note the use of social media in hiring processes, and in Chapter 6: **Monitoring and Analysis of the Safety Climate of the School**, we note social media outlets as platforms to measure climate.

## OVERVIEW OF THE BOOK

In the 1800s, classrooms were one-room schoolhouses with chalkboards in the front of the classrooms and student desks neatly arranged in rows complimented by the teacher's desk at the front of the room. It has been argued that there have been many technological advances in business and industry. Although there have been advances in classrooms and education, the advances have not been as rapid as in other entities like business and industry. Throughout this book, specific technological tools are discussed to assist school principals in leading more efficiently – specifically in the areas of instructional leadership, managerial and organizational leadership, and human resource leadership. We stress throughout the publication that the technological tools proposed support school leaders in their roles; however, we are not proposing that the importance of the necessary knowledge, skills, and dispositions are negated. As a matter of fact, in Chapters 2–7, we provide an introduction to the leadership task/s applicable to the chapter. The applicable NELP and PSEL Standards along with ISTE Standard/s are included followed by a preview into the technologies that support the leadership roles in most of the chapters.

It should be noted that not all PSEL, NELP, and ISTE Standards are covered through discussions in Chapters 2–7. However, several of the standards are applicable in all of the work school leaders do. School leaders must be guided by the Mission, Vision, and Core Values (NELP

1 and PSEL 1) of the schools they serve. School leaders must always engage in actions and dispositions that embody ethical principles (NELP 2 and PSEL 2) and Cultural Leadership and Equity (NELP 3) are extremely critical in this era. In many instances, the benefits of the technological tools along with the challenges of the tools are noted. Access to the internet is required to use most tools discussed. There are instances when tools may be used "offline." Generally, this requires downloading of the information prior to attempting to utilize the pertinent tool. Inadequate infrastructure is a challenge in schools in parts of our nation, and we discussed the infrastructure challenges noted by the Office of Technology in the U.S. Office of Education in Chapter 1. The goals of the Office of Technology are included with the tenants outlined in Connect Education. Many of the principles outlined in the leadership and ISTE Standards are included in concepts by the Office of Technology.

The critical work of school leadership and leadership standards are presented in Chapter 1.

Technological tools to assist with facets of instructional leadership are included in Chapter 5 and Chapter 6: instructional leadership pertinent to culture. Technological tools to assist with tenants of management are included in Chapter 2 and Chapter 4: management related to school safety.

In Chapter 3, technological tools to assist with human resource leadership pertinent to personnel and evaluation of employees are presented. In Chapter 7, tools are included to assist with external relationships that school leaders must maintain and nurture. Technological tools to assist school leaders in conducting research are presented in Chapter 8. The focus of Chapter 8 is action research; however, the technology tools and pertinent information are applicable to traditional research. In this chapter, the section – **Technology and the Work of the School Principal** has tools and applications to assist principals in many of their roles which can be included in most of the chapters.

The focus of the tools presented in the section, **Technology and the Work of the School Principal,** is on effective communication. The effectiveness or lack of effectiveness of communication intersects most if not all of the roles of school leaders. The social media outlets are applicable to many of the roles school leaders facilitate and are included in this chapter as well as other chapters. In fact, there is some repetition of tools when necessarily pertinent to specific roles. Delack (2022, January) recommends that Facebook, Twitter, Instagram, and LinkedIn are the platforms for school leaders to use in 2022. An overview of each of the platforms is provided in Chapter 1. The social media mistakes that hurt engagement for schools are included along with practical guidelines to improve the use of each outlet. Additional specificity regarding engagement is included in the Chapter 7 section: **External Relationships: Social Media** along with strategies to improve engagement. Different uses for the social media outlets are included in Chapter 2 for administrative and management roles, Chapter 3 for hiring and recruiting employees, Chapter 4 for cyber challenges, and Chapter 6 for promoting positive school climates and cultures. In Chapter 8, social media outlets are included as tools to collect data from pertinent participants. Strategies are also provided to address negative comments made about schools on social media in several chapters. Learning Management Systems are highlighted in Chapter 5 linked to the instructional roles of school leaders.

In Chapter 2 **Management and Administration**, a weblink is included that includes over 717 tools – which are described as the best school administration software. Most of the top performers from the weblink are included as they are noted as the "2022 shortlist" of products (https://www.capterra.com/school-administration-software/#buyers -guide.) We state throughout the book and have stated in this chapter; our goal is to provide tools for school leaders. It is not our intention in *Effective Technology Tools for School Leadership: Understanding Digital and Data-Driven Strategies* to suggest that the use of technology tools replace the necessary skills, knowledge, and dispositions needed for school leaders. The technology tools presented in each chapter are included in the reference list, and are also included below the references in a technology tool listing. Several chapters include indexes (with weblinks) to review technologies. The EdSurge Product Index is included in the discussion in Chapter 2. Each chapter also includes an abstract to begin the chapter, and in Chapters 2–7, two case scenarios are included to apply concepts and technology tools pertinent to the chapter and other chapters as deemed relevant. In Chapter 8, examples of action research are included utilizing several different action research models presented in the chapter. The goal of the publication is to provide school leaders, aspiring school leaders, and other educators with useful resources.

---

**TECHNOLOGY TOOLS**

Facebook: http://www.facebook.com
Instagram: http://www.instagram.com
LinkedIn: http://www.linkedin.com
Twitter: http://www.twitter.com
Tumblr: http://www.tumblr.com

---

## REFERENCES

Branch, G. F., Hanushek, E. A., & Rivkin, S. G. (2013). School leaders matter. *Education Next*, *13*(1), 62–69.

Davies, P. M. (2010). On school educational technology leadership. *Management in Education*, *24*(2), 55–61.

Delack, M. (2022, January). 4 social media platforms your district should be using in 2022. https://www.finalsite.com/blog/p/~board/b/post/top-social-media -platforms-for-districts.

Dunlap, J., Li, J., & Kladifko, R. (2015). Competencies for effective school leadership: To what extent are they included in Ed.D. Leadership programs? *Educational Leadership and Administration: Teaching and Program Development*, *26*, 14–26.

Dutta, V., & Sahney, S. (2016). School leadership and its impact on student achievement. *International Journal of Educational Management*, *30*(6), 941–958. https://doi-org.libezp.lib.lsu.edu/10.1108/IJEM-12-2014-0170.

Edmonds, R. (1979). Effeective schools for the urban poor. *Educational Leadership*, *37*, 15–24.

Facebook. http://www.facebook.com.

Faria, A.-M., Greenberg, A., Meakin, J., Bichay, K., & Heppen, J. (2014). *Replicating the relationship between teachers' data use and student achievement: The urban data study and the data dashboard usage study.* Society for Research on Educational Effectiveness. Society for Research on Educational Effectiveness.

Graham, J. W. (1991). Servant-leadership in organizations: Inspirational and moral. *The Leadership Quarterly*, *2*(2), 105–119. https://doi.org/10.1016/1048 -9843(91)90025-W.

Greer, C. (1972). *The great school legend: A revisionist interpretation of American public education.* Basic Books.

Håkansson Lindqvist, M., & Pettersson, F. (2019). Digitalization and school leadership: On the complexity of leading for digitalization in school. *International Journal of Information & Learning Technology*, *36*(3), 218–230. https://doi-org .libezp.lib.lsu.edu/10.1108/IJILT-11-2018-0126.

Instagram. http://www.instgram.com.

International Society of Technology of Education. https://www.iste.org/standards/ for-education-leaders.

Jones, L. (2017). *The relevance of the leadership standards: A new order of business for principals.* Rowman & Littlefield Publishing.

Jones, L. (2020). *The relevance of instructional leadership.* Cognella Publishing.

Jones, L., & Kennedy, E. (2015). *A guide to data-driven leadership in modern schools.* Information Age Publishing.

Koyama, J. (2014). Principals as "bricoleurs": Making sense and making do in an era of accountability. *Educational Administration Quarterly*, *50*(2), 279–304.

Krueger, N. (2021, December). 3 questions to ask before choosing a new Ed tech tool. https://www.iste.org/explore/education-leadership/3-questions-ask -choosing-new-edtech-tool.

Lachat, M. A., Williams, M., & Smith, S. C. (2006). Making sense of all your data. *Principal Leadership*, *7*(2), 16–21.

Leithwood, K., Jantzi, D., & McElheron-Hopkins, C. (2006). The development and testing of a school improvement model. *School Effectiveness and School Improvement*, *17*, 441–464.

Leithwood, K., Patten, S., & Jantzi, D. (2010). Testing a conception of how school leadership influences student learning. *Educational Administration Quarterly*, *46*, 671–706.

Liebowitz, D. D., & Porter, L. (2019). The effect of principal behaviors on student, teacher, and school outcomes: A systematic review and meta-analysis of the empirical literature. *Review of Educational Research*. https://doi.org/10.3102 /0034654319866133.

LinkedIn. http://www.linkedin.com.

Major, M. (2019a, October). How to use Facebook groups to connect your school community. https://www.finalsite.com/blog/p/~board/b/post/facebook-group -strategies-for-schools.

Major, M. (2019b, November). *12 social media mistakes hurting engagement.* https://www.finalsite.com/blog/p/~board/b/post/school-social-media-marketing -mistakes.

Major, M., & Doverspike. (2020, October). How to manage your school's social media comment. https://www.finalsite.com/blog/p/~board/b/post/how-to -manage-school-social-media-comments.

Mangold, L. Top 5 concerns schools have about social media (and why you should stop worrying. https://www.finalsite.com/blog/p/~board/b/post/top-5-concerns -schools-have-about-social-media-and-why-you-should-stop-worrying.

Marsh, J. A., Bush-Mecenas, S., & Hough, H. (2017). Learning from early adopters in the new accountability era: Insights from California's CORE waiver districts. *Educational Administration Quarterly, 53*(3), 327–364.

Mitani, H. (2018). Principals' working conditions, job stress, and turnover behaviors under NCLB accountability pressure. *Educational Administration Quarterly, 54*(5), 822–862. https://doi-org.libezp.lib.lsu.edu/10.1177/0013161X18785874.

National Educational Leadership Preparation (NELP) Standards. https://www .naesp.org/communicator-november-2018/nelp-standards-approved-how-affects -you.

National Policy Board for Educational Administration (2015). Professional Standards for Educational Leaders 2015. Reston, VA: Author.

New Leaders. (2011). Urban excellence framework. *New Leaders.* http://search .ebscohost.com.libezp.lib.lsu.edu/login.aspx?direct=true&db=eric&AN =ED532072&site=ehost-live&scope=site.

Odom, A. L., & Bell, C. V. (2017). Developing PK-12 preservice teachers' skills for understanding data-driven instruction through inquiry learning. *Journal of Statistics Education, 25*(1), 29–37.

Ogle, T. (2002). *Technology in schools: Suggestions, tools, and guidelines for assessing technology in elementary and secondary education.* National Center for Education Statistics.

Pfeffer, J., & Sutton, R. (2000). *The knowing doing gap: How smart companies turn knowledge to action.* Harvard Business Publishing School.

Rai, A., & Prakash, A. (2014). In pursuit of effective schools: From Western perspective. *Journal on Educational Psychology, 7*(4), 41–49.

Reynolds, D., & Teddlie, C. (2000). *The international handbook of school effectiveness research.* Rutledge Publishers. https://doi.org/10.4324 /9780203454404.

Siccone, F. (2012). *Essential skills for effective school leadership.* Pearson Education.

Schmoker, M. J. (2011). *Focus: Elevating the essentials to radically improve student learning.* ASCD.

Sepuru, M. G., & Mohlakwana, M. A. (2020). The perspectives of beginner principals on their new roles in school leadership and management: A South African case study. *South African Journal of Education, 40*(2), 1–12.

Sorensen, L. C. (2019). "Big data" in educational administration: An application for predicting school dropout risk. *Educational Administration Quarterly*, *55*(3), 404–446. https://doi.org/10.1177/0013161X18799439.

Tan, C. Y. (2018). Examining school leadership effects on student achievement: The role of contextual challenges and constraints. *Cambridge Journal of Education*, *48*(1), 21–45. https://doi-org.libezp.lib.lsu.edu/10.1080/0305764X.2016.1221885.

Teddlie, C., & Stringfield S. (1993). *Schools make a difference: lessons learned from 10-year study of school effects*. Teachers College Press.

Thannimalai, R., & Raman, A. (2018). The influence of principals' technology leadership and professional development on teachers' technology integration in secondary schools. *Malaysian Journal of Learning and Instruction*, *15*(1), 203–228.

Towers, J. M. (1992). Twenty-five years after the Coleman report: What should we do? *Clearing House*, *65*(3), 138. https://doi-org.libezp.lib.lsu.edu/10.1080/00098655.1992.10114184.

Tumblr. http://www.tumblr.com.

U. S. Department of Education. Office technology. https://tech.ed.gov/netp/leadership/.

Wayman, J. C. (2005). Involving teachers in data-driven decision making: Using computer data systems to support teacher inquiry and reflection. *Journal of Education for Students Placed at Risk*, *10*(3), 295–308. https://doi-org.libezp.lib.lsu.edu/10.1207/s15327671espr1003_5.

# CHAPTER 2

## Management and Administration

**ABSTRACT**

The managerial and administrative responsibilities of principals are often time-intensive and accompanied by lots of paper copies, which have been referred to as "paper trails." In Chapter 2, the authors discuss technology tools that can be used for multiple administrative tasks (communication, school board business, scheduling, and monitoring of student data,) budgeting and financing, resource and supply management, maintenance of facilities, and transportation. Advantages associated with technology tools are offered, and references are made to weblinks of tools with explanations of the functionalities of the tools. For several of the technological tools, there are options to use the tools through mobile applications, such as tablets. We begin with a discussion of the managerial/administrative tasks linked to the leadership standards and technology standards. The interrelationship between instructional leadership and administrative/managerial leadership is also addressed.

### MANAGERIAL AND ADMINISTRATIVE TASKS LINKED TO LEADERSHIP STANDARDS

In Chapter 1, we noted that many of the leadership roles from a standards-based approach can be categorized as managerial or instructional. The instructional roles are noted in Chapter 5, and the management processes of school leaders are discussed in this chapter. The managerial processes include managing the school budget, surveying the availability of instructional materials and supplies, overseeing course scheduling, teacher assignments, and attendance, etc. We have noted that there is an interrelationship between instructional leadership/instructional

DOI: 10.4324/9781003269472-2

roles and management. Neither role can be performed in a vacuum. For instance, the goals of an instructional leader should be reflected in budgeting; the opposite is also true.

In both the National Education Leadership Preparation (NELP) standards and Professional Standards for Educational Leaders (PSEL), the interrelationship between instructional leadership and management is embedded. Standard 6: Operations and Management of NELP has a focus on management and operation; however, the success of teachers and students is also included, which is the instructional leadership link. A similar argument can be made of PSEL Standard 9. The management of schools is accounted for with a focus on the academic success of students – which is clearly instructional.

In Jones' *The Relevance of the Leadership Standards* (Rowman and Littlefield, 2017), there is a discussion regarding the interrelationship between instructional leadership and management in the standards:

PSEL Standard 9: Operations and Management along with PSEL Standard 10: School Improvement has more standard elements than the other Standards of PSEL. In *Passing the Leadership Test*, *2nd Edition*, Kennedy and I wrote the following about operations and management for school leaders. Many of these notions align with principles in the 2015 Operation and Management Standard. The alignments will be noted in pertinent sections.

"Although great emphasis is placed on the role of school leaders as instructional leaders; it is vital for leaders to be knowledgeable of efficient management techniques and strategies. Furthermore, many managerial decisions are critical to facilitating effective teaching and aspects of the learning environment." For instance, both knowledge and effective use of knowledge of budgeting (PSEL 9: Element 4), human resources, and other resources are advantageous to staffing schools with the pertinent teachers and other individuals in/for the most appropriate classrooms (PSEL 9: Element 2); purchasing materials and equipment; funding professional development activities; and maximizing the use of resources that are available.

Effective leaders must employ technology to improve the quality and efficiency of operations and management (PSEL 9: Element 6). Both managerial and instructional leadership tasks require the use of databases and technological systems. Employing databases and other technologies are important for record-keeping and making data-driven decisions. In *A Guide to Data-Driven Leadership in Modern Schools,* Jones and Kennedy (Information Age Publishing, 2015) discuss the importance of leaders creating a culture for data-driven decisions; using data in school management; and using data in instructional leadership and evaluations.

The importance of data-driven decisions is discussed as such from *A Guide to Data-Driven Leadership in Modern Schools* – A systems approach, as advocated by Kennedy (2003), suggests that data-driven decision-making starts by viewing the school as a complex, multi-layered organization with many subtleties. Data collected in one setting may have little validity in a second setting and may be little more than the preverbal "busy" work which drains resources to no tangible benefit. A data-driven decision-making plan must reflect the unique cultural context of each school, in all its aspects and idiosyncrasies.

The one notion embedded more specifically and empathetically in PSEL is the attention to ethics in the management of resources (monetary and nonmonetary). Both Standard 2: Element 1 and Standard 9: Element 4 state that effective leaders are stewards over the monetary and nonmonetary resources in schools. As previously alluded to, many of the skills and notions pertinent to management in the standards are critical to instruction.

In Element 1 of PSEL 9; it is noted that the mission and vision of the school should be promoted through the management and monitoring of administrative systems. As previously discussed, implementing the vision is critical to promoting academics – teaching and learning in K-12 schools. As a matter of fact, a model provided by the Chicago Public Schools entitled "Five Fundamentals of Success," identifies resource management as critical to instructional leadership and whole-school improvement."

The key indicators of excellence in resource management are:

- The instructional leadership team effectively allocates and manages the school resources – people, time, funds, and materials – to address school priorities and students' needs (PSEL 9: Element 2).
- The school community evaluates and plans school programs and policies based on their contributions toward reaching school goals (PSEL 9: Element 3); and
- Teachers use other staff, classroom volunteers, and family resources at home to maximize the number of individualized instructions students receive. (Chicago's public Schools); (PSEL 9: Element 3).

(http://www.npbea.org/)

Elements 11 and 12 of PSEL 9 include that in working toward the vision and mission, governance processes must be managed relative to internal and external politics. The school leader must take the lead and actively push for the vision in order for the credibility of the vision to remain vital. Action steps become as critical as continuous communication

(Weiss, 1995). Communication and collaboration are important among all "stakeholders," and the principal is continuously the promoter and chief investigator to work through politics.

Below are all the elements of PSEL 9 including competencies in 2 and 3 previously noted,

Effective Leaders:

a) Institute, manage, and monitor operations and administrative systems that promote the mission and vision of the school.

b) Strategically manage staff resources, assigning and scheduling teachers and staff to roles and responsibilities that optimize their professional capacity to address each student's learning needs.

c) Seek, acquire, and manage fiscal, physical, and other resources to support curriculum, instruction, and assessment; student learning community; professional capacity and community; and family and community engagement.

d) Are responsible, ethical, and accountable stewards of the school's monetary and nonmonetary resources, engaging in effective budgeting and accounting practices.

e) Protect teachers' and other staff members' work and learning from disruption.

f) Employ technology to improve the quality and efficiency of operations and management.

g) Develop and maintain data and communication systems to deliver actionable information for classroom and school improvement.

h) Know, comply with, and help the school community understand local, state, and federal laws, rights, policies, and regulations so as to promote student success.

i) Develop and manage relationships with feeders and connecting schools for enrollment management and curricular and instructional articulation.

j) Develop and manage productive relationships with the central office and school board.

k) Develop and administer systems for fair and equitable management of conflict among students, faculty and staff, leaders, families, and community.

l) Manage governance processes and internal and external politics toward achieving the school's mission and vision.

(http://www.npbea.org/)

In addition to PSEL 9 and 10, elements in NELP 6 are also relevant. There is also an interrelationship between PSEL 9 and NELP 6. Technology tools are introduced in this chapter which support leaders with aspects of governance mentioned in Components 6.1 and 6.2 of NELP 6. The Visionary Planner Standard of ISTE includes applications for Administration and Management as well. The core of the standard is to establish a vision, strategic plan, and ongoing evaluation cycle for transforming learning and technology.

Below are Components 6.1, 6.2, and 6.3 of NELP 6:

Component 6.1: Program completers understand and demonstrate the capacity to evaluate, develop, and implement management, communication, technology, school-level governance, and operating systems that support each student's learning needs and promote the mission and vision of the school.

Component 6.2: Program completers understand and demonstrate the capacity to evaluate, develop, and advocate for a data-informed and equitable resourcing plan that supports school improvement and student development.

Component 6.3: Program completers understand and demonstrate the capacity to reflectively evaluate, communicate about, and implement laws, rights, policies, and regulations to promote student and adult success and well-being.

(http://www.npbea.org/)

The ISTE Standard and competencies which align with management and administration is System Designer. The competencies address operations and systems. The focus of the Systems Designer Standard is team building and system building to implement, sustain, and continually improve the use of technology to support learning. The competencies are:

Lead teams to collaboratively establish robust infrastructure and systems needed to implement the strategic plan.

Ensure that resources for supporting the effective use of technology for learning are sufficient and scalable to meet future demand.

Protect privacy and security by ensuring that students and staff observe effective privacy and data management policies.

Establish partnerships that support the strategic vision, achieve learning priorities, and improve operations.

(https://www.iste.org/standards/for-education-leaders)

## TECHNOLOGICAL TOOLS APPLICABLE TO MANY ADMINISTRATIVE TASKS

### Communication and School-Board Specific Technologies

According to a recent review, modern school administrative technology applications provide solutions for essentially all aspects of school administration (Capterra, 2019). Key features of these systems are their security protocols, accessibility, and analytics. Using contemporary tools, school principals can predict student achievement, teacher retention, and a host of other outcomes. Because these systems store data in digital formats, they offer a potential store of information on the inner workings of schools that can be of great value to researchers (Shkurina, 2018, November).

Technology has significantly changed the ways in which many tasks are accomplished (Ogle, 2002). In Chapter 1, social media outlets for communication are included. Delack (2022, January) is cited in Chapter 1 (**Technology and the Work of the School Principal**) noting that Facebook, Twitter, Instagram, and LinkedIn are the social media platforms that should be used in schools. Specific features of each of the previously listed platforms are discussed. We noted that the social media platforms appeal to different audiences, and they are good ways to communicate information regarding schools as well as market school events. Suggestions are provided to strengthen positive messaging on social media and avoid missed opportunities. In this chapter, we discuss other platforms and technology tools for communication as well as tools for other tasks.

ParentLocker is a powerful "instant" channel of communication between home and school. With social media platforms, the messaging is generally to all of the followers/friends/audience. School leaders have the option to email/text selected groups using ParentLocker. Recipient groups are generated based on school information: grade level, class, and course; admission status; SIS fields, staff members, or administration. Other groups may also be created. The communication access is available from the dashboard. The dashboard is discussed more in detail pertinent to other functions of the platform in the remainder of the section. There is a feature to schedule the time of the email or text, or they may be sent immediately. Logs are maintained of the messages sent and the number of individuals reading messages (https://www.parentlocker.com/go/email-blast).

According to Shkuria (2018, November), PARENTLOCKER streamlines all aspects of school administration. It is a web-based school management and communication software package and is described as a Learning Management System. It provides a vehicle by which school principals can "seamlessly" exchange important information for purposes of monitoring student progress. ParentLocker has features for school leaders, teachers, parents, and students. At the link https://www.parentlocker.com/go/, there is an illustration of how to research information on a student. The student displayed on the home screen is Adam Apple, an 8th grader. The attendance of the student is visible along with general information and parental contacts (name of parent, cell, work number, and address). The general information includes the grade level, gender, date of birth, age, cell, allergies, sweatshirt size, and attachments of performance indicators (https://www.parentlocker.com/).

From the page referenced above, the parent or teacher can be emailed. Along the top of the screen, there are options to connect to the school's Student Information System or another database. The school leader may also select courses, grades, attendance, notes, admissions, and financial information. Teachers and others may have access to enter information depending on the nature of the information. Obviously, teachers should have access to enter grades and attendance. Clerks may also have access to enter attendance. The online forms and application option is also convenient for parents, teachers, and school leaders. Forms must be pre-populated by the staff of schools with available information on families and students. Data imputed by parents' imports to the database of ParentLocker (https://www.parentlocker.com/).

When parents enter data online, school staff do not have to duplicate entering the data. Payments may be accepted online as well. The add-ons may be supplemented as needed. Google Forms has the same option. Text inputs, file inputs, drop-down boxes, large text boxes, and other options are available for customizing forms. Below, we will discuss how fields can be customized. Forms can be customized also. Fields can be made mandatory to be filled, and sections may appear if a certain answer is provided for a question. School leaders have access to view form submissions in the submissions inbox. The status of a form is shown as well – "started," "in-progress," "submitted," or "imported." In Chapter 7, we discuss **Leadership for External Relationship**. Parents are members of the external stakeholder group for school leaders. ParentLocker has many features that are advantages for the work schools do with parents (https://www.parentlocker.com/).

As described on the ParentLocker website, https://www.parentlocker.com/go/features, users have the option to customize fields so that school leaders may store any information desired. "Fields can be set as file-uploads" allowing school leaders to upload documents and images to SIS. Data is safe in ParentLocker; a log of edits is maintained to ensure the integrity of the data. Daily backups occur, which ensures that data from a previous year is available. Robust reports may be customized in ParentLocker and exported with filters by grade level, course, class, and graduation year. Filtering is also available for fields such as student allergies and student bus lines. Reports may be printed or downloaded in PDF or Excel formats. The reporting feature is invaluable in this area of accountability. Attendance is a metric in many accountability systems. If a school leader desires to identify attendance trends, reports can be generated to review the specificity of students with consecutive absences, frequent absences, absences by class, tardiness by class, and perfect attendance can be highlighted.

In addition to the improvement of the ability of school leaders to execute their management role more effectively with the use of technology, an additional result of this digitalization of management is that data is retained and stored in formats that make it accessible for analysis. Through electronic communications and video and audio records of meetings and events, school administrators generate a significant amount of data while they function as managers. The obvious advantage for school leaders in using ParentLocker is the many functions that can be performed along with the data storage capabilities of the tools. Another huge advantage of ParentLocker is it is an integrated system. It integrates all modules. When changes are made in ParentLocker, changes automatically synchronize in other systems. The major disadvantage is when the internet is unavailable, there is no access to any of the tools or data (unless the data is stored on the computer's hard drive). In addition, some parents and other stakeholders may be unfamiliar with technology use (https://www.parentlocker.com/).

We highlighted features of ParentLocker pertinent for school leaders performing administrative and managerial roles such as communication and SIS functions; however, we previously mentioned that ParentLocker is also a Learning Management System. Several learning platforms are presented in the Chapter 5 section, **Providing Professional Development and Support for Teachers**. In Learning Management Systems, there are powerful tools for teachers to facilitate instruction through synchronous or asynchronous means. Lesson plans and photo albums are among the features available to teachers and school leaders in ParentLocker.

BoardDocs provides principals and other leaders with resources to help manage meetings with school boards. The features of this system include calendar management, collaboration, document management, electronic signatures, member directory, minutes management, polls/voting, and role-based permissions. The specific features for managing board meetings include action item tracking, agenda management, attendee management, board meetings, committee meetings, internal meetings, materials management, meeting preparation tools, minutes management, post-meeting tools, scheduling, travel management, and voting management. BoardDocs markets itself as a school board governance resource, and it empowers leaders with the technology to "fuel good governance." A student success kit and financial tools are also embedded within the system (https://www.boarddocs.com).

BoardDocs is an affiliate of Diligent (http://www.dilligent.com). One of the focuses of Diligent is modern governance. Diligent markets its modern governance component on transforming how leaders and boards work together. The software helps leaders save time with the digitalization of materials for boards, and school leaders and boards work together with access to data within the system. The streamlining of data helps leaders provide pertinent data to the right stakeholders and helps leaders facilitate strategic planning. Diligent has a component to benchmark compensation practices of work environments against peers.

### Scheduling Function, Monitoring Attendance, and Enrollment Management

In the **Managerial Tasks** section of this Chapter, we discussed the interconnectivity between instructional leadership roles and managerial leadership. Scheduling, monitoring attendance, and enrollment management are managerial tasks of school leaders with direct implications for instructional leadership. As previously mentioned, many schools and/or districts include attendance in accountability metrics. The current accountability metrics are the results of the *Every Student Succeeds Act* (ESSA). ESSA (2015) is the nation's most recent law addressing equal opportunity for students. We cited in Chapter 1 that the first act was passed over 50 years ago in 1965 – the *Elementary and Secondary Education Act (1965)*. The 1965 legislation was followed by the 1983 – *A Nation at Risk*. *A Nation at Risk* was followed in 2001 by the *No Child Left Behind Act*.

Scheduling, attendance monitoring, and enrollment management are generally addressed through one software program at schools. In the previous section on **Communication and School-Board Specific Technologies,** we discussed features of ParentLocker to assist school leaders in communication, data collection, and reporting. Scheduling of meetings, monitoring attendance, and enrollment management can be achieved with ParentLocker. Teacher and student schedules can easily be created on ParentLocker. School leaders must create formats and periods; the times and days each course meets must be selected; then, schedules are created automatically based on courses of enrollment for students. Schedules of teachers populate with the courses they teach. Conflicts are also identified within the system. Because the attendance module is integrated into the schedule module, attendance is streamlined. Attendance reports allow for the identification of trends. Meetings and conferences can be managed with ease. Parents gain access to the available times as soon as the times are posted in the system. There is an admissions dashboard as well. Applicants and potential applicants are tracked on the admissions dashboard. The following are the tenants of the admissions dashboard:

- The dashboard classifies students according to their status in your admissions process, for example, prospective, applied, interviewed, accepted, etc., as well as applying year and grade level.
- Applicants are moved between stages as their admissions status updates. Internal notes, as well as demographic data, can be added to the applicant's admissions portfolio.
- The dashboard includes easy-to-read stats and charts, complete with updated numbers, helping your admissions staff analyze real-time admissions data.

(http://www.parentlocker.com)

*DeansList* is another option for monitoring attendance. The *DeansList* software is one such program that tracks academic and non-academic student data. According to http://deanslistsoftware.com, DeansList supports school leaders in the implementation of school systems. DeansList advertises on its website its commitments to school leaders, teachers, and families and students. For school leaders, the commitment is "to design tools and provide services that are tailored to schools." The commitment aligns with the impetus of this book. The developers of DeansList are also committed to respecting the time of teachers and enhancing the ways schools communicate with students and families.

Applications of DeansList are operational through cell phones, tablets, and computers. The applications are available through the Student Information Systems from/of schools or through the web; and DeansList synchronizes with Student Information Systems. Therefore, the information does not have to be entered in multiple places. When logging on to DeansLists, the options to select are communication, referral, attendance, class attendance, and system behavior. Under the section "My Roster," users may search for a specific student and access student information. We did not discuss the communication feature relative to a communication tool. As a part of the family engagement feature, text messaging, emails, call logs, and parents apps are available.

The family engagement feature of DeansList includes a family portal. The family portal is an "up-to-speed" way to keep families engaged. Daily behavior tracking, attendance tracking, school news and updates, and notifications to parents are available. Weekly reports can be electronically signed, and paychecks and report cards can be viewed. The communication with parents may also be logged giving staff the potential to review any information entered by other staff. This feature is very advantageous for behavior reporting (http://deanslistsoftware.com).

Attendance can be taken in DeansList rather quickly. As the attendance is logged and students are absent, parents are sent text notifications, which are automatically customized. Absence and tardiness letters may be generated on DeansList in the preferred language of families. This is an important feature in schools where there is a high influx of English as a Second Language Learners. An "automatically scaled up response and intervention" may be sent to parents when students reach thresholds linked to absences. Congratulatory messages and letters may be sent to acknowledge students with great attendance (http://deanslistsoftware.com).

As reported on their website, http://deanslistsoftware.com, DeansList is a way to get the "whole school on the same page." Behaviors can be tracked as they occur across schools and within classrooms. The system identifies data trends such as negative or positive behaviors. The rules for rewards and consequences can be built into the system allowing for tiers for Positive Behavior Interventions and Supports (PBIS) or Multi-Tiered Systems Support (MTSS). Another feature of DeansList is that it allows school leaders to set alerts based on the most important information for the school. The alerts occur without logging into the system. DeansList is discussed in Chapter 6 as a means to promote positivism in the cultures of schools.

**BUDGETS AND FINANCES**

Budgeting and finances are important functions for districts as well as schools. School finance and budgeting are also very complex issues – state and local governments have major responsibilities in attempting to provide adequate educational opportunities for all students. Increasing student performance with the maximum use of resources is a critical challenge for school finance. The Government Finance Office Administrators have developed a series of Best Practices in School District Budgeting, which clearly outline steps to developing a budget that best aligns resources with student achievement goals (www.gfoa .org). The budgeting process presented in these Best Practices is focused on optimizing student achievement within available resources. It encompasses the following steps for school leaders:

*Step 1. Plan and Prepare. The budgeting and planning processes begin with key stakeholders, collecting information on academic performance and other costs, and establishing principles and policies to guide the budget process.*

*Step 2. Set Instructional Priorities. The budget needs to be grounded in the priorities. We often say that the budget must align with the academic goals.*

*Step 3. Pay for Priorities. Current expenditures must be analyzed to allocate funding to the instructional priorities.*

*Step 4. Implement Plan. The "strategic financial plan" serves as a road map for implementing the instructional priorities.*

*Step 5. Ensure Sustainability. The planning and budgeting process should be reviewed pertinent to progress* www.gfoa.org.

Other important challenges include seeking funding options to taxes, addressing the issue of education overburden, adapting site-based decision-making, and adapting full state funding. These challenges are compounded with additional school issues. Schools are facing increasing enrollments with more diverse student populations. The disabled student population has increased; the English as a Second Language population has increased; and the population of students affected by drugs and alcohol has increased. The quality of educational programs is definitely linked to the quality of teachers – districts are experimenting with expanding human resource offices and pay measures as a means to attract the best teachers. States will be forced to look critically at budgeting and spending to maintain a high quality of education for the nation's children. The concept of equity and adequacy are challenged further by budgetary constraints (Garfield et al., 2019).

Gutterman (2021, June) notes that inequities in education are "deeply rooted" and "longstanding." Jonathan Kozol (2012) detailed the inequities in two publications – *Salvaged Inequalities* and *Same on American Schools*. Guterman convened a "cross-disciplinary team of experts" to determine ways technology can play a role in improving equitable experiences for school children. The team developed five design principles to promote equity education driven by technology. The principles are to meet students where they are; "support students by providing relevant information," support students, as they are going through educational processes, who have complex challenges by helping them stay on track, be clear and concise because some students are navigating processes on their own, and design systems for collaboration.

Equally important for school leaders pertinent to budgeting from the operational side is the maintenance of accurate records and accounting procedures. The leadership style of budgeting practiced in the district will determine the role and the extent of the role that the building level principals as well as other stakeholders play in budgeting. There are five leadership styles of budgeting – planning-programming-budgeting (PPB), zero-based budgeting (ZBB), site-based budgeting (SBB), strategic planning

(SP), and total quality management (TQM). Regardless of the leadership style of budgeting in place, districts and schools should follow the budget calendar, and the budget should contain the necessary items. The two major components in the budget are the revenue (where the money comes from) and the expenditure (how the money is being spent). Most of the revenue is derived from taxes, and money is spent on both instructional and non-instructional costs! The accounting procedures are also very important due to internal and external auditing (Garfield et al., 2016).

Budgeting and finances are areas where technology software and tools have long been in use. Serving as a school leader in the late 1990s, tools such as QuickBooks were used in collaboration with Excel sheets. The following link has a list of budgeting and financial resources among others – https://www.capterra.com/school-administration-software/. We previously discussed applications of BoardDocs as a tool to improve interactions of school leaders as they work with school boards. Through Diligent (https://www.diligent.com), there is a School Board Financial Toolkit, which includes best budgeting practices; there are also Modern Risk and Modern Audit components. The audit component drives efficiency with internal auditing. The following are key benefits of using Diligent:

- Reduce costs by minimizing duplicate work, rationalizing low-risk or non-key controls, and harmonizing controls that comply with multiple regulations;
- Increase assurance by automating your manual and repetitive internal controls work;
- Engage process owners and the first line of defense to test controls and remediate issues in a single platform; and
- Share real-time updates on compliance issues, remediation tasks, and certification status.

(https://www.diligent.com)

Processes with internal auditors are also addressed by using Diligent. Using Diligent aids in simplifying, centralizing, and accelerating organizations. The following are the key benefits:

- Create a strong control environment improve your relationship with external auditors, and reduce your risk of penalties and fines;
- Integrate risk and control definitions, assessments, and testing to gain a better understanding of your SOX compliance efforts;
- Get up and running quicker and maintain consistency across your program with pre-configured SOX templates and frameworks; and
- Provide immediate insight into your SOX compliance status to executives and control owners with one-click reporting for better assurance and total peace of mind.

(https://www.diligent.com)

It is worth noting that there are commonalities in financial processes in higher education and K-12 schools. Leaders in both entities must be cautious regarding how purchases are made and the sources of funding used for purchases. In both entities, there are funds that are categorized as student allocation. Funds with such categorizations must only be used on things that fit/benefit students. In both entities, there are also pre-approval processes in which the funding must be justified or linked to an area of benefit for students (or for whatever their use). Purchases are generally included in the internal and external auditing processes.

Quicken is financial software that is web-based and has been around for years as an option for school leaders. However, there are currently many technological advances. Quicken is noted by *Top 5 Accounting Software* as one of the top three accounting software applications (which is dated February 2022). NetSuite and FreshBooks are two other applications that are frequently recommended. Most accounting software is similar in nature. The benefits are improved time management, increased professionalism, reduced human error, and instant tracking of finances. Time is saved by accounting software because estimates and invoices can be arranged in seconds, expenses and payments can be logged quickly, and repetitive tasks can be programmed for automatic completion. Professionalism is increased as invoices are customized, terms and conditions are added to invoice templates, and invoices can automatically occur for long-term customers. The accuracy of the record-keeping, automatically set tasks, and access to financial information in one place reduce human error. Finances are instantly tracked as all financial information is readily available (https://top-accounting software.com/?gclid=CjwKCAiAx8KQBhAGEiwAD3EiPxzNF64 A8PhVoG3sEe4KS7f4ICB0oaGrzh3r0aZci3a5THsW0vydtxoCb4 MQAvD_BwE).

Cloud accounting, automation, and collaborative accounting are the 2022 trends in software accounting. With cloud accounting, companies own the software subscription, and this is becoming the norm. Automation is also becoming the norm. There is no need for human intervention with automation. Collaborative accounting allows for globalization; individuals enter data in one location and the data is instantly integrated for individuals at other locations to use. The "must have" accounting software features are online payment processing, visually appealing reporting, dashboards, cloud-based access for multiple users, third-party integration, and expense management (https://top-accountingsoftware.com/?gclid=CjwKCAiAx8K QBhAGEiwAD3EiPxzNF64A8PhVoG3sEe4KS7f4ICB0oaGrzh3r0aZci3a 5THsW0vydtxoCb4MQAvD_BwE).

As noted on the Quicken website (https://quicken.com/), starter, deluxe, and premier packages are available. Quicken provides a consolidated view of finances, an account of where monies are allocated and spent; a dashboard for bill payments; and a monitoring system of all finances. Through the bill tracker, bills are readily available to make payments; inconsistent bills are more manageable; and bills can be paid online in one place. Quicken markets itself as a money management tool. It is connected to over 14,000 financial institutions; and desktops, mobile devices, or web applications can be used to view accounts and transactions. Transactions can be searched and tracked by amount, payee, or type. Illegitimate transactions can be rescinded. Receipts and invoices may also be stored in Quicken. Bill.com and www.domo.com are among the other web applications for managing funds.

There are many software packages and technological tools for assisting school leaders with financing and other roles. Capterra includes a buyer's guide of software packages at https://www.capterra.com/school -administration-software/#buyers-guide. According to the guide, the benefits of most software packages are that there is improved record-keeping, ease of accounting, and an improved platform for parental involvement. Eliminating paperwork and providing a central data repository accessible through mobile applications or on computers are the ways record-keeping is improved. The database serves as a general ledger which eases the accounting through recording automatically.

In Chapter 7, the importance of parental involvement is discussed pertinent to an aspect of external relationships for school leaders; however, one of the advantages of many software packages is that parents can often monitor information about their children and have access to teachers readily. We point this out as a feature in the Learning Management Systems discussed in Chapter 5 as well as in ParentLocker previously discussed in this chapter. Other technologies from the previously referenced link will be presented near the end of this chapter.

## RESOURCES AND SUPPLIES

*One-to-One Plus* is one of the software packages that can be used for resources and supplies as well as many other administrative and managerial tasks. Schools and districts have internal and external auditing processes in place around budgeting, finances, and other processes to ensure fidelity. To streamline and improve auditing processes, computer software such as One-to-One Plus can be used to ensure resources and supplies are purchased and accounted for appropriately. Brimley, Verstegen, and Garfield (2016) is one of the resources that address efficiency linked to the application of all processes of resources and supplies.

## MAINTENANCE OF FACILITIES

There are varying perspectives and resources on the importance of maintaining school facilities. Geiger (2002) provided a list of seven priorities school districts need to consider in developing a high-quality school maintenance program:

1. A commitment on the part of the board, the superintendent, and senior staff to facility maintenance.
2. Development of a comprehensive preventative maintenance program.
3. Adequate funding for both preventative maintenance and capital improvement.
4. A willingness to consider new ideas for the construction and maintenance of facilities.
5. A continual search for new and different ways to pay for maintenance and construction needs.
6. A careful review of district goals and policies to make sure facility management receives the appropriate levels of funding in the annual budget cycle.
7. A plan to link academic programs to facility needs.

There are several software technologies to assist with the maintenance of facilities. *Fiix* is one that addresses the management of facilities – https://www.fiixsoftware.com/cmms/industry-solutions/school-maintenance-software/.

The following are the features of Fiix software:

- Track, communicate, and control maintenance costs and activities.
- Simplify inspection rounds – check off tasks as you complete the inspections in real-time.
- Have your facilities and machines trigger work orders automatically.
- Build custom preventative maintenance work orders.
- Assign users to specific sites, facilities, and equipment.
- Organize and view machinery, systems, and facilities in an intuitive hierarchy.

Like many of the other technological tools, the applications of Fiix are available through mobile applications and computer applications. On the dashboard, the work orders and all pertinent information can be accessed. By selecting a work order, administrators can prioritize specific tasks and alert individuals regarding completing the task. Emails, text messages, and calls can be made to pertinent individuals https://www.fiixsoftware.com/cmms/industry-solutions/school-maintenance-software/. When the dashboard opens, it includes the scheduled compliance percentages, open and closed work orders along with the current online assets, overdue work orders, and work requests. Additional widgets can be added to the dashboard as deemed necessary. When selecting specific options, the specificity pertinent to the option is detailed. For instance, if the open work orders are selected, the details about each open work order are noted https://www.fiixsoftware.com/cmms/industry-solutions /school-maintenance-software/.

## TRANSPORTATION

There is currently a national shortage of school bus drivers, as cited by surveyed transportation coordinators. Furloughs of drivers due to COVID 19 and safety concerns of drivers linked to the lack of vaccines and vaccine administration among school-age children, along with the complexities of bus driver licensing procedures (including Department of Motor Vehicles office closures) are among the reasons for the challenge (Kamenetz, September 2021). The following weblink is a tool to assist with software management in transportation – https://www.capterra .com/school-bus-routing-software/. According to https://www.track-schoolbus.com/blog/managing-school-transport-effectively/, the critical elements to managing transportation effectively:

- Bus transportation must be convenient, time-saving, cost-effective, and fuel-efficient;
- Bus stations must be convenient and accessible for students;
- Bus timing must be managed;
- Fee slots must be viable and feasible;
- Routes must be allocated to staff and students;
- Student attendance must be managed;
- Safety of students must be ensured;
- Techniques must be in place to track groups;
- GPS devices must be integrated;
- Necessary reports must be generated; and
- Video surveillance must be enabled.

Like most departments in district and school offices, there are many regulations and safety protocols for transporting children. Safety is among the top priorities.

In the section **Budgets and Finances,** we mentioned Capterra as a buyer's guide of software packages at https://www.capterra.com/school -administration-software/#buyers-guide. There are over 717 products listed. We will list and briefly describe the products applicable for K-12 schools that made the "2022 shortlist" of products.

- Alma (developed by Alma SIS): Alma is a student information tool. Daily processes are included along with community-wide communication capabilities and state reporting features. It is marketed as a tool for optimizing school operations.

- Gradelink (developed by Gradelink): Gradelink is web-based, and staff may work from any location. Google Classroom, lesson planning, communication tools, and reporting are integrated into one system. The platform is user-friendly.
- Sawyer (developed by Sawyer): Sawyer is designed for schools with after-school programs, camps, and development classes. The program can be customized and includes "top-rated support teams."
- iGradePlus (developed by Corvus Education Systems): iGradePlus is a "user-friendly" school management system that is web-based. It features attendance and behavior tracking, custom report generation, student and parent communication features, and student, class, and grade management.
- PikMyKid (developed by PikMyKid): PikMyKid is a cloud-based product. Its features include dismissal automation, carline management, school bus tracking, parent messaging, and an emergency 'Panic Button' for school staff.
- EDficiency (developed by EDficiency): EDficiency is a web-based scheduling software for response to intervention and multi-tiered system supports. It automates daily rosters to increase teacher and student instructional time.
- MyStudentsProgress (developed by MyStudentsProgress): MyStudentsProgress is a student information management system. Critical school processes are integrated into a cloud-based platform.
- Sandbox ChildCare Management (developed by Sandbox Software): Sandbox ChildCare Management includes a comprehensive child care management system; but the software is also useful for camps, afterschool, and enrichment programs.
- SchoolCues (developed by SchoolCues): SchoolCues is a school management system for smaller schools. The features include communications, online admissions, and student information systems.
- Skyward Student Management Suite (developed by Skyward): Skyward Student Management Suite serves schools abroad and in the United States. Administration automation tools and communication tools are the features.
- LifeCubby (developed by LifeCubby): LifeCubby is used by child care centers but the management software has features applicable to before/after school programs.
- ClassReach (developed by DeyoGroup): ClassReach is a "one stop" product that meets the management needs at schools. Calendar/

announcement features are included. In addition, there is an integrated financial suite, and the forms are easy to create and use.

- Illumine (developed by Illumine Labs): Illumine is a management software for childcare centers; however, its features may be used in after-school and enrichment programs. The software allows for managing day-to-day activities such as attendance and the enhancement of parent-teacher communication.
- Classter (developed by Veritech): Classter is cloud-based and includes student information systems, student management systems, and learning management systems.

There are also school administration tools, which are "free and open source." Classter which is listed above is one of those tools. The other free and open source software listed by capterra.com are: feKara, Gibbon, OpenEduCat, and OpenSIS (Upadhyay, April 2021),

- FeKara (developed by FeKara): FeKara is available on the web and through mobile applications. System administrators or teachers can manage the app. It is a database system, which integrates third-party video conferencing.
- Gibbson (developed by Gibbson): Gibson is a school management system. It is cloud-based and includes a wide range of feature offerings – planners, attendance, behavior tracking, assessment capabilities, library management, and gradebooks for teachers and students. Additional features can be added.
- OpenSIS (developed by OpenSIS): OpenSIS is a school management and student information software. Calendar management applications are embedded, and online schooling can be facilitated by integrating video conferencing and calendar management.

Upadhyay (2021, April) provides guidelines to school leaders on selecting the "right school administration software." Capterra also has a school administration software catalog. In Chapter 1, we also referenced EdSurge Product Index (which is an index for technology users to search and compare products. Upadhyay suggests the following approach:

- Compare the user limit. Seek tools that provide the greatest number of users in the free edition.
- Review which features are free.
- Review the customization options in the free edition.
- Compare support and training services that are offered with the free edition.

Upadhyay (2021, April) also noted common questions for school leaders to ask in the selection of free school management software; they include:

- Is free software customization offered?
- What is the quality of the technical support?
- Are there integration capabilities offered by the product?
- What access and deployment options are available?

---

**SCENARIO 1: A SCHOOL-LEVEL CHALLENGE
ON IMPROVING NEGATIVITY**

Laurel Valley School District serves 5,000 students and is in a rural part of the country. According to a 2010 census, the population of the district is approximately 23,000. The district was established in the early 1800s with the first settlers being French and Spanish. Sugar cane is the major industry in the area. There are over 200,000 acres in the district with over 21,000 of the acres being water. The school district is the major employment entity and most households are impacted by the district through the employment of family or enrollment of students in schools. Members of the leadership team and school board members of the district have a long-standing culture of attempting to serve the needs of the students with efforts to build relationships within the community. When there are challenges or conflicts parents tend to discuss school-related issues with board members and the central office level personnel prior to school-based employees.

Laurel Valley Schools was one of the last districts in the southern states of the United States to integrate. *Brown vs Topeka Board of Education* was decided in 1954 (Delinder, 2004). It was ruled that "racial segregation in public schools violated the equal protection clause of the Fourteenth Amendment, effectively overturning the 1896 *Plessy* v. *Ferguson* decision mandating 'separate but equal'." According to Delinder (2004,) five court cases involving school desegregation were heard in the Supreme Court. The cases were: 1949: *Briggs et al.* v. *Elliott et al.* (South Carolina); 1950: *Bolling* v. *Sharpe* (District of Columbia); May 1951: *Davis et al.* v. *County School Board of Prince Edward County, Virginia, et al.* (Virginia); June 1951: *Brown* v. *Board of Education of Topeka* (Kansas); October 1951: *Gebhart et al.* v. *Belton et al.* (Delaware).

Before the *Brown* ruling, segregated school districts maintained two-school systems within a district. It was documented in all of the previously cited cases that there was inadequate funding in the black schools. Segregated schools were impacted in 21 States. In 1954, there were 17 States with segregated schools required by law – Texas, Oklahoma, Missouri, Arkansas, Louisiana, Mississippi, Alabama, South Carolina, Georgia, Florida, North Carolina, Tennessee, Kentucky, Virginia, West Virginia, Maryland, and Delaware. In four other states, the laws permitted segregated schools (not required) – Kansas, Arizona, New Mexico, and Wyoming. The first integrated high school graduation occurred in Laurel Valley Schools in 1974. Over 30 years ago, a group of parents began meeting to develop a plan to end the segregated proms. Two years after the parent group was formed the school held its first integrated prom. Several racial dilemmas in the Laurel Valley Schools have sparked state-wide attention.

Like other districts in the state, there are measures in place to address the culture of the district as a whole and the individual cultures of schools. Several of the schools are using more technology tools to increase efficiency in the schools and improve communication with staff, parents, and stakeholders. The heightened accountability measures in the state force school leaders and teachers to be more conscientious of student performance, attendance, and disciplinary infractions. Laurel Valley Middle is one of the schools utilizing several technology tools, and it is one of the higher-performing middle schools in the district. The school leader is in her second year and appears to be very personable with staff and parents.

One of the parents, who has a history of being conscientious about the academic performance of her child, is suggesting to the superintendent that there are challenges with the messaging that comes from the automatic messages sent to parents. She suggests that too many of the messages have negative overtones. The parent also suggests that information from the school has been limited. What are the challenges for the school leader? Which technology tools when used appropriately can help to alleviate such challenges?

## SCENARIO 2: A SCHOOL-LEVEL CHALLENGE ON PARENTAL INVOLVEMENT

Jones Creek Elementary is located in a rural area in Louisiana and houses grades Pre-K to 4th Grade. Due to COVID 19, the accountability rating is not current. The score was a B prior to COVID 19.

Jones Creek has 500 students with 70% of the school's population categorized as a minority. The school community of Jones Creek has had challenges as the community has been divided on school board issues linked primarily to funding. Overall, parents are very involved in all aspects of the school.

The principal of Jones Creek is Dr. Hampton. Dr. Hampton is a 30 year veteran of education and has been a school leader for 10 years. He engages in professional development regularly and attended one of Dr. Epstein's professional development conferences on parental involvement. Keany (2019, Oct) highlighted Dr. Epstein's work on the effects of family and community involvement on student achievement. Dr. Epstein has six kinds of parental involvement. Kearny noted Epstein's parental involvement types:

- Parenting: Support the home environment and strengthen families so as to support students at school.
- Communicating: Create effective modes of school-to-home and home-to-school communications regarding school programs and child progress.
- Volunteering: Recruit parents to support school endeavors.
- Learning at Home: Share information regarding ideas for learning at home, as well as what is going on in the classroom to support family–school alignment regarding educational endeavors.
- Decision-Making: Empower parents to be leaders, and involve them in school decision-making.
- Collaborating with Community: Identify and integrate resources and services from the community to strengthen school programs, family practices, and student learning and development.

Jones Creek Elementary includes parents in parenting, communicating, volunteering, learning at home, decision-making, and collaborating with the community initiatives. Although parental involvement is high and the school had a score of B prior to COVID 19, the relationship between the school and the school community became questionable during COVD 19 as challenges developed over attendance. Some teachers marked students as present for the entire week if they attended two of the three mandatory in-person days, and others did not. Teachers felt that there was no clear direction from Dr. Hampton, and information was not communicated to teachers or parents.

In addressing the challenges, Dr. Hampton felt that the culture was in question. Teacher morale appeared to be impacted, and there was concern in the community regarding the inconsistencies pertinent to the attendance policy and how attendance was recorded in the electronic system. As the students returned in January 2021 to a five-day schedule, parents began bombarding Dr. Hampton with requests to meet. Dr. Hampton could not fulfill all of the requests. A group of parents organized a group and referred to themselves as *Parents on the Move*. The group held a virtual meeting with no representation from Jones Creek Elementary for three weeks. What are the major challenges for Dr. Hampton? Are there technology tools which can be used to assist Dr. Hampton?

## SUMMARY

The roles and responsibilities of principals have become more and more complex. In Chapter 1, the roles of school leaders are presented from a standards-based approach. We begin Chapter 2 with a discussion of the interrelationship of the instructional and managerial roles. In Chapter 5, the importance of the instructional leadership role of principals is reviewed with the technologies to support leaders as instructional leaders. In this Chapter, the managerial tasks of leaders are discussed including technologies to support the managerial role of leaders. ParentLocker and BoardDocs are among the tools discussed to assist school leaders with communication and school-board specific tasks. A reference is made to the Chapter 1 section, **Technology and the Work of the School Principal** as the social media outlets are described as forms of communication.

DeansList is presented as a tool to assist school leaders with scheduling, monitoring attendance, and enrollment management. The advantages of accounting software systems along with the "must have" features are discussed. The most pertinent of the *Top 5 Accounting Software* are cited; they are Quicken, NetSuite, and FreshBooks. The accounting software discussion is included in the section on **Budgets and Finances**. Several tools are noted to assist school leaders with managing resources and supplies, maintenance of facilities, and transportation. Prior to the scenarios in this chapter, a listing of tools is provided from https://www.capterra.com/school-administration-software/#buyers-guide. The guide has over 717 tools; we list and provide a brief overview of the tools cited as "top performers." The developers of the tools are included along with primary applications of the tools. The advantages of the technology tools are included in the discussion throughout Chapter 2.

---

**TECHNOLOGY TOOLS**

Alma: https://getalma.com/?utm_campaign=sa&utm_source=capterra
BoardDocs: https://www.boarddocs.com
Capterra: https://www.capterra.com/school-bus-routing-software/
Classter: https://www.claster.com
DeansList: https://www.deanslistsoftware.com/features
EDficiency: https://www.edficiency.com
Fiix: https://www.fiixsoftware.com/cmms/industry-solutions/school-maintenance-software/
Gradelink: https://www.gradelink.com/capterar/?utm_sourcecaptera=capterra
iGradePlus: https://www.igradeplus.com
Illumine: https://www.illumine.app
LifeCubby: https://www.lifecubby.com
MyStudentsProgress: https://www.MyStudentsProgress.com
ParentLocker: https://www.parentlocker.com/
PikMyKid: https://www.pikmykid.com/
Sawyer: https://hiswayer.com
SchoolCues: https://www.schoolcues.com
Skyward Student Management Suite: https://www.skyward.com

---

**REFERENCES**
BOARDDOCS. https://www.boarddocs.com.
Captera. (2019). School administrative software. https://www.capterra.com/sem-compare/school-administration-software?gclid=EAIaIQobChMI8qj8xubr4QIVma_ICh1AmAstEAAYAyAAEgLDkPD_BwE.
Classter. https://www.claster.com.
Deanslist. https://www.deanslistsoftware.com/features.
Delack, M. (2022, January). 4 social media platforms your district should be using in 2022. https://www.finalsite.com/blog/p/~board/b/post/top-social-media-platforms-for-districts.
Delinder, J. V. (2004, Spring). Brown v. Board of education of Topeka. *Prologue Magazine*, 36(1). Retrieved from https://www.archives.gov/publications/prologue/2004/spring/brown-v-board-1.html.
EDficiency. https://www.edficiency.com.
Elementary and Secondary Education Act. (1965). https://www2.ed.gov/documents/essa-act-of-1965.pdf.

Every Student Succeed Act (ESSA). (2015). https://www.everystudentsucceedsact.org/.

Fiixsoftware. https://www.fiixsoftware.com/?ads_cmpid=986797149&ads_adid=455
94361661&ads_matchtype=p&ads_network=g&ads_creative=615917217512&u
tm_term=fiix&ads_targetid=kwd-301799839366&utm_campaign=US%7CGS
N%7CB%7CREG%7CS4%7C-brand&utm_source=google&utm_medium=cp
c&ttv=2&utm_mcamp&gclid=EAIaIQobChMI-rat1NGH-gIVTnxvBB0KmQ04
EAAYASAAEgIdsvD_BwE.

Garfield, R., Verstegen, D., & Brimley, V. (2016). *Financing education in a climate of change* (12th ed.). Pearson Education Company.

Garfield, R., Verstegen, D., & Brimley, V. (2019). *Financing education in a climate of change* (10th ed.). Pearson Education Company.

Geiger, P. E. (2002). Deferred school maintenance creates national crisis. *School Business Affairs*, 68(1), 43.

Gradelink. https://www.gradelink.com/capterar/?utm_sourcecaptera=capterra.

Gutterman, A. (2021, June). 5 tech design principles to promote equity in education. https://www.salesforce.org/blog/tech-design-principles-equity-in-education/.

iGradePlus. https://www.igradeplus.com.

Illumine. https://www.illumine.app.

International Society of Technology of Education. https://www.iste.org/standards/for-education-leaders.

Jones, L. (2017). *The relevance of the leadership standards: a new order of business for principals.* Rowman & Littlefield Publishing Group.

Jones, L., & Kennedy, E. (2015). *A guide to data-driven leadership in modern schools.* Information Age Publishing.

Kamenetz, A. (2021, September 21). National survey finds serve and desperate school bus driver shortage. *NPR.* https://www.npr.org/sections/back-to-school-live-updates/2021/09/01/1032953269/national-survey-finds-severe-and-desperate-school-bus-driver-shortage.

Keany, M. (2019, October). Framework on six types of parent involvement. *School Leadership.* https://schoolleadership20.com/m/discussion?id=1990010%3ATopic%3A333993.

Kennedy, E. (2003). *Raising test scores for all students: an administrator's guide to improving standards tests performance.* Corwin Press.

Kozol, J. (2012). *Salvaged inequalities: Children in America's schools.* Crown Publishers LifeCubby. https://www.lifecubby.com.

MyStudentsProgress.com. https://www.MyStudentsProgress.com

National Educational Leadership Preparation (NELP) Standards. https://www.naesp.org/communicator-november-2018/nelp-standards-approved-how-affects-you.

National Policy Board for Educational Administration. (2015). Professional Standards for Educational Leaders 2015. Author. Retrieved from **http://www.npbea.org/**.

No Child Left Behind. (2001). https://www.everystudentsucceedsact.org/.

Ogle, T. (2002). *Technology in schools: Suggestions, tools, and guidelines for assessing technology in elementary and secondary education.* National Center for Education Statistics.

ParentLocker. http://www.parentlocker.com.

PikMyKid. https://www.pikmykid.com/.

Professional Standards for Educational Leadership (PSEL) Standards. http://www.npbea.org/.

Sawyer. https://hiswayer.com.

SchoolCues. https://www.schoolcues.com.

Shkurina, E. (2018, November). List of 10 best school management software solutions. https://blog.youragora.com/list-of-8-best-school-management -software.

Skyward Student Management Suite. https://www.skyward.com.

TOP 5 ACCOUNTING SOFTWARE. https://top-accountingsoftware.com/?gclid =CjwKCAiAx8KQBhAGEiwAD3EiPxzNF64A8PhVoG3sEe4KS7f4ICB0oaG rzh3r0aZci3a5THsW0vydtxoCb4MQAvD_BwE.

Upadhyay, A. (2021, April 28). 5 free and open source school administration software. https://blog.capterra.com/top-free-school-administration-software/.

Weiss, C. H. (1995). The four I's of school reform: How interests, ideology, information, and instruction affect teachers and principals. *Harvard Education Review, 65,* 571–592.

# CHAPTER 3

## Personnel and Evaluation

**ABSTRACT**

It is becoming more and more challenging to staff schools. Certain teaching positions (such as teachers for Mathematics and Special Education) have historically been difficult to fill while other areas are becoming more difficult to staff, including bus drivers and other support staff. The U.S. Department of Education maintains has a database of teacher shortage areas, aggregated by state and content area at https://tsa.ed.gov/#/reports. We begin Chapter 3 with a discussion of the Leadership and Technology Standards linked to School Personnel and Evaluation Concepts. We discuss general concepts of Human Resource Management followed by processes and procedures for Hiring Non-Instructional and Instructional Personnel. It is important for school leaders to follow protocols in hiring processes. We include guidelines for the hiring process for school leaders applicable to school law from the Civil Rights Acts and American Disabilities Act. Included in the section on Hiring Non-Instructional and Instructional Personnel are strategies to retain teachers. Evaluating Instructional and Non-Instructional Personnel is discussed, and the range of technological tools available to support school leaders with personnel and evaluation areas are included. Two case scenarios are included at the end of the chapter.

## SCHOOL PERSONNEL AND EVALUATION CONCEPTS LINKED TO THE LEADERSHIP STANDARDS

In Chapters 2 and 5, managerial/administrative and instructional roles of leaders are discussed respectively. The interrelationship of

DOI: 10.4324/9781003269472-3

the roles is also noted. In this chapter, we point out that leadership, with respect to school personnel, entails both managerial/administrative skills as well as competencies, with respect to instruction. This is reflected in various standards for school leaders. For example, PSEL Standards 6 and 7 and Standard 7 of NELP specifically include tenets for School Personnel. As cited in Chapter 1; PSEL 6 includes: "Effective educational leaders develop the professional capacity and practice of school personnel to promote each student's academic success and well-being." PSEL 7 includes: "Effective educational leaders fostering a professional community of teachers and other professional staff to promote each student's academic success and well-being."

The competencies in PSEL 6 are:

Effective leaders:

a) Recruit, hire, support, develop, and retain effective and caring teachers and other professional staff and form them into an educationally effective faculty.

b) Plan for and manage staff turnover and succession, providing opportunities for effective induction and mentoring of new personnel.

c) Develop teachers' and staff members' professional knowledge, skills, and practice through differentiated opportunities for learning and growth, guided by an understanding of professional and adult learning and development.

d) Foster continuous improvement of individual and collective instructional capacity to achieve outcomes envisioned for each student.

e) Deliver actionable feedback about instruction and other professional practices through valid, research-anchored systems of supervision and evaluation to support the development of teachers' and staff members' knowledge, skills, and practice.

f) Empower and motivate teachers and staff to the highest levels of professional practice and to continuous learning and improvement.

g) Develop the capacity, opportunities, and support for teacher leadership and leadership from other members of the school community.

h) Promote the personal and professional health, well-being, and work-life balance of faculty and staff.

i) Tend to their own learning and effectiveness through reflection, study, and improvement, maintaining a healthy work-life balance.

(http://www.npbea.org/)

The competencies included in PSEL 7 are:

Effective leaders:

a) Develop workplace conditions for teachers and other professional staff that promote effective professional development, practice, and student learning.
b) Empower and entrust teachers and staff with collective responsibility for meeting the academic, social, emotional, and physical needs of each student, pursuant to the mission, vision, and core values of the school.
c) Establish and sustain a professional culture of engagement and commitment to shared vision, goals, and objectives pertaining to the education of the whole child; high expectations for professional work; ethical and equitable practice; trust and open communication; collaboration, collective efficacy, and continuous individual and organizational learning and improvement.
d) Promote mutual accountability among teachers and other professional staff for each student's success and the effectiveness of the school as a whole.
e) Develop and support open, productive, caring, and trusting working relationships among leaders, faculty, and staff to promote professional capacity and the improvement of practice.
f) Design and implement job-embedded and other opportunities for professional learning collaboratively with faculty and staff.
g) Provide opportunities for collaborative examination of practice, collegial feedback, and collective learning.
h) Encourage faculty-initiated improvement of programs and practices.

(http://www.npbea.org/)

The ISTE Standard that has a component pertinent to the evaluation of personnel is the Vision Planner Standard. The core of the

Visionary Planner Standard is to establish a vision, strategic plan, and ongoing evaluation cycle for transforming learning and technology. The first competency is:

- Engage education stakeholders in developing and adopting a shared vision for using technology to improve student success, informed by the learning sciences.
(https://www.iste.org/standards/for-education-leaders)

## HUMAN RESOURCE MANAGEMENT

There are primarily two positions that govern the managerial operations in organizations. One of those perspectives is the bureaucratic perspective. An organization that functions as a bureaucracy uses hierarchical control, for example, subordinates report to a direct supervisor. A school district is highly bureaucratic when there is a "straight line–order chain of command!" Each employee follows the chain of command. For instance, if a teacher is having a problem, she reports to the assistant principal. If the assistant principal cannot solve the problem, the teacher reports to the principal. The problem is then reported to the principal's supervisor – ultimately to the superintendent. A bureaucratic organization follows and enforces written rules and procedures thoroughly.

The other perspective for managerial operations in a work environment is the human resources development perspective. An organization that functions using this perspective is characterized by a staff focus with collaboration and participation from employees. A school that embraces this perspective empowers teachers, parents, and other staff members to have input into decisions. The administration enforces the rules allowing for flexibility when necessary. The human resource perspective is also characterized by group values and beliefs. Theories of motivation regarding human behavior are also important to organizations. Leaders must understand principles of motivation and how the principles impact the work of employees in organizations. There are six theories of human behavior related to motivation discussed by Hoy and Miskel (2013) – Maslow's Hierarchy of Needs, Hertzberg's Hygiene-Motivator Theory, Goal-Setting Theory, Attribution Theory, Equity Theory, and Intrinsic and Extrinsic Motivation Theory.

Maslow's Hierarchy of Needs focuses on levels of satisfaction necessary in an organization for workers to attain maximum performance. Before an employee can gain maximum attainment in an organization, workers need to feel safe, secure, and have a sense of belonging in addition to other values pertinent to motivation. Hertzberg's theory focuses on concern for people as compared to concern for production – suggesting that individuals are motivated by this concern exemplified by the employer. According to Lunenburg and Ornstein (2000), Goal-Setting Theory suggests that values, emotions, and desires influence goals. As goals evolve, they affect behavior – directing the attention and actions of individuals. Goals motivate the development of strategies that will be helpful to perform. The Attribution Theory is a goal-oriented theory as well. The Equity Theory, inherent in the work of Porter–Lawler, emphasizes the need for equitable treatment in the workplace. Individuals are motivated by the belief that there is fairness in the work environment. Intrinsic and Extrinsic Motivation Theory differentiates between the sources of motivation of individuals. Theorists who embrace the notion that individuals are motivated by internal beliefs, values, and morals embody internal motivation. Individuals who are internally motivated perform in work environments based on their value systems. In contrast, extrinsic motivation suggests that individuals are motivated by rewards – money, certificates, etc. This perspective proposes that individuals must be provided with rewards to be motivated in the work environment.

Because motivation impacts performance, motivation is directly linked to the human resource approach to management. Evaluation tools and analytics reporting have direct implications for human resource management. We mention throughout the book that using technology tools is a way to assist school leaders to work more efficiently; however, the use of the tools does not replace the necessary knowledge, skills, and dispositions needed for leadership. There are specific functions for school leaders (linked to the importance of staffing schools and central offices) that must include strategies to recruit, select, and retain highly qualified employees. Other important functions for human resources include:

- Assisting in the planning for needed personnel,
- Developing job descriptions for each position within the district,
- Assisting in the planning for needed personnel,
- Developing job descriptions for each position within the district,
- Recruiting of certified and classified personnel,
- Selecting of certified and classified personnel,
- Providing an induction program for new personnel,
- Assisting with the appraisal/evaluation process,
- Working closely with the business department regarding compensation,
- Ensuring due process for all personnel,
- Assisting with a plan to retain personnel, and
- Providing information to personnel and other departments (Seyfarth, 2008).

From the human resources tasks of school leaders listed above, we focus on the hiring aspect of the human resources function (which touches on planning for needs; having job descriptions; selecting; retaining through induction, staff development, and mentoring; and evaluating personnel.)

## HIRING OF NON-INSTRUCTIONAL AND INSTRUCTIONAL PERSONNEL

Seyfarth (2008) notes in *Human Resource Management for Effective Schools, Fifth Edition*, that there is a need for leaders to plan for the staffing needs of schools; prepare for personnel selection; obtain information and evaluate applicants; and select the pertinent personnel. In planning for staffing needs, Seyfarth (2008) suggests strategic planning which begins with the school leaders and members of the strategic planning team beginning with the vision (accounting for and re-assessing) and engaging in needs assessment to determine what the critical needs of the schools are. Priorities must be established for staffing based on strategic planning and needs assessments. Additional data points such as enrollment projections must be considered as well. The extensiveness and level to which school leaders and strategic planning committees collect information and engage in hiring practices depend on the nature of the position – instructional or non-instructional.

Most school districts use websites for a portion of the recruiting that leads to the hiring of employees. Google Documents, Talent.com, SchoolSprings, TopSchools.com, the Frog Jobs, K12JobSpot, and the actual websites of the school districts are among the resources for advertising/recruiting and application processes for employees. In Chapter 1: **Technology and the Work of the School Principal**, social media platforms are presented – Facebook, Twitter, Instagram, and LinkedIn. These platforms are another manner for school leaders and districts to advertise and recruit. Schools have traditionally recruited through paper and print news outlets. Journals and newspapers are now available online. We noted the staffing shortages at the beginning of Chapter 3 which makes recruiting critical in this era.

The job description is needed to begin the advertising. Most jobs require advertisements for designated periods of time as noted in school district policies manuals. It is important to note that advertising and recruiting are critical to the selection process. The nature and depth of information submitted for jobs depend on the roles – instructional or non-instructional. Due to liability issues linked to the selection of personnel, it is vital to have policies and procedures in place. Potential employees cannot be discriminated against on the basis of race, gender, disability, or any variable when applicants are qualified for the position. Essex (2015) notes the constitutional, federal, and state statutes prohibit discriminatory practices in hiring on the basis of race, sex, age, color, or religion. Much of the legislation was enacted during the 1960s and 1970s.

The *Civil Rights Act of 1964* is "one of the most extensive federal employment laws." It has two parts – (1) it is an unlawful practice for an employer to: deny hiring individuals on the basis of race, religion, sex, or national origin; (2) it is an unlawful employment practice for an employment agency to fail or refuse to refer individuals on the basis of race, religion, sex, or national origin. An additional federal employment law with intensity is the Americans with Disabilities Act. The intent of the Americans with Disabilities Act is to provide equal access to employment opportunities for individuals with disabilities. Individuals with disabilities cannot be denied employment, training, compensation, promotion, fringe benefits, and terms and conditions for employment on the basis of disabilities. Essex (2015) notes these principles regarding the ADA that are applicable to schools:

- When there are 15 or more employees, discrimination is prohibited by ADA,
- Non-discriminatory policies should be developed by school districts,
- Individuals with disabilities should not be segrateged or limited in job opportunities,
- Standards with discriminatory effects should not be promoted,
- Reasonable accommodations should be provided for disabled individuals,
- The skills of disabled individuals should be identified in comparison to the impairments,
- Appropriate measures should be taken to protect the confidentiality of medical records of disabled individuals, and
- Compensatory and punitive damages may be assessed for deliberate discriminatory acts against disabled individuals.

Essex (2015) also provides practical tips centered on preventing discrimination in hiring practices in other areas (in addition to disabilities) which may be very helpful for school leaders. The following are the tips:

- The impact of federal and state statutes on hiring should be clearly understood,
- The burden of proof of discrimination falls on the teacher,
- Principals may not use pregnancy against female teachers,
- Correctable disabilities such as impaired vision, hypertension, etc. are not covered under the Americans with Disabilities Act,
- Schools must not show a preference for one religion over another,

- Sexual harassment is a form of discrimination,
- Sexual harassment must be reported to the district level,
- Students must be informed of behaviors and policies regarding sexual harassment,
- School leaders must participate when necessitated in discriminatory investigations, and
- Discriminatory behaviors must be documented and forwarded to the appropriate individuals.

Most districts will apply for initial screenings to make certain that applicants are qualified. For instance, if an applicant is applying for a Secondary Mathematics position, human resource officers will check the certification and licensure requirements along with the degree requirements. In many schools, employee applications are submitted through online portals. After reviewing the website of several school districts, most of them require users to create a user name and password to log into a portal. In addition, applicants must not have criminal records. Background checks may also be completed online using https://www.safehiringsolutions.com/safeschool-solutionslike or similar applications. Safe school solutions provide several services for maintaining safety and security in schools, and global background checks are available. In some instances, individuals who are listed as references are notified, and checklist-type assessments are completed online. There are various software solutions available for reference checks; however, Reflynk is noted as innovative and comprehensive (https://www.safehiringsolutions.com/safeschool-solutions).

If applicants are satisfactory for the initial screening, they will progress to the interview. The applicants must submit applications, transcripts, references, tests, and pertinent information. School leaders and school strategic planning teams must select the applicant that best fits the position – the individual who aligns with the vision of the school. Many districts are embracing the site-based management philosophy and participatory decision-making styles. Interview teams may include the administration of the school, lead teachers, parents, and other pertinent stakeholders (possibly students). The Pre-Employment Inquiry Guide has possible interview questions (Seyfarth, 2008). There are a number of resources available to select interview questions. School leaders can draw on their own experiences in developing questions, the experiences of other teachers, and conduct web searches for ideas for questions.

In this era of COVID 19, interviewing that was traditionally done in person is often done through Zoom, Google Meet, or other electronic platforms. The electronic submissions do not negate that principals and human resource directors must follow appropriate policies and regulations pertinent to hiring. Applicants must possess the appropriate credentials; applicants must be submitted timely; and applications must also be complete. The additional layer is the selectivity of the most appropriate candidate.

FreshSchools, ParentLocker, and BoardDocs are among the tools that can be used to store employee data electronically (which were introduced in Chapter 2). Google Drive, at http://www.drive.google.com, is another option that can be used for storing employee data. Google Drive is located at google.com, and individuals have access to Drive after establishing a Gmail email account. With the Gmail creation, a drive can be accessed by selecting the nine dots (next to the Gmail and images at the top right-hand corner of the webpage). Drive is one of the options that can be selected. Some of the other options are account, search, maps, YouTube, Gmail, and calendar.

Folders are created in Google Drive by selecting the new option (marked with a plus sign) on the left-hand column. There is the option to add a new folder, upload a file, upload a folder, create a Google document, sheet, slide, form, or other Google options. There is also the feature that allows for folders and/or individual documents to be shared with an individual or multiple individuals. Simply right-click on any folder or document, share with is one of the options. An email address or multiple addresses can be added to share documents/folders. Microsoft Outlook has an application called SharePoint which is very similar to Google Drive. Private groups can be created to share documents among the participants. There is also an option to create notebooks and hold conversations among the group within SharePoint. Another application available through Microsoft Office is OneDrive. Files can be uploaded and organized in OneDrive like Google Drive and SharePoint and shared with other participants as well. Users of Google Drive, SharePoint, and OneDrive may search for files on the respective platforms.

DocuSign at http://www.godocusign.com is an electronic tool that may be used by personnel in hiring, assessing/evaluating, and managing workloads and assignments for both instructional personnel as well as non-instructional personnel. As noted at http://www.godocusign.com, DocuSign allows documents to be signed from anywhere, from any device, and the documents are as secure as paper. The process is three steps for the individuals sending documents to be signed. For Step 1, upload the document (which can be a Word, PDF, or another popular file type from a computer or any file-sharing site.) For Step 2, the email address of the recipients and signers is added. Step 3 is to drag and drop the DocuSign fields where the signature, initial, and/or date are needed. The document is ready to send. The recipients will receive an email link to access the document. Once completed, the document is easily retrieved and stored securely.

Adobe Acrobat (http://www.acrobat.com) is another tool that is available for electronic signing. One feature of Acrobat is users are allowed to convert PDFs to Word and work across different file types. To sign a file in Acrobat, the file should be opened in the Adobe Acrobat software. Once the file is open, the user must select certificates from the tools option (along the top toolbar in Adobe Acrobat). On the certificates screen, there is the option to digitally sign. The user will be prompted to scroll the mouse over the area needed for the signature. The user will be prompted to continue with one of the following options: use a signature creation device, use a Digital ID from a file, or create a new Digital ID. Once the selection is made, the document is stored with the selection. In the Chapter 2 section **Technological Tools Applicable to Many Administrative Tasks: Communication and Board Specific Technologies**, we include in the discussion about BoardDocs that one of the features of BoardDocs is electronic signing.

We previously mentioned that Acrobat has a feature in which users can work across file types. There are other useful features that may be very helpful for school leaders pertinent to managing personnel and other tasks. According to https://icts.uct.ac.za/acrobat-pro-dc-features, The most useful features of Acrobat are:

- Combine multiple files (of different types, e.g., images, Word documents, or other PDFs) into a single PDF.
- Extract sections of a PDF for separate use or insert files or pages into a pre-existing PDF.
- Split a PDF into separate chapters/files for easier distribution and reading.
- Create portfolios of multiple files (even using differing file types such as images, videos, and documents) for a stunning presentation.

## File Type Conversion:

- Convert webpages to interactive PDFs, complete with links.
- Turn PDFs into editable Microsoft Word, Excel, or PowerPoint files or image files (JPEG, TIFF, or PNG formats) with improved accuracy.
- Convert scanned paper documents into searchable PDFs and fillable forms with selectable and editable text.

## Sharing and Mobile Devices:

- Create interactive forms which can be distributed and collected by the application.

- Work on touch-enabled devices and store and share files online.
- Fill in, sign, and send forms from your computer or mobile device in a flash.

## Editing:

- Edit photos in your documents and move the text and images around in your PDF to optimize flow.

In this era of accountability, retaining highly qualified teachers is critical. We mentioned shortages in the abstract/introduction to this chapter as well as in this section. The shortages are prevalent for teachers and other school staff. Because of the shortages, this makes it extremely important to retain teachers as well as other staff members. There have been alarming statistics released by the State Departments of Education and National Teacher Organizations on teacher retention. One district in Louisiana improved its retention of teachers by 50% through the use of a structured induction program developed by Annette Breaux. Seyfarth (2008) defines induction as "an organized process to assist personnel in adjusting to the new position, and it is a process that helps create a sense of belonging." Some view induction as a focused professional development opportunity for teachers. There are many types of induction programs including district-wide, school-based, consortium programs, and university-district collaboration programs. Some of the concepts discussed relative to professional development/staff development and induction are applicable to teachers and other school personnel but the primary focus in Chapter 3 is on teacher retention.

Castetter and Young (2004) suggest that necessary components of induction programs include:

a) Sending a letter of welcome to the new employee,
b) Providing information regarding benefits,
c) Providing a tour of the facility,
d) Providing a tour of the community,
e) Introducing new employees to appropriate personnel,
f) Assigning a buddy or mentor to the new employee,
g) Setting up a personal meeting,
h) Explaining the appraisal/evaluation process,
i) Designing an orientation to acquaint the new employee with the policies and procedures, resources, and pertinent forms, such as forms for field trips, requisitions, etc.,
j) Providing copies of both teacher and student handbooks,

k)  Providing information regarding central administration responsibilities, and

l)  Developing a procedure or form to evaluate the induction program.

There are many variations of induction programs throughout the literature; however, most teachers will agree (after reflecting on their early experiences as teachers) that it is very important to have a mentor who can answer questions, provide advice, and share strategies. One of the roles of the principal as an instructional leader is to "build teacher leaders" who can provide assistance and support to beginning teachers and teachers needing assistance. Pawlas and Olivia (2007) suggest that all teachers need staff development. Teachers should be provided opportunities to engage in life-learning opportunities that can be utilized in the classroom and shared with colleagues. According to Seyfarth (2008), effective components of staff development include: determining the needs of the personnel, designing and implementing the programs, and evaluating the effectiveness of the program.

The staff/professional development implemented in a school should be based on the needs of the staff; teachers should also have autonomy as it relates to the staff development activities pertinent for participation. One mistake that school districts make is a lack of staff development opportunities for paraprofessionals and other support staff members who must assist with the implementation of instruction and other programs. As staff development is designed and implemented, district and school-based administrators should consider:

• Why is the program needed?
• What is to be learned?
• How will it be delivered?
• Where should it be held?
• Who should attend? Mandatory or voluntary?
• Who can provide the service?
• What cost is involved Seyfarth (2008)?

Another specific kind of professional development that helps teachers focus on student learning is professional learning communities. The following is an excerpt from Jones and colleagues (2013, May) on professional learning communities:

*There are obvious challenges to developing and sustaining professional learning communities. According to Fullan (2009) in his observations of schools, many educators suggest their schools have professional learning communities, and the cultures in the schools are not reflective of sharing and other essential attributes. Collaboration and collegiality are obviously necessary attributes of learning communities.*

*It is more important for concepts like professional learning teams to be applied in schools rather than simply using the verbiage. Unfortunately, conceptualization and thinking do not travel as rapidly as the verbiage in most school settings. Dufour and Colleagues (2006) suggest in the second edition of the Learning by Doing: A Handbook for Professional Learning Communities at Work that the terms – professional learning communities- have been used too loosely recently to describe any "loose coupling of individuals who share a common interest in education."*

*The concept of professional learning communities initiated in business. The verbiage "learning organization" was first used by Senge in 1990 for the purposes of businesses. The educational context was translated by Sergiovanni in 1994 from Senge's work. It was not until 1997 that Shirley Hord used the terms – professional learning communities in her work with the Southern Educational Research Laboratories (SEDL). The following are the five descriptors of Professional Learning Communities suggested by Hord:*

- *Supportive and shared leadership;*
- *Shared values and vision;*
- *Collective learning and application;*
- *Shared personal practice; and*
- *Supportive conditions.*

*Hipp and Huffman (2010) elaborated on Hord's perspective of professional learning communities and defined each of the previously cited components. Since 1990, multiple perspectives of learning communities have been presented. The assertions made by Dufour and Colleagues (2006) about characteristics of learning communities are emphasized in the perspective of Blankstien. Blankstien (2010) suggests that there are six principles essential in schools with Professional Learning Communities –*

- *Principle 1 – Common mission, vision, values, and goals;*
- *Principle 2 – Ensuring achievement for all students;*
- *Principle 3 – Collaborative teaming focused on teaching and learning;*
- *Principle 4 – Using data to guide decision making and continuous improvement;*

- *Principle 5 – Gaining active engagement from family and community; and*
- *Principle 6 – Building sustainable leadership capacity.*

*Dufour and colleagues (2006) contend that commitment to the learning of each student is key in learning communities. This notion parallels Blankstien's (2010) Principle two. Principle four reflects the need for educators to use data to inform practice (Blankstien, 2010). It has been our experience that there is a great deal of data prevalent in schools. The challenge for educators is using the data in relevant ways. Student data must be used to inform instructional decisions of educators.*

*A second noted principle by Dufour and Colleagues (2006) is that there is a shift of focus from teaching to learning. Teacher behaviors were once a focus in classrooms. When observations were conducted by supervisors of teachers in the 90s; supervisors noted the behaviors and dispositions of teachers. Engaging students has become the critical focus. This notion corresponds with Principle three of Blankstein (2010).*

*There is much value in teachers collaborating as it relates to instructional strategies and practices focusing on the needs of learners. School leaders play a critical role in creating cultures where collaboration can take place. In some instances, school leaders should facilitate the collaboration.*

*The advantages of including professional learning communities have been well documented in the literature since the 80s. There have been varying ways to approach the concept of professional learning communities and adjustments to the concept since the eighties. It is also noteworthy that several professional associations have noted the importance of professional learning communities including the National Commission on Teaching and America's Future, the National Education Association, The American Federal of Teachers, and the National Association of Elementary School Principals.*

*According to the Anneberg Institute (2003,) the following are the key benefits of professional learning communities:*

- *Building productive relationships that are required to collaborate, partner, reflect, and act to carry out school-improvement programs;*
- *Engaging educators at all levels in collective, consistent and context-specific learning;*

- *Addressing inequities in teaching and learning opportunities by supporting teachers who work with students requiring the most assistance; and*
- *Promoting efforts to improve results in terms of school and system culture, teacher practice and learning.*

*Obviously, the fundamentals of professional learning communities must be present for the communities to function and to be sustained. PLCs can be an effective form of professional development facilitated by school leaders when all of the previously discussed principles are present in schools. Darling-Hammond and colleagues (2009) suggest that professional learning communities work when they are sustained, school-based, and embedded in the daily work of teachers.*

*Providing opportunities for effective professional development is one way for school leaders to begin embedding professional development into learning communities. Hord (1997) emphasizes the role of the leader in sharing decision-making with teachers. Professional development can be most effective when the school leader involves teachers in setting individual goals rather than dictating the parameters for teachers. Leaders must also share power and authority with teachers (Hord, 1997).*

*One example of a need to embed professional development in the daily work of teachers is that during informal conversations and class discussions with practicing teachers, many suggest that professional development in their districts is not necessarily linked to the needs of the teachers. For example, it is common for districts to sponsor large, "beginning of the year" professional development programs wherein teachers across all grade levels and disciplines meet in an auditorium for an entire day with an expert on a topic deemed important. The problem is the training may not be specific enough to meet the needs of individuals or groups of teachers from very different schools. There is so much information in the literature on differentiating instructional needs for students. It is also important to differentiate the professional development needs for teachers.*

*There are other instances when professional development is scheduled at the end of the work day when teachers have been frustrated by the complexity of challenges of the day. The most effective time for professional development is during working hours particularly when teachers are energetic and can work. Effective professional development planning should allow time during the instructional day for teachers to discuss the critical components of lesson planning; what is working and what is not working; and pertinent issues linked to the needs of the students.*

*Experience has taught us that the following concepts are critical for meaningful professional development: time and organization, relevance, follow-up. Many districts have the first days of school calendars designated for professional development. Although this may appear as an appropriate and logical time, most teachers are most concerned with classroom organization; the classes that they will be teaching; etc. Therefore, the focus on professional development becomes rather limited. Timing is critical.*

*Previously, we cited and discussed the need for a shift to occur in the thinking of educators with a focus on learning. As educators focus on the learning of students, it is fundamental for educators to observe assessment data. Professional learning communities during the school day is an excellent opportunity for educators to analyze and re-direct instruction based on the findings of data. There is an important component of data analyses for focusing on individual students, and there is a component for focusing on whole class performances.*

*Brady and McColl (2010) noted the relevance of educators shifting their thinking to the learning of students. To truly use data well while focusing on learning, educators should have clear definitions of assessments with clear purposes of assessments. There is a tendency for teachers to constantly test and/or assess students. Assessments should be meaningful with clear expectations for students.*

*Many schools and school districts are beginning to use data rooms or data walls. Typically, there are more forms of assessments in elementary schools. In data rooms or on data walls, teachers can view the scores of an entire class on EAGLE or DIBELS. When an entire class is under-performing on a skill, this is an indication for the teacher to re-teach the skill in comparison to one or two students in a class under-performing.*

*Schmoker (2011) discusses the importance for educators in the teaching and learning process for/of students as simplicity, clarity, and priority in Focus. He feels that there are three elements that educators should approach with diligence and simplicity - what is taught; how it is taught; and authentic literacy. We raise these notions because Schmoker (2011) specifically emphasizes the importance of learning communities for educators as educators focus on what is taught, how it is taught, and authentic literacy.*

*Assessments for educators of students in the learning process of what is taught and how it is taught are crucial. Educators must*

collect data and/or reflect on the prior knowledge levels of learners, learning styles of learners, and other pertinent variables. This
information must also be used in the way it is taught.

Schmoker (2011) discusses the – what is taught as the curriculum. He notes that the curriculum should be coherent with
topics and standards. The Common Core is presently being
adopted in many states across the country, and the Partnership
for Assessment of Readiness for College and Careers (PARCC)
assessments are the standardized measures of the Common Core.
Grade level expectations are currently in place in many states.
One of the premises of the Common Core is to "raise the bar"
on what is taught at each grade level. Competencies that were in
fifth grade are in third grade for the Common Core (http://www
.corestandards.org/).

Schomoker (2011) describes The How We Teach as "ordinary,
structurally sound lessons that employ the same basic formula
that educators have known for decades but few implement consistently." Again, it is important for educators to use data pertinent to students' needs to inform methodology.

Revisiting the concept of professional development at the
beginning of the school year – relevance is always a critical variable. When all teachers and other professional staff gather at one
location, it is very difficult to have the individuals focus on what
is relevant for the school year. Teachers are most distracted by
reacquainting with colleagues after the summer break. We have
experienced many district-wide initiatives like the adopting of
reading programs, special education programs, and computer-
based programs. However, it is difficult for district-wide training
to be facilitated that is relevant for all teachers across disciplines
and/or grade levels. There is typically a great need for specificity
for schools and teachers.

To ensure effectiveness with implementation of professional
development, it is vital to have follow-up. The most practical kind
of follow-up is for professionals in the building or at minimum
within the district to be able to answer pertinent questions for
teachers. It does not matter how effectively professional development is facilitated; teachers will have questions as implementation
is occurring. And, it is necessary for teachers to be able to obtain
feedback quickly.

The research findings of Fullan (2009) support the dis-connec-
tivity of the work of teachers with their professional development.
He suggests that only ten to twenty percent of teachers experience meaningful professional development. Furthermore, ninety

*percent of teachers have participated in short term conferences or workshops. Engaging teachers in meaningful discussions linked to practices based on the pertinent student populations is a challenge for professional learning communities.*

*Schlager and Fusco (2003) made similar assertions regarding school-based professional development. They suggest that misaligned pedagogical content can be a challenge when teachers are unable to connect professional development with teacher practices. It is so important for planning to accompany professional development so that there are no gaps and redundancies in training. We note that the school leader as an instructional leader plays a critical role in ensuring that professional development is aligned with teacher practices; is meaningful and organized; and that the relevant follow-up occurs.*

*It is critical for staff/professional development activities to be evaluated. We feel that another critical mistake made in schools is the lack of follow-up! As the instructional leader and leader of the school, principals should be able to evidence the effectiveness of staff development activities in the school (classroom for class-based activities.) Principals should also seek feedback from teachers. Mentors and lead teachers can also provide assistance with staff development initiatives by modeling best practices and supporting other teachers.*

Mentoring is mentioned in the discussion above as a part of induction programs, and mentors are discussed as a way to facilitate staff development. However, it is important to emphasize that it is advantageous for individuals serving in supervisory capacities in any work environment to assign mentors to assist professionals in their roles, especially in schools. In Chapter 6, we focus on aspects of school climates and how school leaders should promote positive climates. Providing staff/professional development and mentors for teachers and staff is monumental in supporting teachers or staff and helping to promote positivism in the climates of schools. Seyfarth (2008) suggested the following points that support the need for professional development and supporting teachers:

- Teachers with mentors are less likely to leave jobs.
- Male teachers have higher attrition rates.
- Attrition rates are higher at schools with diverse populations.
- Attrition rates are higher when teachers do not receive support from the administration.

## EVALUATING INSTRUCTIONAL PERSONNEL (TEACHERS AND NON-CLASSROOM TEACHERS WHO SUPPORT INSTRUCTION)

The principles, concepts, and applicable standards of Instructional Leadership are presented in Chapter 5, through the lens of classroom observations. It is as important for school leaders to begin observations with the state and local level policies that include the evaluation requirements for teachers and other staff. Under the 10th amendment of the U.S. Constitution, the responsibility of governance of educators flows to states and locals.

Creating teacher evaluation systems appears to be a challenge for many states and locals. We have mentioned and cited reform efforts throughout this book. However, the *Every Student Succeeds Act* (ESSA) grants states flexibility to revise evaluation systems (Aragon and Colleagues, 2016). According to the Education Commission of States, 16 states enacted/adopted policies to address teacher evaluations as a result of ESSA. The states opting to address the policies sought to address the following areas and answer the following questions:

- Purpose: Why do teacher evaluations exist, and what purpose do they serve?
- Design: Who is responsible for conducting the evaluations, and when and how often do evaluations take place? What metrics and rating categories are used to measure and classify teacher performance?
- Authority: Subject to some safeguards, should some or all elements of the evaluation design be left up to school districts? Should evaluation procedures be subject to collective bargaining?
- Progress: Is the current evaluation system meeting its intended purpose? Do districts have the support they need to ensure proper implementation?

Aragon and Colleagues (2016) also noted the trends regarding Teacher Evaluations. In 2009, a report from The New Teacher Project (TNTP) conveyed that 99% of teachers were rated good or great by evaluation systems which indicates that the systems are not meaningful. TNTP recommended student growth as a measure of teacher effectiveness. From 2009 through 2012, Race to the Top grants were issued by the federal government. The initiative urged states and districts to revise outdated evaluation systems. One of the requirements to receive a waiver from the No Child Left Behind Act (NCLB) from 2011 to 2014 was the revision of the teacher evaluation systems. The notion of attaching student growth to teacher evaluations re-surfaced. In 2014–15, states were granted additional time by the U.S. Department of Education to prepare teacher evaluation systems to align student learning objectives and assessments. The waivers granted for revising teacher evaluation systems between 2011 and2014 as a part of NCLB were rescinded as a part of ESSA.

The focus on teacher evaluation systems was heightened in accountability initiatives which affirmed the need for effective teaching and school leaders supporting such processes. The roles that leaders play in supporting teachers are discussed in Chapter 5. Effective teaching is at the core of the work in schools.

It is essential for technology tools to support such processes. Many of the observation tools that were once paper-and-pencil are now electronic; some school leaders use mobile devices while conducting observations. Danielson also has both electronic and paper-and-pencil forms of observations at http://www.mybookezzz.org/danielson-formal-classroom-observation-form/.

Danielson and Maranzo are included on the *iObservation* website. According to the website, iObservation "is a comprehensive data collection and management system that reports real-time data from classroom walkthroughs, teacher observations, self-assessments, instructional rounds, and evaluations." It is a convenient, web-based program accessible on any computer with an Internet connection. Offline functionality is also available for buildings and locations without wireless access.

Using efficient electronic tools and research-based content resources, iObservation enables administrators to focus on instructional leadership while helping them stay compliant with state and district requirements. Feedback can be sent to teachers immediately following the classroom visits for a transparent and effective process.

*Whether leaders prefer to collect teacher data using the school's current walkthrough or observation forms or decide to take advantage of existing research-based and expert models in iObservation, we offer solutions that advance – not interrupt – your mission and goals.*

(http://www.iobservation.com/iObservation/classroom-observation/)

iObservation improves the classroom observation process in several ways:

Increase efficiency with an automated and systematized process,
Create focus for busy instructional leaders using content resources like "exemplary classroom,"
Videos that identify effective practices,
Remove the burden of paper-based documentation,

Make data-based decisions informed by real-time reports, aggregated or
    disaggregated,
Send effective feedback to teachers that encourages reflection and sup-
    ports growth,
Choose your language of instruction: digitize your own content, use the
    iObservation research-based framework, or adopt an expert frame-
    work from Charlotte Danielson or Dr. Robert Marzano,
Enjoy convenient wireless, offline, or mobile access.
Information is available at: http://www.iobservation.com/iObservation
    /classroom-observation/#sthash.HaJd9SW0.dpuf and http://www
    .iobservation.com/iObservation/classroom-observation/

Additional information and resources are included in Chapter 5, on the
role of the school leader as an instructional leader. A model is discussed
to provide instructional support to teachers while facilitating instructional leadership and observing classroom instructions. Chapter 5 does
not address processes when teachers are underperforming and in need
of remediation. It may be argued that non-tenured teachers and other
staff who are non-tenured should not be provided the opportunity to
improve prior to termination. Essex (2015) argues that non-tenured
teachers have:

- No expectation beyond an annual contract for employment,
- No right to an explanation of termination,
- No right to due process, and
- No hearing.

However, it is critical to follow policies and procedures as previously
alluded to when evaluating teachers and other personnel. In most
instances, an evaluation system is in place, and protocols should be followed to remedy ineffectiveness.

Essex (2015) suggests that school districts should have "well documented" policies and procedures to follow regarding teacher evaluations.
School leaders must maintain documentation of the evaluations and
inform teachers of pending evaluations. In the event that teachers desire
to rebut evaluations, such opportunities should be provided. Leaders
must communicate to teachers that a rebuttal does not imply that the
evaluation is off the record. The rebutted observation remains on record.
In addition, the standards and expectations of teachers should be clearly
articulated; evaluation results must be of high quality, to the greatest
extent. A thorough improvement plan with support is an essential element of the process. When assistance has been provided and improvement
does not occur, dismissal procedures must be followed. The legalities of

evaluating and terminating must always be considered. Essex (2015) provides guidelines for teacher evaluation. He suggests that criteria should be communicated to teachers consistently and fairly, teachers should be made aware of the use of evaluations when they are used for factors other than performance, and support from administration is essential in the development of an improvement plan (Essex, 2015).

Tenured teachers and employees are also entitled to due process (students who are suspended or expelled are also entitled to due process). According to Essex (2015) tenured teachers have substantive and procedural considerations involved with due process. Procedural due process implies that teachers cannot be deprived of life, liberty, or property. Substantive due process implies that the state must have reasonable grounds to deny teachers the right to procedural due process rights. In order for teachers to be dismissed districts must demonstrate in due process hearings that teachers have been incompetent, neglected duty, have failed to obey reasonable requests from the administration, and/or have acted immorally. Essex provides the following guidelines regarding tenure for teachers:

- Tenured and non-tenured teachers are entitled to fundamental fairness,
- Tenure is not a protective measure for ineffective teachers,
- Tenured teachers may only be dismissed with documented evidence,
- Due process must be followed for tenured teachers, and
- Non-tenured teachers are not entitled to due process unless there is an alleged constitutional violation.

There are also instances where teachers and/or other employees may file grievances.

Grievances can be formal or informal; however, the purpose of the grievance process is to resolve complaints and conflicts in the work environment. Obviously, there is less structure involved in the informal grievance procedures. Recommended strategies to address informal grievances procedures include placing suggestion boxes at various locations on campuses, developing personnel networks, and conducting exit interviews with employees who left because of conflict. Because of the nature of educators, we believe conflict is inevitable; however, effective communication is a means to minimize conflict. There are proactive strategies that the administrator can exhibit to minimize conflict. Maintaining a TRUE open door policy and being visible in schools are definitely effective in working with employees.

Castetter and Young (2004) discuss the process for formal grievance procedures. The employee initiates the grievance in writing to the principal; the principal then responds within the time parameters (Step 1). If the employee doesn't feel that the principal has resolved the grievance, the employee must submit the grievance form to the human resource director or assistant superintendent (Step 2). If a resolution is not derived in Step 2, the employee appeals to the superintendent of schools (Step 3). Step 4 is an appeal to the Board of Education. Binding arbitration is involved in Step 5 if a resolution is not reached in Step 4. It is important for districts to have policies in place regarding grievances, and there should be no reprisals for employees invoking grievances.

Like teachers, non-classroom instructional staff can be evaluated with the support of technology tools. It is important to note that leaders must use all appropriate protocols (when using technology to support the evaluation processes). Seyfarth (2008) suggested that personnel should be evaluated based on their job performances as defined in the job descriptions. The Marzano Center has a teacher evaluation model and a model for evaluating non-classroom support personnel. These are the individuals who support instruction and include: guidance counselors, psychologists, therapists, media specialists, and other personnel who are required to hold a teaching or technology certificate.

The Marzano Focused Non-Classroom Instructional Support Personnel Evaluation Model has four domains for evaluating:

- Domain 1: Planning and Preparing to Provide Support,
- Domain 2: Supporting Student Achievement,
- Domain 3: Continuous Improvement of Professional Practice, and
- Domain 4: Professional Responsibilities.

Within Domain 1, the competencies for the professionals include establishing clear goals for the supporting services, helping the school/district to achieve goals, and using available resources.

Supporting student achievement: Domain 2 is in most if not all of the job descriptions of non-classroom instructional personnel. Professionals must demonstrate knowledge of students and help students meet achievement goals. If required, professionals must also plan standards-based lessons, identify critical content, use questioning strategies, facilitate groups, manage student behavior, and use engagement strategies. Professionalism is critical for all professionals. For Domain 3, reflecting and evaluating personal performance and using data and feedback to support changes to professional practice is essential. The importance of professional responsibilities is essential to the cultures of schools. For Domain 4, non-classroom instructional staff must demonstrate knowledge of practice, promote positive interactions with colleagues and community, adhere to school and district policy, and support and participate in school and district initiatives. Like the teacher evaluation model, the observations for non-instructional personnel can be conducted by using the technology-based iObservations (Marazano (2018)

The following link has instruments that can be used in electronic format:

https://www.education.pa.gov/Teachers%20-%20Administrators/
    Educator%20Effectiveness/Pages/Non-Teaching-Staff.aspx

## EVALUATING NON-INSTRUCTIONAL PERSONNEL

Loeb (2016, January) reported that half the people working in schools are not classroom teachers, and some of the non-teaching adults play critical roles in helping schools focus on students. We listed the following professionals above – guidance counselors, psychologists, therapists, and media specialists. There are also aides/paraprofessionals, clerical staff, nurses, social workers, food service personnel, custodial, maintenance, and security personnel. Several of the concepts discussed in the previous section, **Evaluating Instructional Personnel** are relevant to this section pertinent to evaluating staff. Policies and procedures should be followed in conducting evaluations, and initiatives should be in place to support individuals perform their jobs.

Seyfarth (2008) notes that the evaluations of employees should be guided by the "Priority Actions:" which actions they perform and the "Results Sought:" what the intended results are. The "Results Sought:" is the expected outcomes that employees are expected to achieve. In some instances, teachers and principals evaluate the performances of non-instructional staff. Teachers and principals both have some working knowledge of the roles of individuals in maintenance and transportation. There is a great deal of variability in evaluation systems across states and school districts. Seyfarth (2008) suggests that the following questions be considered:

• What is the intent of the system?
• How well is the system performing the functions it is intended to perform?
• Is the system credible?
• Is the data being used appropriately?

Although collective bargaining frequently invokes controversy, it is viewed as a means by educators to have opportunities to achieve greater roles in management and operations in the education system. Collective bargaining gained legal protection in 1930 and became popular in education in the 1960s. As membership in national organizations has increased, there has been an increase in strike activity. This is another area for school leaders to be versed in as it relates to employee processes. There are three steps involved in collective bargaining.

In Step 1, the district's personnel offices need to:

- Develop bargaining structures,
- Analyze current contract,
- Analyze anticipated issues,
- Forecast financial outlook,
- Cost potential of contract changes,
- Compare regional contracts,
- Review reports from unit administrators,
- Prepare a bargaining notebook,
- Anticipate union proposals, and
- Formulate strategy and tactics.

In the Step 2, the following actions take place:

- Establish ground rules,
- Exchange proposals,
- Evaluate union proposals,
- Prepare proposal response,
- Plan for impasse resolutions,
- Ready strike arrangements (the portion depends on the state; a right-to-work state does not permit strikes, but rather sick-outs, etc. occur), and
- Approve agreement.

In Step 3, the final step, the human resource director or designee:

Communicates agreement details,
Instructs administrative personnel,
Implements the grievance system,
Resolves contract disputes, and
Monitors contract validity, effectiveness, and adequacy.

The modes of negotiating behavior are collaborative, competitive, and subordinate. In the collaborative model, both sides are satisfied. Adversarial relationships are developed through competitive models. This is a win–lose method of negotiating. In the subordinate model, one group makes subordinate to the other group.

## SCENARIO 1: ARE THINGS OKAY AS THEY ARE?

Mr. Douglas began his new assignment as principal of the largest high school in his hometown. Summerfield High School is located in Summerfield, Alabama. He spent most of his career in the northern part of Alabama in a supervisory role in a central office, but decided to finish his career at home to be close to his family and friends. He had not lived in the town since moving away to college but everything seemed familiar to him; however, he did not stay in touch with many of his friends.

On entering the office for the first day, he began reviewing files. His goal was to assess the school aligned with objectives for the State. The State's objectives include:

> All students should show continuous improvement and perform at proficiency levels or above.
> All students succeed.
> All students must graduate high school.
> Students must graduate high school prepared (college and/or career ready).

The strategies for learners include:

> Develop and adopt college and career-ready aligned standards in core subject areas.
> Develop and disseminate a model curriculum framework.
> Create and implement meaningful assessments.

The Support Systems

> Students will attend school daily and engage in rigorous learning.
> Students will develop a sense of civic and personal responsibilities to ensure that learning environments are safe.
> Students will be provided opportunities for individual and group counseling.
> Students will enter 9th grade with a plan to address academic needs and interests.
> Students will be provided healthy meals.

The objectives for professionals include:

> Children are taught by highly prepared and qualified educators.
> Schools are led by effective leaders.
> School systems are led by visionary instructional leaders.

The test scores appeared average; the disciplinary records painted an overall positive picture in that Summerfield High School recorded referral rates below most of the middle schools in the district with only two expulsions for the entire year. Like the disciplinary records, the attendance records painted a rosy picture. The attendance rates were slightly above the average for the state.

Mr. Douglas' assessment of the test results is that their test scores were mediocre. The dropout rate is high; but on all of the metrics for standardized tests, Summerfield is performing at the State's average consistently. The performance on the standardized assessment resembles the same rating year after year for the past five years. Many of the students do not attend college and seek employment at the local manufacturing plants. The administration at the local plants often applauds Summerfield High School for the number of employees the plant acquires from the high school.

The major concern that Mr. Douglas has is that as he walks through the school, he notices that many of the teachers appear unengaged in classes. The school has a college-preparatory section, a non-college preparatory section, a special education section, and a vocational section. When looking into the advanced classes, all the students appear to be engaged. The students in the other sections' rooms appeared to be engaging in conversations, and many had their heads down on their desks. Mr. Douglas also noticed the make-up of the classrooms. The college preparatory classes were primarily white students while the other sections of the school were primarily minority students.

Mr. Douglas had a discussion with Mr. Ken (a high school friend who has taught at the school for most of his career) about his assessments and observations. After sharing what he observed, Mr. Ken shared with Mr. Douglas that he felt the school was doing well academically and along the lines of all metrics. Mr. Ken further explained that his sentiment represented the sentiment of the school and school community. Mr. Douglas wondered if Mr. Ken's assessment was accurate.

Where does the school leader begin with the formal observation processes of teachers?

## SCENARIO 2: ENSURING ACADEMIC INTEGRITY

CASE 5: In Chapter 8; written by Dr. Obie Cleveland Hill and Dr. Gregg Stall: Ensuring Academic Integrity

Jones, L. and Kennedy, E. (2012). *Passing the Leadership Test* (2nd Edition). New York: Rowman and Littlefield Publishing.

Hilly High School is the only high school in the Kenny district; there are about 1,200 students in grades 9–12. Hilly High School has a mixture of experienced and inexperienced teachers. Mr. Obie is in his third year as a school leader, and the district experienced several major initiatives since his assuming the role –the elementary and middle schools were restructured as linked to grade-level confirmations with some rezoning; the district adopted mathematics and reading initiatives; and the district has adopted a new model for meeting the needs of special needs students.

Kenny district has also experienced several leadership shifts. The superintendent is in her second year, and half of the central office has retired. Furthermore, most of the school leaders have been reassigned at the request of the school board. The superintendent and central office staff have been promoting the philosophy of site-based management and budgeting, providing opportunities for school leaders to have additional autonomy.

Mr. Obie is a huge advocate of professional learning communities. One of the activities addressed for several school improvement goals for Hilly High School is professional learning communities. Mr. Obie feels that this is one way to achieve and sustain academic growth in high schools. Hilly High School is departmentalized, like most high schools in the region, and the teachers in the same departments have common planning. In addition, there are professional development activities where teachers plan with colleagues in different disciplines.

Mr. Obie has also encouraged teachers to supplant instruction with technology. Many of the students at Hilly High School have access to technology. Some of the classes are web-based for students who attend school for half of the day; the faculty members also embrace this notion because it grants them more freedom. In one of the professional learning community meetings, one of the more experienced teachers, Ms. Apple shared with the staff that one of her courses is listed as a traditional course, but the course is held during the last hour of the day, and she allows students to leave the campus and complete the work online.

Mr. Obie is made aware of the situation with the online versus "face-to-face" challenges and conferences with Ms. Apple about it. Ms. Apple informs Mr. Obie that she does not see a problem with providing students the option because it is the last hour of the day and students are performing exceptionally well in the applied mathematics course. Ms. Apple has been teaching at the school for about five years, with mediocre ratings. However, she has 20 years of teaching experience in mathematics. What should Mr. Obie do?

## SUMMARY

In Chapter 3 we discuss leadership and technology standards linked to personnel and evaluation. Prior to discussing the specifics of hiring instructional and non-instructional personnel and evaluating personnel, general principles of human resources management are discussed. Protocols for hiring and evaluating instructional and non-instructional staff in schools are included from Seyfarth (2008). School leaders must have a knowledge of human resources management and policies and procedures. Guidelines are presented for hiring protocols based on the Civil Rights Act and the Americans with Disabilities Act. The importance of supporting staff through professional development and mentoring is discussed as it is becoming more and more difficult to staff schools because of teacher and other staff shortages. We stress throughout the chapters that the technology tools are included to assist school leaders and their roles and do not replace the necessary knowledge, skills, and dispositions school leaders need. Various technological tools are included to support the personnel and evaluation processes school leaders perform. In the conclusion of this chapter, two scenarios are presented for the application of content and tools from Chapter 3 and other chapters.

### TECHNOLOGY TOOLS

Adobe Acrobat: http://www.acrobat.com
BoardDocs: https://www.boarddocs.com
DeansList Software: https://www.deanslistsoftware.com/features
DocuSign: https://www.godocusign.com
FreshSchools: https://www.freshschools.com
Google Drive: https://www.google.com
iObservations: http://www.iobservation.com/iObservation/class-room-observation/#sthash.HaJd9SW0.dpuf
ParentLocker: https://www.parentlocker.com/go/
Safe School Solutions: https://www.safehiringsolutions.com/safe-school-solutions

### REFERENCES

Adobe Acrobat. https://www.abode.om.
Annenberg Institute. (2003). Retrieved February 6, 2013, from http://annenberginstitute.org/pdf/proflearning.pdf.
Aragon, S. et al. (2016, August). *ESSA: Quick guides on top issues.* Education Commission of the States. https://www.ecs.org/wp-content/uploads/ESSA-Quick-guides-on-top-issues.pdf.

Blankstein. (2010). *Failure is not an option*. Corwin Press.

BOARDDOCS. https://www.boarddocs.com.

Brady, L., & McColl, L. (2010). *Test less assess more: A K-8 guide to formative assessment*. Eye on Education.

Castetter, W. B., & Young, I. P. (2004). *The human resource function in educational administration* (8th ed.). Prentice Hall.

Darling-Hammond, L., Meyerson, D., LaPointe, M., & Orr, M. (2009). *Preparing principals for a changing world: Lessons from effective school leadership programs*. Jossey-Bass.

DeansList Software. https://www.deanslistsoftware.com/features.

DocuSign. https://www.godocusign.com.

Dufour, R., Dufour, R., Eaker, R., & Many, T. (2006). *Learning by doing: A handbook for professional learning communities at work*. National Education Service.

Essex, N. (2015). *A teacher's pocket guide to school law*. Allyn & Bacon Educational Leadership.

Fullan, M. (2009). *Motion leadership: The skinny on becoming change savvy*. Corwin at SAGE Company.

Google Drive. https://www.google.com.

Hipp, K., & Huffman, J. (2010). *Demystifying professional learning communities: School leadership at its best*. Rowman & Littlefield Education.

Hord, S. (1997). *Professional learning communities: Communities of continuous inquiry and improvement*. Retrieved July 20, 2012, from Southwest Educational Developmental Laboratory at http://www.sedl.org/pubs/change34/welcome.html. (1998). *School professional staff as learning community*. Southwest Educational Developmental Laboratory.

Hoy, W., & Miskel C. (2013). *Educational administration: Theory, research, and practice*. McGrawhill.

https://www.education.pa.gov/Teachers%20-%20Administrators/Educator%20Effectiveness/Pages/Non-Teaching-Staff.aspx

International Society of Technology of Education. https://www.iste.org/standards/for-education-leaders.

Iobservations. http://www.iobservation.com/iObservation/classroom-observation/#sthash.HaJd9SW0.dpuf.

Jones, L., & Kennedy, E. (2012). *Passing the leadership test* (2nd ed.). Rowman and Littlefield Publishing.

Jones, L., Stall, G., & Yarbrough, D. (2013, May). The importance of professional learning communities for school improvement. *Creative Education*, 4. Retrieved May 13, 2013, from http://www.script.org/journal/ce.

Loeb. (2016, January). Half the people working in schools aren't teachers - So what? https://www.brookings.edu/research/half-the-people-working-in-schools-arent-classroom-teachers-so-what/.

Lunenburg, F., & Orstein, A. (2000). *Educational administration: Concepts and practices*. Wadsworth.

Marzano, R. (2018). Marzano focused non-classroom instructional support personnel evaluation model. learning sciences international. https://www.marzanocenter.com/wp-content/uploads/sites/4/2018/10/MC08-01-Focused-NCIS-Eval-Map-052518.pdf.

National Educational Leadership Preparation (NELP) Standards. https://www.naesp.org/communicator-november-2018/nelp-standards-approved-how-affects-you.

National Policy Board for Educational Administration. (2015). Professional Standards for Educational Leaders 2015. Reston, VA: Author. http://www.npbea. org.

Pawlas, G., & Olivia, P. (2007). *Eight edition: Supervision for today's schools.* John Wiley & Sons Inc.

Safe School Solutions. https://www.safehiringsolutions.com/safeschool-solutions.

Schlager, M., & Fusco, J. (2003, July). Teacher professional development, technology, and communities of practice: Are we putting the cart before the horuse. *The Information Society, 19*(3), 203–220. https://doi.org/10.1080/01972240309464.

Schmoker, M. (2011). *Focus: Elevating the essentials to radically improve student learning.* Association of Curriculum and Development.

Senge, P. M. (1990). *The fifth discipline: The art and practice of learning organizations.* Currency Doubleday Publishers.

Sergiovanni, T. J. (1994). *Building community in schools.* Jossey-Bass.

Seyfarth, J. (2008). *Human resources management for effective schools.* Allyn and Bacon Publishing.

# CHAPTER 4

## School Security and Safety

**ABSTRACT**

In recent decades, headlines of school shootings, disruptive behavior by parents, visitors to school grounds, etc., have eroded public confidence and led to demands for increased safety for all involved in schools. Administrators have responded with increases in security officers, updates to facilities, and integration of various security technologies designed to increase school safety. Recommendations for improving school safety using technology are noted in the chapter, and guidelines for comprehensive safety and emergency planning are included. We also review technologies related to five aspects of school operations: information technology systems, transportation, school buildings and facilities, school grounds, and electronic communication. In each instance, we describe various types of technologies and present criteria for evaluation. We begin the chapter with a discussion of how the school leader's role regarding safety and security is linked to the Leadership Standards and ISTE Standards.

### SCHOOL LEADER'S ROLE IN SCHOOL SECURITY AND SAFETY LINKED TO THE STANDARDS

The importance of the role of school leaders in establishing and maintaining the safety of the environments of schools is noted in each of the three sets of standards – PSEL, NELP, and ISTE. We list the applicable standards below:

PSEL 9: National Educational Leadership Preparation (NELP) Standards: https://www.naesp.org/communicator-november-2018/nelp-standards-approved-how-affects-you

DOI: 10.4324/9781003269472-4

Effective educational leaders manage school operations and resources to promote each student's academic success and well-being. Effective leaders:

a) Institute, manage, and monitor operations and administrative systems that promote the mission and vision of the school.

b) Strategically manage staff resources, assigning and scheduling teachers and staff to roles and responsibilities that optimize their professional capacity to address each student's learning needs.

c) Seek, acquire, and manage fiscal, physical, and other resources to support curriculum, instruction, and assessment; student learning community; professional capacity and community; and family and community engagement.

d) Are responsible, ethical, and accountable stewards of the school's monetary and nonmonetary resources, engaging in effective budgeting and accounting practices.

e) Protect teachers' and other staff members' work and learning from disruption.

f) Employ technology to improve the quality and efficiency of operations and management.

g) Develop and maintain data and communication systems to deliver actionable information for classroom and school improvement.

h) Know, comply with, and help the school community understand local, state, and federal laws, rights, policies, and regulations so as to promote student success.

i) Develop and manage relationships with feeders and connecting schools for enrollment management and curricular and instructional articulation.

j) Develop and manage productive relationships with the central office and school board.

k) Develop and administer systems for fair and equitable management of conflict among students, faculty and staff, leaders, families, and community.

l) Manage governance processes and internal and external politics toward achieving the school's mission and vision.

The NELP Standard and standard competencies that align with safety and security are below:

Standard Six: Operations and Management
Program completers who successfully complete a building-level educational leadership preparation program understand and

demonstrate the capability to promote the success and well-being of each student, teacher, and leader by applying the knowledge, skills, and commitments necessary for (1) management and operation; (2) data and resources; (3) communication systems; and (4) legal compliance.

Component 6.1 Program completers understand and demonstrate the capacity to evaluate, develop, and implement management, communication, technology, school-level governance, and operating systems that support each student's learning needs and promote the mission and vision of the school.

Component 6.2 Program completers understand and demonstrate the capacity to evaluate, develop, and advocate for a data-informed and equitable resourcing plan that supports school improvement and student development.

Component 6.3 Program completers understand and demonstrate the capacity to reflectively evaluate, communicate about, and implement laws, rights, policies, and regulations to promote student and adult success and well-being.

The ISTE Standard and competencies which align with management and administration is System Designer. The competencies address operations and systems. The focus of the Systems Designer Standard is team building and system building to implement, sustain, and continually improve the use of technology to support learning. The competencies are below:

Lead teams to collaboratively establish robust infrastructure and systems needed to implement the strategic plan.

Ensure that resources for supporting the effective use of technology for learning are sufficient and scalable to meet future demand.

Protect privacy and security by ensuring that students and staff observe effective privacy and data management policies.

Establish partnerships that support the strategic vision, achieve learning priorities, and improve operations.

(http://www.iste.org/standards/for-education-leaders)

These standards point to the important role of the administrator in school safety. Further evidence is shown in the emphasis on safety in educational leaders' training. Throughout the coursework, administrators are taught how to develop policies and procedures that promote safety and security for all involved in schools. These involve policies that control access to school facilities, monitoring behavior on school grounds and inside school buildings, and securing transportation and communications.

The Global Alliance for Disaster Risk Reduction and Resilience in the Educational Sector has a Comprehensive School Safety framework. We believe that the need for safety and security (both physical and cyber) is heightened across the world for obvious reasons/incidents that can be listed one by one, and safe learning environments are critical to the foundation of learning. The purpose of the comprehensive safety framework is:

- To improve all children's equitable and safe access to a quality, inclusive, and integrated basic education,
- To monitor and evaluate the progress of initiatives for reducing disaster and conflict risks,
- To increase the availability of and access to hazard-related evidence, such as multi-hazard early warning systems' data and disaster risk information,
- To promote risk reduction and resilience in the education sector, including a clear focus on major international agreements (e.g., Sustainable Development Goals and Sendai Framework for Disaster Risk Reduction 2015–2030),
- To strengthen coordination and networks for resilience from all levels, local to international,
- To strengthen education governance and local participation, and
- To strengthen conflict risk reduction in order to implement integrated, inclusive measures to prevent and reduce hazard exposure and vulnerability to disaster, increase preparedness for response and recovery, and strengthen resilience.

  (https://gadrrres.net/what-we-do/gadrrres-global-activities/comprehensive-school-safety-framework)

The principles listed above from the Global Alliance for Disaster Risk Reduction and Resilience in the Educational Sector align with the *Guide for Developing High-Quality School Emergency Plans* released by the national government. In Chapter 1, we included goals from the national level pertinent to technology from the Department of Education. The federal government also suggests that comprehensive emergency plans should be in place in schools. These guidelines govern the parameters for school and district leadership for emergency preparation. The tenants at the federal level are:

Prevention means the capabilities necessary to avoid, deter, or stop an imminent crime or threatened or actual mass casualty incident. Prevention is the action schools take to prevent a threatened or actual incident from occurring.

Protection means the capabilities to secure schools against acts of violence and manmade or natural disasters. Protection focuses on ongoing actions that protect students, teachers, staff, visitors, networks, and property from a threat or hazard.

Mitigation means the capabilities necessary to eliminate or reduce the loss of life and property damage by lessening the impact of an event or emergency. In this document, "mitigation" also means reducing the likelihood that threats and hazards will happen.

Response means the capabilities necessary to stabilize an emergency once it has already happened or is certain to happen in an unpreventable way; establish a safe and secure environment; save lives and property; and facilitate the transition to recovery.

Recovery means the capabilities necessary to assist schools affected by an event or emergency in restoring the learning environment. (https://rems.ed.gov/docs/School_Guide_508C.pdf)

In the federal guidelines for School Emergency Operations Plans (*https://rems.ed.gov/docs/School_Guide_508C.pdf*), planning is stressed. It is first noted that planning should be supported by leaders at senior levels in schools and districts. Second, ongoing and comprehensive assessments should guide the customizations of planning. Assessments allow for the unique characteristics of schools to be accounted for. Third, a wide range of threats are noted in planning. The needs before, during, and after an incident are considered. Fourth, it is critical for planning to address access to the "whole school community." The planning should accommodate functionality to/for students, parents, teachers, and all necessary stakeholders. Fifth, all the settings and times of schools and related events must be accounted for in planning. This includes events on- and off-campus and during and outside of operational hours. Finally, collaborative processes should be a part of planning in which revisions are made on the basis of the collaboration.

According to the *Guide for Developing High-Quality School Emergency Plans* (CreateSpace Independent Publishing Platform, 2014), management planning and the development of Emergency Operation Plans are not one and the same. Stakeholder involvement is critical during planning processes. Local emergency management staff, public mental health officials, and first responders should be involved in planning processes. Six steps are proposed in planning, and the steps can be used to develop plans, review plans comprehensively, and conduct periodic reviews. The steps are:

- Form a collaborative planning team,
- Understand the situation,
- Determine goals and objectives,
- Plan development,
- Plan, prepare, review, and approve, and
- Plan implementation and maintenance.

In identifying the core planning team members we previously noted that stakeholder involvement is needed from the community – local emergency management staff, public mental health officials, and first responders. Obviously, school personnel should be included. Administrators, teachers, school psychologists, nurses, facilities managers, transportation managers, food services managers, and family services managers should be included. In addition to students and parents, individuals representing special interests of various diverse groups should be included. The teams should be small enough to facilitate collaboration but large enough to diversify the workload (U.S. Department of Education, 2013).

For Step 2, the situation should be understood. This requires the identification of possible hazards and risks along with assessing the vulnerabilities posed by hazards and threats. Site assessments, cultural and climate assessments, school threat assessments, and capacity assessments provide the necessary information to identify potential risks and hazards which should be consolidated after all assessments are completed. Information obtained from the assessments should be organized and prioritized as high, medium, or low risk. Step 3 is to determine goals and objectives. From the "high risks" threats and possible others identified in Step 2, planning teams formulate goals and objectives based on the risks the planning teams decide to prioritize. Functions should be compiled from the objectives. For each function, planning teams must also decide the desired outcomes before, during, and after the function is completed (U.S. Department of Education, 2013).

In Step 4, a course of action is developed. Courses of action must be developed for each objective in Step 3. We noted that the objectives are derived from the goals which originate from the threats and hazards. Functions are developed for threats and action. Protocols support the course of action. In developing the course of action, the following questions should be answered:

- What is the action?
- Who bears the responsibility for the action?
- When will the action take place?
- What is the projected time for the action?
- What should happen before?
- What should happen after?
- What is needed to perform the action?
- What are the implications of the actions on a specific individual?
  (U.S. Department of Education, 2013)

The plan preparation, review, and approval occur in Step 5. Effective plans should be user-friendly including three sections: the basic plan, functional annexes, and threat and hazard-specific annexes. The primary audience of the basic plan is the school, community, and local emergency officials, and the basic plan guides the development of operational annexes. The functional annexes include the courses of action (communication, evacuation, recovery,) goals, and objectives that apply across multiple threats or hazards. The threat and hazard-specific annexes address specific threats or hazards like hurricanes or active shooters.

In 2018, a Federal Commission on School Safety was created. The commission recommended that the federal government create a clearinghouse "to provide school safety strategies and serve as a central location for federal resources." The website https://www.schoolsafety.gov serves as a "central location of federal resources." It launched in February of 2020. Some of the areas previously addressed in this chapter and areas that will be addressed are included on this website. These areas include: bullying and cyberbullying, cybersecurity, emergency planning, infectious diseases and public health, mental health, school climate, targeted violence, and threat assessment and reporting.

In the past, administrators have relied on incident reports (e.g., fights among students) by students and teachers, trends in data on problems and threats, and climate surveys (U.S. Department of Education, 2013) to gauge the safety climate of their school. Modern technologies offer many additional ways of obtaining information on school safety issues as well as analytics which can be used to find associations and patterns, and formulate predictions. In a recent report, Schwartz et al. (2016) identified 12 categories of technology used in school safety. These include (a) entry control: electromagnetic door locks; (b) identification: visitor badges, palm scanners; (c) surveillance: cameras, video recording, video motion detection system; (d) communication: walkie talkies, phones, radios; (e) alarm and protection systems: scream alarms, motion/sound/heat detectors; (f) emergency alerts: automated text messages or emails; (g) metal detectors: hand-held and walk through; (h) anonymous tips: toll-free hotline, voice mail systems; (i) tracking systems: smartphone apps, GPS devices; (j) GIS mapping: maps of school bus routes; (k) violence prediction: data software; and (l) social media monitoring: scans of online content for bullying. A RAND Corporation study was highlighted by Schwartz et al. which suggest that violence permeated three-fourths of American public schools in the 2009–2010 school year. We have divided these into five basic categories: access to facilities, transportation, school grounds, within-building activities, and communications and social media. In each instance, we describe technologies administrators might employ. The goal is not to promote a particular application or platform, but to identify features of various technologies that could be considered. Because of the widespread and increasing use of technology in school operations, we start with an overview of strategies and issues in maintaining the security of a school's information technology system.

## SECURITY OF SCHOOLS' INFORMATION TECHNOLOGY SYSTEM

Ransomware attacks, identity theft, data breaches, and a host of other technology security challenges increasingly face organizations at every level, including schools. Hackers, criminals, and others may view the personal information and files available at schools as a commodity to trade or exploit for profit. A common challenge for school administrators is to develop plans that can keep their school's technology system secure? Specifically, a question that confronts many school leaders is "What vulnerabilities and threats should be planned for?"
(Firch, n.d.)

## Understanding Digital Security

Cybersecurity is a term that has become commonplace in the digital age. It refers to strategies and techniques individuals and organizations can undertake to protect their information technology resources from exploitation and abuse. These breaches and attacks take on many forms.

Malware is perhaps one of the most familiar cybersecurity threats and includes a variety of different types of software and applications that gain access to a system and can corrupt or destroy files, share personal information, etc. Some of the more common types of malware are as follows:

**Viruses**. A virus is the most common type of malware attack. In order for a virus to infect a system it requires a user to click or copy it to media or a host. Most viruses self-replicate without the knowledge of the user. These viruses can be spread from one system to another via email, instant messaging, website downloads, removable media (USB), and network connections. Some file types are more susceptible to virus infections – .doc/docx, .exe, .html, .xls/.xlsx, .zip. Viruses typically remain dormant until it has spread onto a network or a number of devices before delivering the payload.

**Keyloggers**. Keylogging, or keyboard capturing, logs a user's keystrokes and sends data to the threat actor. Users are typically unaware that their actions are being monitored. While there are use cases for employers using keyloggers to track employee activity, they're mostly used to steal passwords or sensitive data. Keyloggers can be a physical wire discreetly connected to a peripheral device, such as a keyboard, or installed by a Trojan.

**Worms**. Similar to a virus, a worm can also self-replicate and spread full copies and segments of itself via network connections, email attachments, and instant messages. Unlike viruses; however, a worm does not require a host program in order to run, self-replicate, and propagate. Worms are commonly used against email servers, web servers, and database servers. Once infected, worms spread quickly over the internet and computer networks.

**Trojan Horses**. Trojan horse programs are malware that is disguised as legitimate software. A Trojan horse program will hide on your computer until it's called upon. When activated, Trojans can allow threat actors to spy on you, steal your sensitive data, and gain backdoor access to your system. Trojans are commonly downloaded through email attachments, website downloads, and instant messages. Social engineering tactics are typically deployed to trick users into loading and executing Trojans on their systems. Unlike computer viruses and worms, Trojans are not able to self-replicate.

**Ransomware/Crypto-Malware.** Ransomware is a type of malware designed to lock users out of their system or deny access to data until a ransom is paid. Crypto-malware is a type of ransomware that encrypts user files and requires payment within a time frame and often through a digital currency such as Bitcoin.

**Logic Bombs.** Logic bombs are a type of malware that will only activate when triggered, such as on a specific date/time or on the 25th log-in to an account. Viruses and worms often contain logic bombs to deliver their payload (malicious code) at a pre-defined time or when a preset condition is met. The damage caused by logic bombs varies from changing bytes of data to making hard drives unreadable. Antivirus software can detect the most common types of logic bombs when they're executed. However, until they do, logic bombs can lie dormant on a system for weeks, months, or years.

**Bots/Botnets.** Botnet, short for roBOT NETwork, is a group of bots, which are any type of computer system attached to a network whose security has been compromised. They are typically controlled remotely. The Mirai botnet was able to gain control of Internet of Things (IoT) connected devices like your DVR, home printer, as well as smart appliances by entering the default username and password that the devices shipped with. The threat actors deployed a DDoS (Distributed Denial of Service) attack by sending large amounts of data at a website hosting company, causing many popular websites to be taken offline.

**Adware and Spyware.** Adware and Spyware are both unwanted software. Adware is designed to serve advertisements on screens within a web browser. It's usually quietly installed in the background when downloading a program without your knowledge or permission. While harmless, adware can be annoying for the user. Spyware, on the other hand, is a type of malware designed to gain access and damage your computer. Spyware collects user information such as habits, browsing history, and personal identification information. Attackers then sell your data to advertisers or data firms, capture your bank account information, or steal your personal identity. Spyware is often downloaded in a software bundle or from file-sharing sites.

**Rootkits.** Rootkits are backdoor programs that allow a threat actor to maintain command and control over a computer without the user knowing. This access can potentially result in full control over the targeted system. The controller can then log files, spy on the owner's usage, execute files, and change system configurations remotely. While traditionally deployed using Trojan horse attacks, it's becoming more common in trusted applications. Some antivirus software can detect rootkits; however, they are difficult to clean from a system. In most cases, it's best to remove the rootkit and rebuild the compromised system.

(Firch, n.d.)

Insider threats, denial of service attacks, advanced persistent attacks, and man-in-the middle attacks are additional cyber attacks that are becoming more prevalent. Each are briefly described below:

**Insider Threats.** Insider threats are threats from individuals that have legitimate access to the system. In schools, these include students who may be interested in *hacking into the system* to change grades, cancel classes, etc. They can also include current or former employees who may access a system to download files, disrupt communications, etc.

**Denial of Service Attacks.** Denial of Service Attacks are designed to overload a system with traffic, which then has the effect of preventing legitimate users from utilizing it.

**Advanced Persistent Threats.** Advanced persistent threats are attacks in which individuals infiltrate a system and function largely to collect information and make it available to an outside entity. These attacks may not disrupt the operations of a system, but they can prove to be a serious threat to the security of information.

**Man-in-the-Middle Attacks.** Man-in-the-middle attacks are attacks in which an individual gains access to a system for the purpose of intercepting communications between a user and a network. These intercepted communications are then shared with an external actor.

The prevention of cyber threats includes a variety of actions. Some of the more common are the following:

- Ensure that the system is password protected. This can include password-protected networks, password-protected user accounts, encrypted communications, etc. Passwords should be changed regularly and conform to conventions for effective passwords. Additionally, key files should be encrypted and password protected. Finally, multifactor authentication of passwords is recommended in which access to the system is granted only after multiple pieces of evidence (e.g., passwords and mobile phone authentication apps).
- Limit the ability of external devices to pair with the system (i.e., turn off Wi-Fi Protected Setup) and restrict the range of IP addresses permitted to access your system (i.e., disable or limit the Dynamic Host Configuration Protocol).
- Ensure that firewalls, spam filters, and antivirus programs are up-to-date and active.

- Create a Virtual Private Network (VPN) to help secure remote access to the system. VPNs mask IP addresses and create an encrypted and secure connection to the system.
- The system should filter or block access to inappropriate material and material deemed harmful to minors.
- Train staff and students on cybersecurity policies and procedures. For students, these policies should explicitly address cyberbullying, sexting, oversharing, and potential threats from predators. For teachers, they should address
- Perform vulnerability checks on a regular basis

(Firch, n.d.)

An effective strategy for dealing with cybersecurity involves a well-developed plan. Several governmental organizations and professional groups have offered guidelines regarding cybersecurity for organizations, including schools. The following is a sample of these resources:

- U.S. Department of Homeland Security Cybersecurity Education Materials https://www.dhs.gov/stopthinkconnect
- Cybersecurity Training Materials from the National Center for Missing and Exploited Children https://www.netsmartz.org/
- Cybersecurity Training Materials for Teachers, Parents, and Students https://www.consumer.ftc.gov/features/feature-0038 -onguardonline
- The Guide for Developing High-Quality School Emergency Operations Plans https://rems.ed.gov/docs/REMS_K-12_Guide _508.pdf
- A Comprehensive Report on School Safety https://www.ojp.gov/ pdffiles1/nij/grants/250274.pdf
- Information Technology/Cybersecurity Checklist https://opi.mt .gov/Portals/182/Page%20Files/Emergency%20Planning%20and %20Safety/Cyber%20Checklist%20Checklist%20v1.4.pdf
- Top 5 Security Threats for Schools
- https://www.cosn.org/sites/default/files/Top%205 %20Cybersecurity%20Threats.pdf
- U.S. Department of Education Data Security Checklist https://stu-dentprivacy.ed.gov/sites/default/files/resource_document/file/Data %20Security%20Checklist_0.pdf
- Federal Government School Safety Website https://www.school-safety.gov

Cyberbullying is included in several of the weblinks listed above as well as in many comprehensive threat assessment lists. The resources listed above are not only advantageous for information technology systems for schools, but can also be shared with parents and students. Because students spend an increasing amount of time using digital devices such as smartphones, tablets, etc., they are increasingly exposed to potential threats such as cyberbullying. As noted on the U.S. Department of Health and Human Service cyberbullying website (https://www.stopbullying.gov/cyberbullying/what-is-it), cyberbullying is most common on social media, text messaging and messaging apps, direct and instant messaging, online chatting, online forums, email. and online gaming communities. The following are risks of social media apps and sites:

- Screening for harmful content on websites and apps varies widely.
- Content posted can be incorrect, harmful, or hurtful.
- Apps and platforms can be used to share harmful or adult content.
- Apps and platforms can include users of all ages and allow children to connect with adults.
- Apps and platforms can have no moderator for chats, groups, and forums that allow all types of content to be posted or shared.
- Apps and platforms can allow all types of content to be posted or shared.
- Privacy controls over who can view or access posted material vary across apps, and many users are not aware of how to use them effectively.
- Apps that allow for real-time user videos "live streaming" can be used to show bullying, violence, suicide, and harmful acts as they are happening.
- Some apps that include location information can be used to get personal information, such as someone's age, current location, or where someone lives.
- Apps that support telephone calls do not show up on a call log, so parents may not know who their children are talking to.

(https://www.stopbullying.gov/cyberbullying/what-is-it)

It is important for school leaders, teachers, and parents to know the risks and use preventive strategies and supports to assist students and others who are cyberbullied or who are at risk of being bullied. In Chapter 1, we include social media platforms for school leaders to use for communication; the platforms are repeated in the chapters for leadership tasks associated with the pertinent role/s addressed in the chapters. However, we note in Chapter 1 that different outlets have different users by age group. We include the platforms of Facebook, Twitter, LinkedIn, Tumblr, TikTok, Instagram, and YouTube in most chapters. In addition to the previously listed platforms, younger students also use Amino, ASKfm, Calculator%, Chatroulette, Discord, Houseparty, Kik, Linke, LiveMe, MeetMe, Omegle, Reddit, Roblox, Sarahah, Snapchat, Telegram, Twitch, VSCO, WeChat, WhatsApp, Whisper, Yubo (formerly Yellow), and YouNow. It is important to research each platform; the risks and the benefits. Throughout the book, there are indexes provided to research technologies. The EdSurge Product Index is one example of the indexes; it is included in Chapter 2.

## MONITORING TRANSPORTATION

Most school systems in the United States provide transportation for students to and from school. School buses, vans, and other types of vehicles are commonly used. Once a child enters a school-sponsored transportation vehicle, the school system is responsible for their safety. In most cases, school transportation is managed at the district level. However, the behavior or events on a bus or van are of decided interest to building-level school leaders. While in the past, information about incidents on buses was dependent upon reports from drivers or students, the accuracy and completeness of this information could be questioned for many reasons, including the willingness of witnesses or participants to accurately report what was seen. The response in many school systems has been to place cameras on most transportation vehicles. However, contemporary technologies offer many tools beyond videos. These include the following:

**GPS Tracking**. Fleet management systems allow administrators to know where their buses are at all times. In addition, many provide information on speed, stops, and other analytics which can help forestall a problem. In the event of an emergency, some systems will alert authorities and school administrators.

**Driver Assist Technologies**. These tools alert the driver to vehicles that are located in the driver's blind spot, traveling too closely, or making sudden stops. Some will also monitor the driver's movements and eye gaze toward the end of identifying drivers that may be distracted or exhibiting signs of being impaired or drowsy.

**Entry–Exit Monitoring**. These systems keep track of people entering or exiting the bus. Some may utilize facial recognition or ID tag technology and verify that persons entering the bus are part of a school's database. Some will alert the driver when a child remains on the bus after it has stopped. They can also help locate young students who may have exited at the wrong stop.

**Video and Audio Monitoring**. Far beyond simply capturing images of behavior on the bus, contemporary technologies include analytics which help identify potentially problematic behavior such as bullying, and monitor conversations for keywords or phrases which suggest potential threats or other issues which may have safety considerations.

**Stop-Arm Technology.** An often tragic problem occurs when drivers ignore the stop-arm of a bus, resulting in them striking the bus or a child. Radar and other technologies have been incorporated into these systems which alert the bus driver when a vehicle is in danger of running through the stop-arm of a bus. Other technologies such as 360° viewing systems monitor motion around the bus and alert the driver when a child may be at risk of being struck by the bus itself.

(Schwartz et al., 2016)

These are just a few of the technologies that are currently being incorporated into school bus safety. In the first case scenario below, we present an example of the technology components of a school transportation safety system. It is noteworthy that the U.S. Department of Transportation promotes a Safe Routes to School (SRTS) program. According to the weblink (https://www.transportation.gov/mission/health/Safe-Routes -to-School-Programs), 10–14 % of car trips occurring during rush hour are for school travel. SRTS promotes walking and bicycling to school. Promoting these strategies helps to address chronic diseases, increases physical activity, improves safety, reduces motor vehicle–related injuries and fatalities, and reduces transportation's contributions to air pollution. Another layer of safety protocols must be implemented by school leaders when students are walking and riding bikes to school. There is an entity, Safe Routes Partnership which provides guidance to school leaders for this component of safety.

## MONITORING ACCESS TO SCHOOL BUILDINGS AND FACILITIES
Controlling who can enter school grounds is perhaps one of the first strategies for keeping schools safe. Limiting the ability of armed intruders, criminals, and others to gain access to school grounds is critical to maintaining a safe environment. Technologies for doing so have never been greater. They include the following:

**Electronic Locks on Doors and Windows.** These permit security personnel to monitor the security of the facility around the clock and without being physically in the facility.

**Surveillance Cameras and Motion Detectors.** The sophistication of these devices permits recording during the day and night. Images can be detected and compared to databases.

**Motion-Activated Lights.** While it may not be practical to keep lights on continuously, motion-activated lights can be activated when there is motion.

**Facial and Voice Recognition.** These systems can quickly scan an individual's face and compare it to various databases, including those that should not be permitted on school grounds. These scans can be synced with door locks, cameras, security turnstiles, etc.

**Smart Cards and IDs.** These systems can electronically identify and record entry and exit to the school grounds. They can automate attendance and reduce the amount of time needed for reviewing attendance rosters and other ways of checking attendance. Further, they can prevent unauthorized persons from entering the facility.

**License Plate Recognition.** Scanning license plates is another technology which has been used to identify individuals who should not be on school grounds and/or record identifying information about a vehicle involved in a school safety incident.

(Schwartz et al., 2016)

## MONITORING ACTIVITY ON SCHOOL GROUNDS

A well-developed system will also focus on activities on school grounds. Visitors can be monitored, and the activities of students and others can be surveilled for behavior or activity that may violate school policies and/or place others at risk of harm. Technologies for doing so include the following:

**Video systems and motion detectors.** Can monitor traffic throughout school grounds, including classrooms, hallways, playgrounds etc. The analytics associated with these systems can detect potential bullying, fighting, stealing, and other types of behavior. A significant advantage is that this level of monitoring can be accomplished with technology and not a major investment in personnel.

**Classroom monitoring systems.** Can provide accurate details about events in classrooms. These include the amount of instructional time, student engagement behaviors, damage to property, threats, etc. These systems also extend to remote learning in which the teacher can view and freeze a student's screen, close tabs, and scan websites the student may have visited.

(Schwartz et al., 2016)

In the event that intruders enter buildings, get onto school grounds, and/or there are emergency situations needing addressing, it is important to have plans in place to make the pertinent individuals aware without alerting the intruder and/or escalating the situation further. In 2008, Aurora's School District In Aurora, Colorado developed a training manual for all employees and provided it to support the training. One of the components that is helpful is a security level guide based on threat assessment ranging from low-risk levels to severe risks:

## GREEN: LOW-RISK LEVEL, LEVEL ONE LOCKDOWN

LOW RISK (Normal day-to-day operations)
Incident Response Team (IRT) on standby status
All exterior doors will be locked and closed
All interior doors will be locked and either open or closed to the hallways
Interior doors which are not classrooms are locked and closed

## YELLOW: POTENTIAL RISK, LEVEL ONE LOCKDOWN

POTENTIAL RISK (A potential threat exists in the neighborhood around the school)
IRT is on ready status to respond to an emergency situation
All exterior doors will be locked and closed
High traffic doors must be monitored by staff members to allow building access to
students, staff, and appropriate visitors to the building
All interior doors will be locked
Bells continue to ring, students attend classes, and classroom activities continue
Teachers on planning time, report to the commons

## ORANGE: HIGH RISK, LEVEL TWO LOCKDOWN

HIGH RISK (An actual threat is in the neighborhoods around the school)
IRT in EOC as needed to respond to an emergency situation
All interior doors will be locked and closed
Exterior window coverings are in the closed position
Parking lots and site driveways/entryways are barricaded or closed
Follow COOP plan in preparing to work at alternative locations if needed
Restrict building access to essential staff only
Interior classroom and office windows covered
Classroom activities continue/students must remain in the classroom
Passing bells are turned off
Teachers on planning time, report to the commons

RED: SEVERE RISK, LEVEL THREE

SEVERE RISK (Threat in the building)
   IRT in EOC to respond to an emergency situation
   All interior and exterior doors will be locked and closed
   Exterior and interior window coverings are in the closed position
   Interior classroom and office windows covered
   Teachers stop teaching; interior lights are off
   Students and staff are in the "duck and cover" position –
INVISIBLE (students and staff attempt to be unseen)
   Follow COOP plan in preparing to work at alternative locations if needed
   (https://rems.ed.gov/docs/repository/REMS_000046_0001.pdf)

## ELECTRONIC COMMUNICATIONS

Finally, a strong safety plan will include monitoring social media and other electronic communications, such as emails. Recent events have shown that social media posts often foreshadow tragic events at schools such as mass shootings. Monitoring these can be a significant part of a comprehensive system of school safety. Similarly, emails and electronic communications can be monitored for particular words or phrases, which may indicate a potential threat to safety.

### Systems for Alerts and Alarms

The final component of a comprehensive system is a process that permits students, parents, and teachers to provide information about potential threats. There are many vendors and providers for technologies in each of these categories. As an example of social media monitoring "Social Net Watcher" is a cloud-based software solution that monitors and alerts school administrators of "dangerous" words posted on Facebook. "Anonymous Alerts" is an app that can be downloaded to mobile devices and used by students and staff of a school to alert the administrator to situations deemed to be dangerous. Capterra has a webpage which lists social media marketing software systems. Automated publishing, content management, conversion tracking, customer segmentation, keyword filtering, multi-account management, and reporting analytics are among the possible features of social media marketing software. Not all software has all the features; but the following software all have the features we previously noted – Sprout Social, Salesforce Marketing Cloud, Agorapulse, and Falcon.io. There is variability in the features provided by HubSpot, #paid, monday.com, Constant Contact, Oktopost, and Sked Social.

   https://gadrrres.net/what-we-do/gadrrres-global-activities/comprehensive-school-safety-framework

## SCENARIO 1: THE SAFE SCHOOL BUS

In this scenario, we describe a video and audio platform used to monitor the behavior of students on school buses. The system includes analytics which offers alerts and provides a record of behavior on buses. We do not describe a particular system, but recommended features of a system and how it might work in practice.

GPS Tracking. The first component of the system is its ability to track the location and speed of the bus at all times. The GPS device located in the bus displays its location on a graphic screen for school administrators and provides a graphic alert if its speed exceeds guidelines. Additionally, the number and duration of stops made are provided in an on-demand set of analytics. Trend data can be provided as well as analytics that will flag buses for "unsafe" driving (e.g., driving beyond recommended guidelines in inclement weather).

Entry and Exit. The second component of the system provides detailed information on who enters the bus and who exits. This component consists of several systems. The door sensors monitor when the door opens, whether a passenger enters or exits, records the time, and keeps count. The facial recognition system captures the face of the passenger upon entry/exit and matches it to the school's database. Passengers who are not in the database are flagged. The final feature of this system will be to flag passengers who exhibit a heightened emotional state (e.g., fear, anxiety, etc.) upon entry or exit to the bus. This information can be used to identify individuals who may be in need of counseling or support from school personnel. Additionally, monitoring entry and exit can help prevent instances in which a child is left on a bus after the driver has completed the route, as has happened when students fall asleep during long bus rides. The system would provide the driver with an alert letting him/her know that the bus was not empty.

Driver Monitoring. Distracted driving, drowsy driving, and a host of other activities by the bus driver can place the passengers at risk.

Passenger Monitoring. A major source of distractions for drivers are bus passengers. Children may be engaged in rough play, games, boisterous communications, and a host of other activities during their time on a bus. Behaviors such as opening windows, walking while the bus is in motion, and seeking the attention of the driver during times while bus is in motion.

Considering the information above, Johnville High is a large school with 1,200 students in a rural school district in the northwestern portion of the United States. The community is rather "close knit." However, two communities have experienced conflicts among parents, which has resulted in feuding among students. On a rainy morning, one of the bus drivers stops and several of the students load onto the bus. Shortly afterward the students enter the bus and a fight breaks out at the back of the bus. The driver pulls to the side of the road to try and control the fight. While on the side, other persons enter the bus, and there is now chaos in the front of the bus. Six high school students from the bus fight experienced severe injuries. The superintendent has requested that the principal along with the director of transportation strategize which technologies would be helpful for investigation purposes and which technologies would minimize the risks of such an incident in the future? The technologies noted above can be of value for both purposes.

### SCENARIO 2: PREVENTION OF SCHOOL BULLYING

Schools of Aurora Focus on Emergency Plans: A training manual to assist district staff in responding to emergent or threatening situations. (2008, February). Aurora, Colorado. Retrieved from https://rems.ed.gov/docs/repository/REMS_000046_0001.pdf

Bullying along with other disciplinary and safety issues are becoming more and more a concern in schools. Use the information below from Aurora's Emergency Plan to Develop a Bullying Plan for the information provided for Hill Middle School.

Beginning in 1999, the US Secret Service and the US Department of Education conducted an extensive study on targeted violence in schools, formally called the "Safe Schools Initiative." Researchers identified 37 incidents of targeted school violence involving 41 attackers that occurred in the United States from 1974 through June 2000. The earliest case which occurred in 1974 was an incident where a student brought guns and homemade bombs to school; set off the fire alarm; and shot at emergency and custodial personnel who responded to the alarm. "Targeted violence" is defined as an incident where a current or recent former student attacked someone at his or her school with lethal means (e.g., a gun or knife); and, where the student attacker purposefully chose his or her school as the location of the attack. (Incidents that were solely related to gang or drug trade activity or to a violent interaction between individuals that just happened to occur at the school were not included.).

There were ten key findings from the Safe Schools Initiative, two of which address targeted violence

INCIDENTS OF TARGETED VIOLENCE AT SCHOOL RARELY ARE SUDDEN, IMPULSIVE ACTS.

Students who engaged in school-based attacks typically did not "just snap." and then engage in impulsive or random acts of "targeted school violence." The attacks examined typically began with an idea, progressed to the development of a plan, moved on to securing the means to carry out the plan and culminating in an attack. However, the time span between the attacker's decision to mount an attack and the actual the incident may be short.

MOST ATTACKERS FELT BULLIED, PERSECUTED, OR WERE INJURED BY OTHERS PRIOR TO THE ATTACK.

Almost three-quarters of the attackers in recent school shootings felt persecuted, bullied, threatened, attacked or injured by others prior to the incident.

Bullying can happen in the home as is reflected in this scenario. Unfortunately as the scenario progresses, we will see that the bullying in the home affected what happened at the school. In an educational setting where there is a climate of "safety," adults and students respect each other. This climate is defined and fostered by students having a positive connection to at least one adult in authority. In such a climate, students develop the capacity to talk and openly share their concerns without fear of shame and reprisal. They try to help friends and fellow students who are in distress, bringing serious concerns to the attention of adults. Young people can find an adult to trust with this information, so that it does not remain "secret" until it is too late. Example: A young man, who brought a rifle to school, killing two students, and wounding several others, told the Secret Service from his prison cell: "I was really hurting. "I didn't have anybody to talk to. They just didn't care."

(Aurora Public Schools, 2008)

Retrieved from https://rems.ed.gov/docs/repository/REMS_000046 _0001.pdf

Using the information above, Hill Middle School is a large middle school in a deeply rural community. The school leadership team, after noting an increase in disruptive behavior, developed a comprehensive plan to address school safety. One aspect of the plan was to detect and respond to bullying before it led to negative outcomes for all at the school. The main portions of the plan include (1) developing a formal set of policies for consequences for bullying. This policy clearly specified the definition of bullying and gave examples of the types of behaviors that would not be tolerated and the consequences for anyone who engaged in those behaviors.

(2) Awareness and Monitoring Plan. The team developed notices (e.g., don't be a bully), posters, and other ways of informing all at the school about bullying. These were posted on the school website, social media, and included in electronic and other correspondences with parents, as well as other stakeholders. (3) Professional Development for School Personnel. The team provided professional development for detecting and responding to bullying for all school staff. Additionally, applications were utilized to detect possible (e.g., keyword search, etc.) on all social media and electronic communications connected with the school. Finally, school safety software designed to detect suspicious behavior was installed in the school security monitoring system. The following is an excerpt from material developed by the team:

> …What we may see as "kids being kids" may have far more long term consequences if action isn't taken. If a child is being bullied, many times they will joke around and act like they are okay but deep inside they are embarrassed and humiliated. If a student is being bullied and sees that an adult in the building has observed the bullying and does nothing about it, the student may turn to other means to stop the bullying as is indicated in several school shootings in the past. The Board of Education recognizes the negative impact that bullying has on student health, welfare and safety and on the learning environment at school. Bullying prevention efforts will be utilized in Aurora Public Schools through school-wide, classroom, and/or individual measures. All programs and efforts will communicate that bullying is not acceptable behavior and will not be tolerated. Bullying by students is prohibited on all district property, at district or school-related activities, in district vehicles, and off school property when such conduct has a connection to school or any district curricular or non-curricular activity. Bullying may imply an imbalance of

power or strength in which one student is victimized by others. Students who are exposed to the negative actions generally have difficulty defending themselves and in specific situations may be helpless against the student or students who harass. Friendly or playful teasing may be considered bullying when such repeated behaviors continue despite clear signs of distress and opposition on the part of the victim.

## SUMMARY

In Chapter 4, we discussed the roles of school leaders in ensuring that campuses are safe. We begin the chapter with the Leadership and Technology Standards, which are aligned to the roles. In this era, school safety has received heightened attention. There have been many school shootings and other incidents. As we consistently write, technological tools can assist principals in all of their roles; but it is still necessary for school leaders to possess the necessary knowledge, skills, and dispositions related to each role. We include technological tools to assist principals related to five aspects of school operations: information technology systems, transportation, school buildings and facilities, school grounds, and electronic communication. In each instance, we describe various types of technologies that might be employed. Guidelines for comprehensive safety and emergency planning are included. We also include https://www.schoolsafety.gov in the discussion as was created in 2020 based on the recommendation of the Federal Commission on School Safety. SafetySchools.gov includes information on bullying and cyberbullying, cybersecurity, emergency planning, infectious diseases and public health, mental health, school climate, targeted violence, and threat assessment and reporting. We addressed most of these tenants in this chapter. Two case scenarios at the end of the chapter are presented for the application of the concepts and tools for this and other chapters as deemed applicable.

## TECHNOLOGY TOOLS

Captera:    https://www.capterra.com/sem-compare/social-media-marketing-software/?utm_source=ps-google&utm_medium=ppc&gclid=Cj0KCQiA95aRBhCsARIsAC2xvfygggeBx-Y36MLzenJ4Th_ISl1fBygrC76ksSlDp5YanpnKDh8DvccaAupkEALw_wcB

*Anonymous Alert - https://apps.apple.com/us/app/anonymous-alerts-reporting-app/id615788135*

*Social Net Watcher- https://explore.meltwater.com/social-media -monitoring-solutions?utm_source=google&utm_medium= ppc&utm_campaign=advertising-google-17329565278_1455 84052468&utm_term=g_kwd-303065760206_p_social%20 monitoring%20tool&utm_content=600175048936&loca- tionid=9025169&device=c_c&matchtype=p&network=g &campaign=US_Search-Social%20Media%20Monitoring %20%26%20Listening&_fct=1&campaignid=17329565278 &adgroupid=145584052468&gclid=EAIaIQobChMI8b2 uxPaF-QIVanxvBB0_rwKtEAAYASAAEgKP4fD_BwE*

Cybersecurity Educational Material

U.S. Department of Homeland Security Cybersecurity Education Materials: https://www.dhs.gov/stopthinkconnect

Cybersecurity Training Materials from the National Center for Missing and Exploited Children: https://www.netsmartz.org/

Cybersecurity Training Materials for Teachers, Parents and Students: https://www.consumer.ftc.gov/features/feature-0038 -onguardonline

The Guide for Developing High-Quality School Emergency Operations Plans: https://rems.ed.gov/docs/REMS_K-12_Guide_508.pdf

A Comprehensive Report on School Safety: https://www.ojp.gov/pdffiles1/nij/grants/250274.pdf

Information Technology/Cybersecurity Checklist: https://opi.mt.gov /Portals/182/Page%20Files/Emergency%20Planning%20and %20Safety/Cyber%20Checklist%20Checklist%20v1.4.pdf

Top 5 Security Threats for Schools: https://www.cosn.org/sites/default/files/Top%205 %20Cybersecurity%20Threats.pdf

U.S. Department of Education Data Security Checklist: https://studentprivacy.ed.gov/sites/default/files/resource_document/ file/Data%20Security%20Checklist_0.pdf

Federal Government School Safety Website: https://www.schoolsafety.gov

## REFERENCES

Captera. https://www.capterra.com/sem-compare/social-media-marketing-software/ ?utm_source=ps-google&utm_medium=ppc&gclid=Cj0KCQiA95aRBhCsARI sAC2xvfygggeBx-Y36MLzenJ4Th_ISl1fBygrC76ksSlDp5YanpnKDh8DvccaAupk EALw_wcB.

Firch, J. (n.d.) 9 common types of malware (and how to prevent them). https:// purplesec.us/common-malware-types/.

Goals of comprehensive school safety; A comprehensive school safety framework (CSSF); by global alliance for diaster risk reduction & resilience in the education sector. https://gadrrres.net/what-we-do/gadrrres-global-activities/comprehensive-school-safety-fr.

International Society of Technology of Education. https://www.iste.org/standards/for-education-leaders.

National Educational Leadership Preparation (NELP) Standards. https://www.naesp.org/communicator-november-2018/nelp-standards-approved-how-affects-you.

National Policy Board for Educational Administration (2015). Professional Standards for Educational Leaders 2015. Reston, VA: Author.

SafetySchool.gov. https://www.schoolsafety.gov.

Schools of aurora focus on emergency plans: A training manual to assist district staff in responding to emergent or threatening situations. (2008, February). https://rems.ed.gov/docs/repository/REMS_000046_0001.pdf.

Schwartz, H. L., Ramchand, R., Barnes-Proby, D., Grant, S., Jackson, B. A., Leuschner, K. J., Matsuda, M., & Saunders, J. (2016). *The role of technology in improving K–12 school safety*. RAND Corporation. https://www.rand.org/pubs/research_reports/RR1488.html.

U.S. Department of Education. (2013). *Guide for developing high quality school emergency operations plans*. https://rems.ed.gov/docs/School_Guide_508C.pdf.

# CHAPTER 5

## Instructional Leadership

**ABSTRACT**

In this chapter, technology tools to support the school leader as an instructional leader are discussed. It should be noted that the role of the principal as an instructional leader evolved with the accountability movements (the *No Child Left Behind Act* and *Every Student Succeeds Act*). A heightened focus on instructional leadership may be linked to increases in accountability mandates. According to the comprehensive guide (manual) of the *Every Student Succeeds Act* (https://www.everystudentsucceedsact.org/), the purpose is to *"provide all children significant opportunity to receive a fair, equitable, and high-quality education, and to close educational achievement gaps."* It is noteworthy that the importance of achievement was the impetus for the first accountability movement in 1965; the *Elementary and Secondary Education Act*. In 1983, *A Nation At Risk* re-emphasized the 1965 movement which was followed by the *No Child Left Behind Act* in 2001 and then the *Every Student Succeeds Act* in 2015.

In Chapter 3, the interrelationship of instructional leadership and management is argued pertinent to the Professional Standards for Educational Leaders (PSEL) and the National Educational Leadership Preparation (NELP) Standards. The concepts are relevant for this chapter as well, and the leadership standards and technology standards most aligned with instructional leadership are noted. Various technologies are discussed to support the instructional leader in monitoring classroom instruction, providing professional development and support for teachers, promoting collaboration and mentoring among teachers and students, facilitating individualized instruction and support for students, and monitoring student achievement. We begin this chapter with a discussion of the Professional Standards for Educational Leadership (PSEL), National Educational

DOI: 10.4324/9781003269472-5

Leadership Preparation (NELP) Standards, and International Society for Technology in Educational (ISTE) Standards which are most aligned to the instructional leadership roles of school leaders.

---

**INSTRUCTIONAL LEADERSHIP LINKED TO THE LEADERSHIP STANDARDS**

The school principal as instructional leader implies that the principal is actively involved in the instructional process of the school. According to Hallinger (2015) instructional leadership surfaced as a "practice-related construct" in the United States in the 1950s. The transformation of instructional leadership into a "theoretically-grounded, research-based construction" occurred in the 1980s. The emergence of learner-centered leadership and leadership for learning began to evolve in 2000. In the *Relevance of Instructional Leadership,* instructional leadership is included as one of the Five Fundamentals for School Success. Tenants of teaching and learning are significantly embedded in Chicago's instructional leadership principles.

Instructional leadership is presented in alignment with the Professional Standards for Educational Leaders (PSEL). Notions pertinent to educational leaders supporting instruction and the academic success of students are encompassed in Standards 4, 6, and 7 of PSEL. Standard 4 is Curriculum, Instruction, and Assessment. "Effective educational leaders develop and support intellectually rigorous and coherent systems of curriculum, instruction, and assessment to promote each student's academic success and well-being." Standard 6 is Professional Capacity of School Personnel. "Effective educational leaders develop the professional capacity and practice of school personnel to promote each student's academic success and well-being." Standard 7 is Professional Community for Teachers and Staff. "Effective educational leaders foster a professional community of teachers and other professional staff to promote each student's academic success and well-being." The most relevant PSEL and NELP Standards for Chapter 5 are PSEL 4 and NELP 4; they are listed below.

PSEL 4
Effective leaders:

a) Implement coherent systems of curriculum, instruction, and assessment that promote the mission, vision, and core values of the school, embody high expectations for student learning, align with academic standards, and are culturally responsive.

b) Align and focus systems of curriculum, instruction, and assessment within and across grade levels to promote student academic success, love of learning, the identities and habits of learners, and a healthy sense of self.
c) Promote instructional practice that is consistent with knowledge of child learning and development, effective pedagogy, and the needs of each student.
d) Ensure instructional practice that is intellectually challenging, authentic to student experiences, recognizes student strengths, and is differentiated and personalized.
e) Promote the effective use of technology in the service of teaching and learning.
f) Employ valid assessments that are consistent with knowledge of child learning and development and technical standards of measurement.
g) Use assessment data appropriately and within technical limitations to monitor student progress and improve instruction.

NELP 4

Component 4.1 Program completers understand and can demonstrate the capacity to evaluate, develop, and implement high-quality, technology-rich curricula programs and other supports for academic and non-academic student programs.
Component 4.2 Program completers understand and can demonstrate the capacity to evaluate, develop, and implement high-quality and equitable academic and non-academic instructional practices, resources, technologies, and services that support equity, digital literacy, and the academic and non-academic systems of the school.
Component 4.3 Program completers understand and can demonstrate the capacity to evaluate, develop, and implement formal and informal culturally responsive and accessible assessments that support data-informed instructional improvement and student learning and well-being.
Component 4.4 Program completers understand and demonstrate the capacity to collaboratively evaluate, develop, and implement the curriculum of the school, instruction, technology, data systems, and assessment practices in a coherent, equitable, and systematic manner.

(http://www.npbea.org/)

As presented in Chapter 1, NELP Standard 4: Learning and Instruction aligns with PSEL 4. The tenants of NELP 4.1, 4.2, 4.3, and 4.4 include evaluating and implementing curricula, implementing high-quality curricular accounting for equity, implementing culturally responsive assessments, and collaborating in a systematic manner pertinent to learning and instructional needs respectively. In addition, learning and instruction are embedded in most of the competencies of the ISTE Standards for Leadership: equity and citizenship advocate, visionary planner, empowering leader, systems designer, and connected learner.

Below we discuss various aspects of instructional leadership, including monitoring classroom instruction, providing professional development and support for teachers, facilitating individualized instruction and support for students, promoting collaboration and mentoring among teachers and students, and monitoring student achievement. It is easy to imagine that performing these roles would have been labor intensive two decades ago, especially with regard to collecting, processing, and acting on data. With modern technologies, the tasks associated with instructional leadership require far less input of resources.

## MONITORING CLASSROOM INSTRUCTION

One of the more critical roles of the school principal is to ensure that effective instruction occurs in classrooms. While there are many ways this could be approached, a traditional strategy is to observe each teacher teach. The results of the observations will indicate to the principal the kinds of skills/competencies the teacher is proficient with or lacking proficiency in. When teachers are proficient, they can serve as mentors or leaders of faculty study groups. When they are lacking proficiency, teachers need to be mentored or placed in groups to be assisted. In the past, observation tools would entail sitting in a classroom and observing the teacher, utilizing an established observation tool for the purpose. Modern technologies allow principals to observe teachers without technically entering the classrooms. In some settings principals may have video-taped a lesson and then reviewed it, again using a tool to structure the observation process. In more recent developments, the use of mobile devices in walk-throughs provides an efficient way to record data. Data from walk-throughs and formal observations can be gathered efficiently using mobile devices regarding the strengths of teachers and areas in need of improvement. It should be noted that current analytics for video data permit analysis of teaching behaviors that were not possible in the past (Sonnert et al., 2018). These data can be analyzed with student performance data. In addition, data can be aggregated and disaggregated by pertinent teacher variables.

An example of a tool that can be used to support school principals in the instructional leadership role is the resource referred to as iObservation (Gonzales and Young, 2014). We discussed iObservations in Chapter 3 when discussing the roles of school leaders in personnel evaluations. There are many other tools, and most observation instruments can be converted to virtual use. iObservation is "a comprehensive data collection and management system that reports real-time data from classroom walk-throughs, teacher observations, self-assessments, instructional rounds, and evaluations." The system is web-based and accessible through an internet connection; however, there is an offline version for buildings without internet access. iObservation improves classroom observations in the following ways:

Increase efficiency with an automated and systematized process,
Create a focus for busy instructional leaders using content resources,
Remove the burden of paper-based documentation,
Make data-based decisions informed by real-time reports (aggregated or disaggregated),
Send effective feedback to teachers that encourages reflection and supports growth,
Choose your language of instruction, digitize your own content, use the iObservation research-based framework, or adopt an expert framework from Danielson or Marzano, and
Enjoy convenient wireless, offline, or mobile access. https://www.iobservation.com/

These and other features of the iObservation application are described on the company's website, https://www.iobservation.com/. As described on their website, other notable features include tabs on the login screen of iObservation are alerts, observations, collaboration, manage, assessment, first time users, and quick start guide. Selecting the observation tab provides the option to conduct the observation (the instrument is available electronically). There is also the option to view previously recorded observations along with the option to start peer observations. The storing capabilities of previous data along with the report generating capabilities are significant advantages of the iObservation system. The Marzano Focused Teacher Evaluation Model is also included in the iObservation application.

As noted several times in earlier chapters, although technology can significantly enhance the efforts to monitor classroom instruction, this does not negate the importance of school leaders possessing pertinent knowledge, skills, and dispositions. It is important for school leaders to align classroom instruction with professional growth for teachers that in turn leads to improved student performance. Oliva and Pawlas (2018) discuss key roles related directly to instruction on how principals can assist teachers.

Those roles are:

- Helping teachers plan for instruction,
- Helping teachers present instruction,
- Helping teachers with classroom management,
- Helping teachers evaluate instruction,
- Helping teachers plan and implement curricula,
- Helping teachers evaluate curricula,
- Helping teachers through in-service programs,
- Helping teachers on a one-on-one basis,
- Helping teachers work together, and
- Helping teachers evaluate their own performances.

The following quotation is from *The Relevance of Instructional Leadership, 2nd Edition* by Leslie Jones (Cognella Academic Publishing, 2020).

Zepeda's model is useful because it can ultimately support the role of the school leader (directly or indirectly) in monitoring classroom instruction, providing professional development and support for teachers, facilitating individualized instruction and support for students, and promoting collaboration and mentoring among teachers and students.

Zepeda (2017) has a model in which she links classroom observations to professional development. In conducting classroom observations, school leaders assume the role of instructional leadership. Professional development should obviously provide the framework for continuous improvement and lead to improved academic performances for students. The is available in the 2nd edition of *The Relevance of Instructional Leadership* (Cognella Academic Publish, 2020).

The facilitation of effective teaching and meaningful professional development are emphasized in the model. The starting point for implementation of the model is with informal observations which lead to clinical supervision. Informal observations are referred to as "snap shots," walk-ins," "pop-ins," "drop-ins" among other names. These are brief visits where school leaders can get an idea of good or bad practices.

The cycle begins with Clinical Supervision. Clinical Supervision entails a classroom observation accompanied with a pre-observation conference and post-observation conference. School leaders generally conduct informal observations and/or pop-ins that lead to the formal classroom observations.

During the post-observation conference, this is an important time for the school leader to provide constructive feedback. Zepeda (2017) identifies characteristics of effective back from leaders to teachers.

The following are the characteristics:

- Supports the teacher in examining both the positive and the not-so-positive aspects of practice.
- Promotes footholds for follow-up.
- Nurtures a sense of worth and positive self-esteem.
- Facilitates self-assessment and self-discovery.
- Focuses on a few key areas.
- Describes accurately what was observed.
- Is authentic and free of meaningless or patronizing platitudes.
- Clarifies and expands ideas for both the teacher and the observer.
- Deals with the concrete examples observed (actions, behaviors, words of the teacher or students).
- Promotes goal setting and the development of strategies.
- Avoids:
  - Making assumptions about teachers,
  - Overloading the teacher with detail after detail after detail,
  - Evaluating the teacher's overall credibility as a teacher,
  - Asserting or making inferences about the teacher, and
  - Judging and labeling a practice as good or bad.
- Guides the teacher to think beyond the lesson observed.
- Accepts and incorporates the points the teacher makes as part of the feedback process.

Zepeda's model suggests that clinical supervision should be coupled with differentiated supervision. The value of differentiated supervision is that teachers are provided opportunities to individualize feedback processes from the school leader and provide evidence of professional growth. After both models of supervision, school leaders and teachers can make decisions about opportunities for mentoring, staff development, and goal setting.

There is great emphasis placed on the value of mentoring. There are obviously some teachers in schools who may serve as mentors and others who need mentoring. One huge advantage of mentoring is that collegiality is promoted. In Chapter 3, the value and importance of collegiality are discussed. Leaders may facilitate larger groups of teachers to work together through professional learning communities.

Professional learning communities facilitated by school leaders can be an effective form of professional development for teachers as well. Darling-Hammond et al. (2009), suggests that professional learning communities work when they are sustained, school-based and embedded in the daily work of teachers. Experiences in school leadership suggest that the following concepts are critical for meaningful professional development: time and organization, relevance, follow-up.

Professional learning communities and mentoring may serve as kinds of professional development. There are obviously other kinds of professional and staff development. The needs of the staff should dictate the kind of professional and/or staff development for engagement. The professional development must align and also lead to individual goal setting – all of which the school leader as an evaluator of teaching facilitates. The cycle begins again with the next observation.

There are many tools available for school leaders for both formal and informal observations. A reference list is provided below.

Resources for School Leaders on Teacher Evaluation Instruments:
http://www4.esc13.net/schoolreadyteam/observation-tools
-admin
http://www.educationworld.com/a_admin/admin/admin400_d
.shtml
http://usny.nysed.gov/rttt/teachers-leaders/practicerubrics/Docs/
SilverStrongTeacherRubric.pdf;
http://www.iobservation.com/
http://www.doe.in.gov/sites/default/files/turnaround-principles/
classroom-walkthrough-development-samples.pdf
http://usny.nysed.gov/rttt/teachers-leaders/practicerubrics/Docs/
SilverStrongObservationRubric.pdf;
http://www.42regular.com/obs/help/documents.pdf
http://www.ascd.org/publications/educational-leadership/dec10
/vol68/num04/Evaluations-That-Help-Teachers-Learn.aspx.
http://www.ncpublicschools.org/docs/effectiveness-model/ncees/
instruments/teach-eval-manual.pdf

We mentioned previously that COVID-19 shifted many classes online in K-12 schools as well as many other work environments to online platforms. Several Learning Management Systems are included in the section **Providing Professional Development and Support for Teachers** below. Technological tools to assist principals in supporting classroom instruction face-to-face and in the virtual platforms are noted throughout this Chapter. It is also essential to highlight that there are features through the Learning Management Systems that allow school leaders to observe classrooms that are face-to-face remotely.

## PROVIDING PROFESSIONAL DEVELOPMENT AND SUPPORT FOR TEACHERS

Evaluating teachers is a key aspect of the work of the school principal. Related to this is providing the needed professional development and support that will address identified needs. Modern technologies are especially useful for supporting teachers. Professional development delivered virtually is a growing trend among classroom teachers (Kennedy and Laurillard, 2019). Williams (2021, February) noted that there are myths about virtual professional development, and she suggested that principals are often convinced that every teacher can teach online. The North American Council for Online Learning revealed that teachers and principals need professional development in how to deliver online learning. We believe this is multidimensional. One aspect is that teachers need to know how to deliver instruction through online platforms like Zoom, Google Meet, etc. Another dimension is for teachers to engage in professional development as learners related to other topics that refine instructional skills. We will discuss a few of the tools for teachers to deliver online instruction. It should be noted that teachers need proficiency in the use of these tools. We will follow the discussion of online delivery instructional tools with the professional development opportunities for teachers related to other topics. As mentioned in Chapter 1, there are technology tools available to educators; here we highlight a selected sample.

Zoom, Google Classroom, Swivel, Blackboard Collaborate, Moodle, Adobe Connect, WizIQ, LearnCube, BigBlueButton, VEDAMO, Newrow Smart, and Samba Live are among the tools and/or Learning Management Platforms for instructional delivery. Ohnigian et al. (2021) advocates that Zoom has become essential due to the pandemic. It is categorized as a "cloud-based peer-to-peer" software platform, and teachers (or participants) can view each other synchronously through the video conferencing feature. Group work can be facilitated using breakout rooms. Participants can share screens, show videos, and record the meeting. In real-time, students and teachers can have synchronous interactions. The application also includes polling options, where instructors might administer learning checks like quizzes. Swivl has fewer features than Zoom; however, it provides the options for students to view teachers and see entire classrooms. Lessons can also be recorded in Swivl (https://swivl.zendesk.com).

Google Classroom has an element called Google Meet; the classroom is obviously the platform used most frequently for educational purposes. It is similar to Zoom in how it appears on the devices of screens. Google Classroom is facilitated through "classroom.google.com" while Zoom is facilitated through an application that can be downloaded to a computer, tablet, or smartphone. In addition to giving and receiving feedback in real-time, watching videos and interacting with peers and instructors like Zoom, Google Classroom allows learners to submit assignments, review and meet academic deadlines, and review class announcements (Ohnigian et al., 2021).

Blackboard Collaborate, Moodle, and Canvas are Learning Management Systems. There are also many other Learning Management Systems. Blackboard Collaborate is an instructional delivery tool with synchronous and asynchronous options. Teachers can engage students with customized course menus; and dashboards for course updates. The menu includes, but is not limited to, announcements, collaborations (discussions, grading, cloud storage, push notifications, tests, and assignments,) what's new, and connect. Blackboard Collaborate includes tutorials and training information within the platform. In Chapter 7, we reference a function of Blackboard Collaborate; Blackboard Connect that allows the user to perform mass messaging (https://www.blackboard.com).

Moodle is the most popular Learning Management System. It is also free; however, there are add-ons/plugins available for purchase. Like Blackboard Collaborate, instructions may be facilitated through synchronous and asynchronous modalities. Collaborative learning may be facilitated through Wikis, Forms, or Workshops. Student progress can be measured through Moodle's Gradebook, which features the capability to send grades directly to students. In addition, the application allows for rewarding student progress with Course Certificates, a Moodle plugin. There are also options for library gamification plugins that reward the accomplishments of students (https://www.moodle.com).

Like Blackboard Connect and Moodle, Canvas has a dashboard. The dashboard on Canvas has a feature for students to email the teachers along with a calendar feature (which may display due dates for upcoming assignments). Although Canvas was designed for asynchronous instruction, synchronous instruction can occur by enabling Zoom on Canvas. Discussion can be facilitated through the discussion board, and the discussions can be collaborative. Like the other Learning Management Systems, quizzes can be administered. There is a gradebook that stores assessment data for students (https://www.instructure.com).

Schoology is a Learning Management System that has 200 educational platforms and tools integrated into it. Because it has so many platforms integrated, it is a useful tool for many of the tasks school leaders perform and is applicable to most of this book's chapters. Schoology has a strong instructional component as well and is marketed as leveling "the playing field, enabling students to be successful in the 21st century, regardless of language, learning deficiency, or background" (https://www.schoology .com/).

Adobe Connect is a tool for administering classes, digital training, webinars, and other virtual experiences. Virtual rooms are created in Adobe Connect that provide customization in the appearances of participants (through the creation of avatars). Instructors create resizable pods which provide functionality that allows for the sharing of multiple screens. There are options for teachers to customize presentations, videos, polls, and room templates (Cappiccie and Desrosiers, 2011). Similar to other tools presented, WizIQ provides a synchronous classroom. WizIQ is used by businesses but has the option for tutoring and is a comprehensive solution for virtual classrooms inclusive of course builders, test and assessment builders, and customized applications (https:// www.adobeconnect.com).

LearnCube is described as a virtual classroom with a synchronous component. According to their website (https://learncube.com), LearnCube is an online environment that "allows teachers and students to communicate, interact, collaborate, and explain ideas." The features of LearnCube include video conferencing, audio conferencing, real-time chat, an interactive online whiteboard, a library of learning materials, and teacher tools. The interactive online whiteboard, library of learning materials, and teacher tools and controls are key features that "transform" the online educational experiences. The interactive whiteboard gives a focus point for teachers and students to collaborate on learning projects. Lesson materials may be included in learning projects.

Many of the platforms discussed in this chapter are categorized as "web-conferencing software" which provides "screen-sharing." The whiteboards offered in LearnCube provide the option for students to write/type/draw on actual pages. Student participation is encouraged, and it is most efficient for teachers to change from concepts to student engagement and then back and forth as deemed necessary. The library of learning material includes digital material comparable to the textbooks, games, exercises, templates, worksheets, and multimedia resources in the physical classroom. The virtual software provides the opportunity for learners to be on the same page with teachers. In LearnCube, the following controls are available for teachers:

- Teacher tools: Text tool, draw tool, eraser, shapes, pen color, zoom.
- Specialist teacher tools: Math tools, instant dictionary, instant verb conjugation tables.
- Save or record: Save learning materials for the student to review later.
- Group class tools: Raise hand tool and breakout rooms for larger groups.
- Control of the student webcam: Helpful if the student has a poor connection and needs to reduce internet bandwidth requirements.
- Control of the student mic: Yes, that means you can finally "mute" your student when required.

(https://www.learncube.com/virtual-classroom-software.html)

BigBlueButton is another synchronous option to provide virtual instruction. Like several of the other options, the use of the breakouts rooms, polling, and chats facilitate student engagement. Slideshows, videos, whiteboards, and recording of lectures. When using the whiteboard, annotations are visible to students, and teachers can zoom in, highlight, draw, and write on presentations (Malone, 2015). Integrated into the Learning Management Systems of Canvas, Google for Education, Moodle, and Schoology, VEDAMO is an online virtual tutoring platform. It is browser-based and requires downloading. Breakout rooms, screen sharing, media sharing, and collaborative whiteboards are available. Newrow integrates seamlessly as well with major Learning Management Systems and has many of the features noted for the other tools. It is entirely web-based with no Flash, and no necessary downloads or installations (Malone, 2015).

As previously mentioned, the growth of virtual classrooms is due to COVID 19 and other weather events. Businesses are also using virtual platforms, and the popularity of virtual professional development is growing. Virtual professional development helps reduce the disruption that is caused when teachers must leave their classroom for an extended period to participate in professional development, and virtual professional development can also reduce costs. Additionally, supporting teachers with video-taped demonstration lectures, computer-based simulations of classroom interactions, and other activities help to promote efforts to continuously improve and refine instructional skills. Web-based technologies facilitate these activities (Smith and Sivo, 2012; Gunter and Reeves, 2017). According to Castelo (2020, July) virtual professional development requires strategic planning. She proposes that clear objectives are set for virtual professional development along with clear expectations and roles. This aligns with in-person professional development.

Like in-person professional development, virtual professional development requires the identification of goals and how the goals will be measured. The goals of professional development should also be aligned with the school and/or district. In Zepeda's model (2017) cited above; we note that professional development should align with the results of classroom observations. This principle ensures the alignment of professional development with the goals of the school and/or district. It is important for the professional development provided to teachers to be meaningful and can be implemented with the work that is done with students and/or other sectors of the job. We previously referenced that there are various modalities of delivering online professional development. Castelo (2020, July) also suggests that it is paramount to select the modality of delivery that best coincides with the objectives of professional development. Other factors to consider include in planning professional development is the number of attendees, the structure of the professional development to facilitate learning opportunities, the nature of the discussion (whole or small group,) and the nature of the feedback.

Live interactions are facilitated through videoconferencing technology. Microsoft Teams, Cisco Webex, Google Meet, and Zoom are platforms to promote live interactions. There are opportunities for teachers to familiarize themselves with the various technological tools through vendors like Google Education that provide free sessions. Because there are challenges in delivering professional development, Castelo (2020, July) indicates that technology should be tested in advance. For in-person professional development, facilitators check to make certain all materials are available. For virtual professional development, it is necessary to check devices like webcams, microphones, and headsets. In-person professional development when facilitated effectively can be effective, useful, and empowering.

When we conducted web searches, attended conferences, and consulted with other professionals, we saw that virtual platforms for professional development in teaching are growing exponentially. Due to COVID 19, many conferences have been and are being held virtually. Fontichiaro et al. (2021, December) recommend webinars for professional development (PD) that engage educators. The advantage of a live webinar or online presentation is the opportunity to chat with other participants as experts present. Archived versions of online presentations provide the opportunity to listen at the participant's convenience. The need to focus on interactivity in professional development through global learning networks is embedded in Indicator 2.1b of the ISTE Standards.

The leadership ISTE Standards are included in Chapter 1 and other chapters. In this section, we are referring to the general ISTE Standards for Educators. Indicator 2.1b is the impetus for the following guidelines to increase interactivity in online professional development.

Fontichiaro et al. (2021, December) note that school leaders and developers of web-based professional development for teachers should:

- Plan with learning outcomes in mind,
- Make webinars a conversation,
- Signal from the start that participants matter,
- Practice, practice, practice,
- 'Goldilocks' your topic,
- Don't be afraid to go off-roading, and
- Remember that interactivity is just one piece of the webinar.

The critical notion in planning for web-based professional development/webinars is that professional development is about the development of colleagues' capacity. The focus should be on what the participants will learn. Moderators and presenters have distinct roles in webinars. Moderators monitor the time along with other protocol-related issues whereas presenters have the responsibility pertaining to planning content and considering interactive opportunities for attendees. The participants should be drawn into the webinar as active participants. Moderators can signal at the beginning of webinars the expectations of participation by welcoming participants by name (Fontichiaro et al., 2021, December.)

A huge benefit for the presenter is practicing. It is important for presenters to anticipate challenges and "hiccups." Repetitive practice with authentic audiences helps presenters build confidence which in turn welcomes the participants to the conversation. As previously noted, moderators can help with time management. Presenters must be conscientious of time as attendees will be frustrated when presenters go through slides too quickly. 5–10 minutes for question-and-answer time provides a cushion for ending the presentation. Giving participants the opportunity to interact with each other and technology tools are powerful interacting strategies. Demonstrating aspects of technology and allowing practice allows for "hands-on" professional development. Although interactivity is meaningful, it is only "one piece of the webinar." It is equally crucial for presenters to know what the non-negotiables are including, what do participants need to know, what are the essential takeaways from my presentation, and where is there room for ideas from participants. The goal of professional development is to leverage its impact (Fontichiaro et al., 2021, December).

## PROMOTING COLLABORATION AND MENTORING AMONG TEACHERS AND STUDENTS

Collaborations and mentoring are important for maximizing learning in school settings (Jones, 2015). This is true for teachers and students. In Chapter 3, Professional Learning Communities are introduced as a retention strategy. Professional Learning Communities (PLCs) have been demonstrated to promote instructional effectiveness, adoption of classroom innovations, and sharing of information and resources among teachers (Hunuk et al., 2019; Thomas et al., 2017). Initiating in business, PLCs were first called learning organizations (Senge, 1990). As early as 1997, Hord noted that in education "PLCs involve infrastructure changes that lead to school improvement," and "the ultimate benefit of PLCs is improved instructional practices which lead to improved student achievement."

Referring to Zapada's model (2017) in the section **Monitoring Classroom Instruction**, mentoring is included as a portion of the classroom instructional process aligning classroom instruction to professional development. Mentoring can be facilitated through PLCs. Web-based resources, such as Moodle promote collaborations among teachers in ways that are difficult to obtain in the past. Among students, web-based collaborations can promote joint learning activities with teachers and students geographically displaced from the local school (Armstrong et al., 2009; Hughes et al., 2018; Rowland et al., 2017). Additionally, these tools can greatly expand the pool of potential mentors as they permit mentoring virtually (Radcliffe and Stephens, 2008).

## FACILITATING INDIVIDUALIZED INSTRUCTION AND SUPPORT FOR STUDENTS

Students often struggle with specific skills and concepts, necessitating tailored instruction opportunities. While this is near impossible in the traditional classroom, with modern technologies intelligent tutoring programs can identify specific areas in which students are struggling and provide targeted learning activities (Koedinger et al., 2015). These systems cannot identify specific concepts that may need re-teaching, but can help identify the learning strategies students are employing that may be leading to a faulty learning outcome. Such support is not possible in traditional classrooms.

It should be noted that all of the tools and technologies noted above can be linked and integrated into databases that can be subjected to analysis. Such data permit examination of learning processes that are often not possible with traditional approaches. An additional complexity for instructional leaders is supporting virtual classrooms. There are various technologies available, Google Classroom, Zoom, etc.; however, the challenge is to ensure that instruction is communicated effectively and learners are engaged.

As early as 2008, Gee (2008, p. 19) discussed the paramount need for online courses to provide students with challenging learning experiences that were in their "regime of competence." It is equally important for students to be supported in their online experiences. Lowes and Lin (2015) echoed the importance of students being provided challenging learning experiences with support. Borup et al. (2018) discussed that there are three challenges for students learning online – a high degree of flexibility, online communication, and technological competence.

In a study of virtual teachers in Michigan with high online student passage rates, teachers provide insight into success. Students are assigned mentors who do not replace the content expert teachers but support students in developing communication skills, organizational skills, and study skills necessary to learn online. Both teachers and mentors facilitate interactions with students, develop caring relationships, motivate students to engage in learning activities, and organize and manage student learning. Students participating in the study perceive that the following are the responsibilities related to instruction: advising students about course enrollment, orienting students to online expectations and learning experiences, and instructing students about the course content.

In Chapter 1, we noted guidelines suggested by ISTE for providing the best learning opportunities for students in a remote and digital environment. The following are the elements cited in Chapter 1:

- Learning environments that allow for rich educator and student collaboration and communication, that may also include collaboration with subject matter experts, instructional support personnel, and peers.
- Digital learning content and interactive learning experiences that engage students in reaching specific learning goals.
- The use of data and information to personalize learning and/or provide targeted instruction.
- A wide variety of computer-based formative and summative assessments.

There are also several weblinks where strategies to improve online learning are noted; the following are a few of the welinks:

https://www.pearsoned.com/9-strategies-for-effective-online-teaching/#:~:text=9%20strategies%20for%20effective%20online%20teaching%201%20Know,maintain%20a%20strong%20presence.%20...%20More%20items...%20

https://www.albert.io/blog/strategies-for-teaching-online/
https://elearningindustry.com/5-strategies-improve-your-online
    -teaching
https://blog.konversai.com/10-strategies-effective-online-teaching/

In Chapter 1, we also noted the EdSurge Product Index referenced by Krueger (2021, December) for comparing and selecting technology products. The "Seal of Alignment" from ISTE was also referenced in Chapter 1. ISTE highlights all technology programs aligned to its standards.

## MONITORING STUDENT ACHIEVEMENT

Traditionally, most school administrators would rely on a combination of teacher-made tests, annually administered standardized tests, and, to a lesser extent, formative assessments provided by test vendors. In most cases, significant investments of time, effort, and resources were required to acquire, administer, score, and report the results of the assessments. Olivia and Pawlass (2018) present monitoring the performance of students as a part of the instructional process. Teachers plan (or have instructional goals), deliver instruction, and assess. Of course, this is most aligned to teacher-made tests and other assessment methods in comparison to standardized tests. Traditional tests, portfolios, journals, observations, and interviews are noted by Olivia and Pawlass (2018) as methods to gather data pertinent to student performance.

Further, the actual collection of the data was a disruptive event, one that typically occurred at the end of the learning process. However, there are methods noted as a means to gather data from students before the instruction occurs in the instructional process and as the instruction is taking place. Story shares, quick writes, values lineup, brainstorming and factstorming, drawings, four corners, peer interviews, and prior knowledge interviews are means to gather data from students prior to instruction implementation. Choral responses, whips, flash cards, finger signals, wipe boards, letter and number tiles, peer coaching, student-led recitation, numbered heads together, toss the ball, talk to your partner, sorts, and partner journals are all means to gather information for students as instruction is taking place (Olivia and Pawlass, 2018).

In contrast to traditional testing, modern testing is increasingly computer-based (Russell et al., 2003). The time between test administration and access to results is reduced to days and not months, costs associated with scoring and reporting are only a fraction of what was required previously, and the analytics available to administrators allow for examining trends in student outcomes on specific learning objectives for specific teachers (Chaney and Gilman, 2005). Finally, as opposed to obtaining information on students at the end of the learning process, analytics associated with online learning and virtual tutors, to name a few, provide data on learning while it is occurring. For example, modern analytics permit investigation of whether or not students are using effective learning strategies (Koedinger et al., 2015; Badger et al., 2019).

Lane (2016, December,) presents several applications to assist teachers daily to inform instruction and measure student performance. GoFormative is a tool that allows for "real-time" interventions so that teachers can provide immediate assistance to students based on their responses. Students can respond to questions and responses in GoFormative by typing, drawing, or submitting images. MasteryContent allows teachers to disaggregate data by performance and mastery levels. The tool can be used in any subject for any performance-based assessment; teachers simply score bubble sheets using webcams and upload their own rubrics to determine mastery standards for performance-based assessments.

Paper clickers provide "checks for understanding." They are not one-to-one; however, teachers import the names of students into classes, scan the room for responses, and a graph view of the responses of students is provided. Teachers can view individual students and question reports. Another resource is the weblink PBS LearningMedia for all subjects and grades which includes over 200,000 digital resources. Teachers are provided the opportunity to create lessons, storybooks, puzzles, quizzes, and there is a quiz-maker option. Quizalize also includes options to deliver quizzes. The quizzes can be administered to individuals or whole classes. Using Quizalize, teachers can identify which students need assistance and in what areas students need assistance (Lane, 2016, December).

Another tool to facilitate quizzes is Quizizz. Teachers have the option to make or use premade quizzes to include text and/or the picture in Quizizz. Students can competitively engage using avatars, leaderboards, themes, music, and memes. Detailed class and student-level data are provided to teachers for immediate student interventions. ForAllRubrics is a tool that can be used by teachers and school leaders conducting teacher observations. Three scoring types are included on ForAllRubrics – badges, checklists, and rubrics. Teachers must create a class list, select a rubric (premade or upload a rubric to the platform), and then grade. Data can be viewed through class reports, weekly progress reports, pre/post reports, and student item analysis (Lane, 2016, December).

In addition to quizzes, the Socrative tool has the option of two different assessments – space race and exit tickets. Space race is a means to promote competition with a quiz bowl. The assessment can become "crowd-pleasing" as the correct answers are provided by individuals or group races. Live results which are saved to an account are provided through the quiz option. Explanations can also be provided for correct answers to students who get the answers incorrect. As with ForAllRubrics, teachers have access to the data through email or downloaded formats (Lane, 2016, December).

Another assessment platform is the Answer Pad. This platform gives teachers the opportunity to provide immediate response feedback. Teachers may align questions to standards and create detailed assessments while also having a space for instructions, formula charts, and proficiency levels. Live results are provided to teachers with several ways to review the data including individual student, group results, or by standard/skill. Data reporting is also facilitated through Nearpod which is a lesson implementation tool. Interactive premade or teacher-made lessons including but not limited to slides, virtual field trips, quizzes, polls, and short answers can be presented by teachers. All of the previously discussed packages are free; for Quizalize, the basic package is free. There are options to purchase upgrades (Lane, 2016, December).

---

## SCENARIO 1: THE CASE OF THE INEFFECTIVE SPECIAL EDUCATOR: INSTRUCTIONAL CHALLENGES OF A FIRST-YEAR PRINCIPAL

Jones, L., & Crochet, F. (2008, July 22). The case of the ineffective special educator: Instructional challenges of a first year principal. *International Journal of Educational Leadership Preparation*, 3 (2) Retrieved from https://files.eric.ed.gov/fulltext/EJ1067150.pdf.

### Background and Demographics

Washington Elementary School is located in Andersonville, Mississippi. Andersonville is a very rural area with a population of about 5,000; it is the seat of the district. Washington Elementary School is the largest of five elementary schools. Andersonville School District also has five middle schools and one high school. The enrollment of Washington Elementary School is 600 students who are taught by 25 teachers, 2 special education teachers, and 15 paraprofessionals. Washington has an 80% free and reduced lunch population with a racial composition of 75% percent African-American, 20% White, and 5% Hispanic.

The Washington Elementary School principal, Dr. Long, is an African-American female. Dr. Long was appointed in the summer prior to the 2007–08 school year. Serving as an assistant principal in another district, Dr. Long's educational experiences include teaching at the college and high school levels. Dr. Long, a native of the district, attended Washington Elementary School as a student and graduated from Andersonville High School. Dr. Long describes her administrative style as authoritarian yet democratic, and she is student-centered.

## Instructional Challenges with a Look at the Inclusion Model

Among the many adjustments for the school year, the staff of Washington Elementary School implemented a reading program and adopted an inclusion model for its special education program. The implemented research-based reading program, Success For All (SFA), was developed by Robert Slavin, then at John Hopkins University, and his colleagues. The program was implemented at Washington Elementary School for two primary reasons (a) the research findings indicated increased student achievement levels of students in schools with SFA and (b) the program was also designed to meet the needs of minorities and at risk students (Campoli, 2000).

Washington Elementary School's instructional challenge regarding special needs students was mandated by the State of Mississippi, which was developed after the most recent reauthorization of the *Individuals with Disabilities Education Act* (Essex, 2006). With the exception of a few special needs students, the state mandated that special education students be educated in the regular education classroom. Prior to the state's mandate, special education students received instruction in self-contained classrooms with all special education students in the same classroom. There were severe cases where students were functioning on first-grade academic levels, and the mandate required that they be placed in fourth-grade classrooms that were closer to the age-appropriate levels of the students. As a result of the mandate, two classrooms at each grade level would have special education students integrated into regular education classrooms.

In the inclusion classroom at Washington Elementary School, the regular education teacher provides direct instruction. One inclusion teacher and a paraprofessional are responsible for two grade levels. The inclusion teacher rotates among four classes spending approximately two hours in each inclusion classroom. The inclusion teacher's main concerns are the progress of special needs students and making certain that special needs students receive necessary accommodations; however, the inclusion teacher may provide one-on-one assistance to any student.

Andersonville School District required special education teachers to maintain the Individualized Educational Plans (IEPs) of special education students, inform the regular education teachers of modifications, and provide instructional assistance to students in the regular education classroom. Special and regular education teachers are required to collaborate. A paraprofessional also provides assistance to students in the inclusion classrooms. Student success is monitored through progress monitoring on a weekly basis as linked to classroom assessments; formal monitoring occurs at the end of the IEP term to determine if students have met goals. Due to the lack of funding, a paraprofessional was also shared among four classes to provide tutorial assistance to students. The inclusion schedule implemented at Washington Elementary School requires the paraprofessional to give assistance to special needs students at a different time from the inclusion teacher allowing for additional time with two adults in the inclusion class.

The two neighboring districts have an inclusion plan that allows for one regular education teacher, one special education teacher, and one paraprofessional in a class with approximately 17 regular education students and a maximum number of five special needs students. In both of the neighboring districts, the special education department experiences better standardized test scores for students. The regular and special education teachers collaborate on lesson planning and engage in team teaching. The paraprofessional's role is to provide tutorial assistance as needed. At Washington Elementary School, the inclusion classrooms contain a maximum of 21 students with approximately five special needs students.

## The Appointment of Special Education Teacher – Ms Jackson

Dr. Long needed a special education in order to begin the school year fully staffed with only three days remaining until the start of school. Dr. Long accepted the recommendation of the personnel director to hire Ms Jackson, a certified regular and special education teacher with 25 years of experience that included a variety of teaching assignments in six other elementary and middle schools in the district. In preparation for the new assignment, Dr. Long assigned Ms. Jackson to attend a six-day special education training that addressed IEP preparation, modifications for special needs students, and provisions of classroom assistance to special needs students.

Dr. Long assigned Ms. Jackson to manage the IEPs and provide classroom assistance to the first- and second-grade students. Dr. Long assigned Ms. Jackson to the younger students because most of her experience was with kindergarten. After doing research, Dr.

Long also discovered that Ms. Jackson had satisfactory evaluations; however, most of the previous principals that she worked with viewed her as a lazy teacher – one that does the minimum and is unmotivated. Mr. Davis, the most recent principal with whom Ms. Jackson worked, stated that Ms. Jackson "makes up excuses when she does something wrong." Ms. Lee was the other special education teacher, and she was responsible for third- and fourth-grade special needs students.

School started on August 17, 2007. At the end of September, Dr. Long received correspondence from the central office regarding 20 IEPs that needed to be updated immediately. The correspondence from the central office indicated that only one third-grade IEP was late – the others were of first- and second-grade students. Dr. Long had also received concerns from first- and second-grade teachers regarding the absence of instructional assistance and the absence of modifications for special education students. Ms. Jackson was not providing instructional assistance in classrooms, she did not follow her daily scheduled visits to classrooms, and she was not maintaining her responsibilities with the IEPS.

Dr. Long scheduled a conference with both special education and regular education teachers. Dr. Long discussed the immediate attention necessary to complete the IEPs requested by the central office, the need for regular education teachers to have modifications in their instructional delivery, and the need for special education teachers to provide classroom assistance. Ms. Lee volunteered to assist Ms. Jackson in updating the necessary IEPs. Ms. Lee confirmed through a phone call to the director of special education at the central office that one third-grade IEP was complete. Both special education teachers and regular education teachers with special needs students received a schedule that included times devoted to preparing IEPs and times for providing classroom assistance. Dr. Long explained to both special education teachers that providing classroom assistance to students was critical because of the new state mandate; some students were in age-appropriate classes but were functioning at lower academic levels.

Approximately a week later, first- and second-grade teachers began expressing to Dr. Long that Ms. Jackson was still not providing classroom assistance to special education students. Dr. Long began following Ms. Jackson's schedule and discovered that Ms. Jackson was not in her assigned classrooms. Dr. Long phoned the special education director who was assigned to Washington Elementary School, Ms. Oncale. Dr. Long informed Ms. Oncale of the present concerns as well as the previous conference that was held with Ms. Jackson. In the previous conference, Dr. Long attempted to outline the responsibilities of the special education teachers. Ms. Oncale requested that another conference with Ms. Jackson was necessary, and Ms. Oncale deemed it necessary to attend. Dr. Long also phoned the personnel director, who suggested that Ms. Jackson be placed on Level I assistance.

## The District's Policy

The Andersonville School District's policy required that teachers be placed on levels of assistance prior to any other actions transpiring. The three levels of assistance are intensive and proactive measures that serve as documentation that efforts were made by administration to provide assistance to teachers in critical need of improvement. Principals are responsible for bi-annual observations of all teachers at their respective schools to determine the quality of teacher performance regarding instructional and non-instructional duties. Teachers placed on Level I assistance are given a list of recommendations to assist in areas needing improvement and have four weeks to demonstrate growth. Teachers that do not demonstrate improvement move to Level II, then Level III. In Level II, teachers are given more intense instructions within four weeks to demonstrate growth. If it is determined that a teacher has not performed satisfactorily at the end of the four-week period in Level II, a teacher moves to Level III. A teacher that is placed on Level III assistance and completes Level III with an unsatisfactory rating can be recommended for dismissal. A conference is held at each level, and documentation of the conference is necessary with the signatures of everyone in attendance. Principals are instructed to phone the central office supervisor assigned to the school to assist teachers who are placed on assistance.

The type of assistance that teachers receive depends upon the areas where teachers are lacking in performance. The general areas for assistance are instructional duties, non-instructional duties, and professionalism (e.g., parent relationships, dress code). Teachers with instructional problems work with a supervisor in lesson planning, developing lesson objectives, and implementing lessons. In the first week of assistance, teachers are required to observe two peers and reflect on the experience in writing prior to being observed by the supervisor. In the second and third weeks of assistance, the teacher is observed three times weekly. The supervisor gives additional recommendations after the first week of observations, and improvement is expected after the third week. In the fourth week, the supervisor reflects on the improvement of the teacher; recommendations are made to the principal by the supervisor.

## Level I Conference

Ms. Oncale, Dr. Long, and Ms. Jackson were in attendance at the conference. Dr. Long began the conference by explaining the purpose and listing the concerns regarding Ms. Jackson's performance. Ms. Jackson admitted that she was not following her schedule and completing the IEPs. Ms. Jackson indicated that she had several personal problems that obviously interfered with her work. Ms. Jackson was given a list of recommendations to assist her in performing her responsibilities, and she signed the documentation of the Level I assistance period. Dr. Long forwarded a copy to the personnel director and kept a copy of the file at Washington Elementary School.

Ms. Jackson began completing IEPs; however, she was not providing classroom assistance to students. Ms. Oncale gave Ms. Jackson a list of strategies that could be utilized in working with students and a daily planner to assist her in following her schedule. Ms. Oncale required Ms. Jackson to spend two days observing/shadowing a special needs teacher at another school with a schedule similar to her schedule. Ms. Jackson was required to write a reflection on the experience, and Ms. Jackson exhibited satisfactory performance during the shadowing period.

## Ms Jackson's Performance after the Shadowing Period

After Ms. Jackson returned from observing/shadowing, Ms. Oncale began observing Ms. Jackson to give additional assistance. Ms. Jackson was not reporting to classes nor did she provide teachers with modifications for special needs students. Attempting to motivate Ms. Jackson to follow her schedule, Ms. Oncale conferenced with Ms. Jackson. After four weeks of assistance, Ms. Oncale recommended that Dr. Long place Ms. Jackson on Level II, then Level III assistance after four additional weeks. Dr. Long kept documentation of all incidents and conferences. Ms. Jackson was placed on Level II, then Level III assistance. As previously cited, Andersonville School District's board policy indicates that a teacher may be recommended for dismissal hearings when a teacher does not receive a satisfactory rating at the completion of Level III.

Ms. Jackson phoned Washington Elementary School the morning following the Level III conference. She asked the secretary to make the principal aware that she was ill and to inform the principal that she would be requesting sick leave for the remainder of the school year.

The school board granted Ms. Jackson the leave, and the personnel director informed Dr. Long that no additional action could be taken regarding Ms. Jackson's performance because she did not complete the Level III assistance period. Ms. Jackson was a tenured teacher with accumulated sick leave. In addition, Ms. Jackson would remain an employee of Washington district for the next academic year. Dr. Long could request that Ms. Jackson be transferred; however, there was no guarantee that a position would be available in another school in the district.

Using the discussion in the chapter, are there ways to assist Ms. Jackson? Are there ways through iObservation and/or other technologies to provide documentation pertinent to Ms. Jackson's situation?

## SCENARIO 2: AN AVERAGE DISTRICT WITH A HIGH PERFORMING SCHOOL

### Sugarland School District's State Performance

Sugarland School District is located in Sugarland Parish in Louisiana. According to a 2010 census, the population of the district is approximately 23,000. The parish was established in the early 1800s with the first settlers being from Germany. Sugar cane is the major industry for the parish. There are over 200,000 acres in the parish with over 21,000 of the acres being water. The office of the School Board is housed in the "seat" of the parish, and the school district serves approximately five communities within the district.

There are nine schools within the district; and the schools within the district have ratings of A, B, C, D, and F by the Louisiana State Department of Education. The School District has a rating of C. Four of the nine schools in the district have a score of B with one school with a C, two schools with a score of D, and another with an F. There are two middle schools with the D rating, and the school with an F is an elementary school.

To meet the 2025 state goal, students scoring basic may need additional academic support.

Thirty-four percent of the students in the district are scoring mastery on assessments for grades 3–8. The state's percentage is 35%. On the Louisiana State Department's website, data are included for minority students, students with disabilities, and the economically disadvantaged. The following are indicators that Louisiana is tracking toward the 2025 vision:

- Louisiana is experiencing an increase in the percentage of students scoring mastery and above statewide since the inception of the new, standards-aligned tests,
- Louisiana has increased the number of students who are scoring 21 or above on ACT since 2012 by 3,896 students,
- Louisiana is increasing the number of students earning credit through advanced placement since 2012,
- Louisiana had the highest percentage of students who completed FAFSA by the priority deadline in 2018,
- Louisiana is experiencing an annual increase since 2012 in the number of students who qualify for TOPS,
- Louisiana's graduation rate in 2017 represented a rate of 78.1% of students – more students than ever before,
- Forty-three percent of Louisiana's Class of 2016 earned college credit,
- Louisiana's college enrollment increased in 2017.

Retrieved from https://www.louisianabelieves.com/docs/default-source/louisiana-believes/statewide-results-one-pager.pdf?sfvrsn=6.

Louisiana's vision for 2025 aligns with ESSA (2015). ESSA is the nation's most recent law addressing equal opportunity for students. The first act was passed over 50 years ago in 1965 – the Elementary and Secondary Education Action Act (1965). The 1965 legislation was followed by the 1983 report *A Nation at Risk* (National Commission on Excellence in Education). *A Nation at Risk* was followed by the 2001 *No Child Left Behind Act*. Obviously, accountability – linked to equal opportunity for students is a focus of our nation. As previously noted, Louisiana is attempting to "raise the bar" as linked to accountability. A full report of how the National Education Association ranks states is included at http://www.nea.org/home/73145.html.

The Louisiana Department of Education uses a cohort graduation rate for this metric. The cohort graduation rate is the percentage of students that graduate in four years once entering high school (9th grade). The district is exceeding both the state and national averages for the percentages of students graduating in four years with a diploma. Ninety percent of the students in the district graduate in four years, 78 % of the students in the state graduate in four years, and 84% of the students in the nation graduate in four years.

Data are included for students of color; students with disabilities, and economically disadvantaged students.

There is variability in the percentage of students scoring mastery on assessments in elementary schools. In the school with an A (Harvest Time Elementary) rating, 55% of the students are scoring mastery on the standardized assessments, and 11% are scoring mastery in the elementary school with the F rating. The percentages of students scoring mastery in the middle schools are 31% in the school with a C rating and 19% in the schools with a D rating. In high school, 44% of the students are scoring mastery on LEAP. As previously cited, 35% of the students are scoring mastery on LEAP in grades 3-8 in the state; and the district's average is 34%. The state's average is 45% for high schools in the state on LEAP and the district's average is 44% for high schools.

## Harvest Time Elementary

In March of 2020, the COVID 19 numbers were increasing rapidly, and the governor closed public schools in the State of Louisiana with a public service announcement. Sugarland's district had a desire to facilitate instruction as best as possible; however, there was limited infrastructure in the Harvest Time community to facilitate instruction. The school year ended with little to no interaction with Harvest Time Elementary and the school community. The next academic year began with face-to-face instruction. Parents expressed concerns about the "missed instructional opportunities" and the need for a plan in the event of another interruption.

Sugarland was able to increase its technology infrastructure providing Harvest Time and other schools with laptops. Internet service providers also provided access points for free internet services. Throughout the 2020–21 academic year, there have been multiple interruptions and parents are more and more concerned about maintaining and/or improving the grade at Harvest Time and the learning for the students. Parents are requesting through their school board members that the Principal; Ms Peachtree explore reliable alternatives for facilitating online instruction. Using information from Chapters 1, 2, and 3, discuss a plan of action that Ms. Peachtree can communicate with parents and present technological alternatives.

## SUMMARY

In Chapter 5, the roles of the school leaders as instructional leaders are presented. Multidimensions of accountability have heightened the emphasis on school leaders as instructional leaders. In the introduction, the NELP, PSEL, and ISTE Standards are presented that most align with the task of the school leader as instructional leader. We discuss the roles of principals toward monitoring student achievement, monitoring classroom instruction, providing professional development and support for teachers, facilitating individualized instruction and support for students, and promoting collaboration and mentoring among teachers and students. The specifics of the roles of school leaders in unifying professional development to classroom observations are discussed using Zepadea's model. Various technologies are included to support the role of the principals as instructional leaders. The features of several Learning Management Systems are included, and the chapter ends with two scenarios for the application of the principles discussed in Chapter 5.

## TECHNOLOGY TOOLS

Adobe Connect: https://www.adobeconnect.com
BigBlueButton: https://www.bigbluebutton.com
Blackboard Collaborate: https://www.blackboard.com
Canvas: https://www.instructure.com.
DeansList software: https://www.deanslistsoftware.com/features
iObservations: https://www.iobservation.com
LearnCube. Virtual Classroom Software. https://www.learncube
.com/virtual-classroom-software.html.
Moodle: https://www.moodle.com
Schoology: https://www.schoology.com/.
Swivel: https://swivil.zendesk.com
Resources for School Leaders on Teacher Evaluation Instruments:

http://www4.esc13.net/schoolreadyteam/observation-tools-admin
http://www.educationworld.com/a_admin/admin/admin400_d
.shtml
http://usny.nysed.gov/rttt/teachers-leaders/practicerubrics/Docs/
SilverStrongTeacherRubric.pdf
http://www.iobservation.com/
http://www.doe.in.gov/sites/default/files/turnaround-principles/
classroom-walkthrough-development-samples.pdf
http://usny.nysed.gov/rttt/teachers-leaders/practicerubrics/Docs/
SilverStrongObservationRubric.pdf

http://www.42regular.com/obs/help/documents.pdf
http://www.ascd.org/publications/educational-leadership/dec10/
vol68/num04/Evaluations-That-Help-Teachers-Learn.aspx.
http://www.ncpublicschools.org/docs/effectiveness-model/ncees/
instruments/teach-eval-manual.pdf

## REFERENCES

Armstrong, G. R., Tucker, J. M., & Massad, V. J. (2009). Interviewing the experts: Student produced podcast. *Journal of Information Technology Education*, 8, IIP-79–IIP-90.

Badger, C., Horrocks, S., Turton, C., & Lewis, H. (2019). Using technology to promote metacognition. *Impact*, *2514–6955*, 52–56.

Blackboard Collaborate. https://www.blackboard.com.

Borup, J., Chambers, C. B., & Stimson, R. (2018). *Helping online students be successful: Student perceptions of online teacher and on-site mentor facilitation support*. Michigan Virtual University. https://mvlri.org/research/publications/helping-online-students-be-successful-student-perceptions-of-support/.

Campoli, P. (2000, April). How do you spell success? *John Hopkins Magazine*, *50*, 10–15.

Canvas. https://www.instructure.com.

Cappiccie, A., & Desrosiers, P. (2011). Lessons learned from using adobe connect in the social work classroom. *Journal of Technology in Human Services*, *29*(4), 296–302. http://doi-org.uhcno.idm.oclc.org/10.1080/15228835.2011.638239.

Castelo, M. (2020, July). 4 tips for effective virtual professional development. *Ed Teach*. https://edtechmagazine.com/k12/article/2020/07/4-tips-effective-virtual-professional-development.

Chaney, E., & Gilman, D. A. (2005). Filling in the blanks: Using computers to test and teach. *Computers in the Schools*, *22*(1/2), 157–168. https://doi-org.libezp.lib.lsu.edu/10.1300/J025v22n01_14.

Darling-Hammond, L., Andree, A., Richardson, N., Orphanos, S., & Wei, R. C. (2009). *Professional learning in the learning profession: A status report on teacher development in the United States and abroad*. National Staff Development Council.

DeansList software. https://www.deanslistsoftware.com/.

Essex, N. (2006). *A teacher's pocket guide to school law*. Pearson Education.

Fontichiaro, K., Kolb, L., Stanzler, J., & Yankson, K. (2021, December). Create PD webinars that engage educators. https://www.iste.org/explore/professional-development/create-pd-webinars-engage-educators.

Gee, J. P. (2008). *Good video games + good learning: Collected essays on video games, learning and literacy*. Peter Lang Publishing.

Gonzales, L., & Young, C. (2014). Grading teachers gets smarter. *Tech & Learning*, *34*(6), 28.

Gunter, G. A., & Reeves, J. L. (2017). Online professional development embedded with mobile learning: An examination of teachers' attitudes, engagement and dispositions. *British Journal of Educational Technology*, *48*(6), 1305–1317. https://doi-org.libezp.lib.lsu.edu/10.1111/bjet.12490.

Hallinger, P. (2015). *The evolution of instructional leadership*. http://doi.org/10.1007/978-3-319-15533-3_1.

Hord, S. (1997). *Professional learning communities: Communities of continuous inquiry and improvement.* Southwest Educational Developmental Laboratory. Retrieved July 20, 2012, from http://www.sedl.org/pubs/chagne34/welcome .html(1998).

Hughes, E. S., Bradford, J., & Likens, C. (2018). Facilitating collaboration, communication, and critical thinking skills in physical therapy education through technology-enhanced instruction: A case study. *TechTrends: Linking Research & Practice to Improve Learning, 62*(3), 296–302. https://doi-org.libezp.lib.lsu.edu /10.1007/s11528-018-0259-8.

Hunuk, D., Tannehill, D., & Levent Ince, M. (2019). Interaction patterns of physical education teachers in a professional learning community. *Physical Education & Sport Pedagogy, 24*(3), 301–317. https://doi-org.libezp.lib.lsu.edu/10.1080 /17408989.2019.1576862.

International Society of Technology of Education. https://www.iste.org/standards/ for-education-leaders.

Jones, L. (2020). *The relevance of instructional leadership.* Cognella.

Jones, L., & Crochet, F. (2008, July 22). The case of the ineffective special educator: Instructional challenges of a first-year principal. *International Journal of Educational Leadership Preparation, 3*(2). Retrieved January from https://files .eric.ed.gov/fulltext/EJ1067150.pdf.

Jones, V. R. (2015). 21st century skills: Collaboration. *Children's Technology & Engineering, 20*(1), 24–26.

Kennedy, E., & Laurillard, D. (2019). The potential of MOOCs for large-scale teacher professional development in contexts of mass displacement. *London Review of Education, 17*(2), 141–158. https://doi-org.libezp.lib.lsu.edu/10.18546/LRE.17.2.04.

Koedinger, K. R., D'Mello, S., McLaughlin, E. A., Pardos, Z. A., & Rosé, C. P. (2015). Data mining and education. *WIREs: Cognitive Science, 6*(4), 333–353. https://doi-org.libezp.lib.lsu.edu/10.1002/wcs.1350.

Krueger, N. (2021, December). 3 questions to ask before choosing a new. *Ed Tech Tool.* https://www.iste.org/explore/education-leadership/3-questions-ask -choosing-new-edtech-tool.

Lane, M. (2016, December). 10 data tracking apps you can use in your class tomorrow. *Education Matters.* https://www.gpb.org/blogs/education-matters /2016/12/13/10-data-tracking-apps-you-can-use-in-your-class-tomorrow.

LearnCube. Virtual Classroom Software. https://www.learncube.com/virtual -classroom-software.html.

Lowes, S., & Lin, P. (2015). Learning to learn online: Using locus of control to help students become successful online learners. *Journal of Online Learning Research, 1*(1), 17–48.

Malone, D. (2015). Using synchronous video within a learning management system from library and information literacy instruction. *Public Services Quarterly, 11*(3), 208–216. http://doi-org.uhcno.idm.oclc.org/10.1080/15228959.2015 .1060146.

Moodle. https://www.moodle.com.

National Educational Leadership Preparation (NELP) Standards. https://www .naesp.org/communicator-november-2018/nelp-standards-approved-how-affects -you.

National Policy Board for Educational Administration (2015). Professional Standards for Educational Leaders 2015. Reston, VA: Author.

Ohnigian, S., Richards, J. B., Monette, D. L., & Roberts, D. H. (2021). Optimizing remote learning: Leveraging zoom to develop and implement successful education sessions. *Journal of Medical Education & Curricular Development*, 1–4. https://doi-org.uhcno.idm.oclc.org/10.1177/23821205211020760.

Olivia, P., & Pawlass, G. E. (2018). *Supervision for today's schools* (7th ed.). Wiley & Sons.

Radcliffe, R., & Stephens, L. C. (2008). Preservice teachers are creating a college culture for at-risk middle school students. *Research in Middle Level Education Online*, 32(4), 1–15. https://doi-org.libezp.lib.lsu.edu/10.1080/19404476.2008.11462057.

Rowland, A., Craig-Hare, J., Ault, M., Ellis, J., & Bulgren, J. (2017). Social media: How the next generation can practice argumentation. *Educational Media International*, 54(2), 99–111. https://doi-org.libezp.lib.lsu.edu/10.1080/09523987.2017.1362818.

Russell, M., Goldberg, A., & O'Connor, K. (2003). Computer-based testing and validity: A look back into the future. *Assessment in Education: Principles, Policy & Practice*, 10(3), 279–293. https://doi-org.libezp.lib.lsu.edu/10.1080/0969594032000148145.

Schoology. https://www.schoology.com/.

Senge, P. M. (1990). *The fifth discipline: The art and practice of learning organizations.* Currency Doubleday Publishers.

Smith, J. A., & Sivo, S. A. (2012). Predicting continued use of online teacher professional development and the influence of social presence and sociability. *British Journal of Educational Technology*, 43(6), 871–882. https://doi-org.libezp.lib.lsu.edu/10.1111/j.1467-8535.2011.01223.x.

Sonnert, G., Hazari, Z., & Sadler, P. M. (2018). Evaluating the quality of middle school mathematics teachers, using videos rated by college students. *Studies in Educational Evaluation*, 58, 60–69. https://doi-org.libezp.lib.lsu.edu/10.1016/j.stueduc.2018.05.006.

Swivel. https://swivil.zendesk.com

Thomas, J., Hutchison, A., Johnson, D., Johnson, K., & Stromer, E. (2017). Planning for technology integration in a professional learning community. *Reading Teacher*, 71(2), 167–175. https://doi-org.libezp.lib.lsu.edu/10.1002/trtr.1604.

William, C. (2021, February 21). Virtual learning professional development for teachers. Center for Student Achievement Solutions. https://www.csas.co/virtual-learning-professional-development-for-teachers/.

Zepeda, S. (2017). *Instructional supervision: Applying tools and concepts.* Eye on Education.

# CHAPTER 6

## Organizational Culture and Climate

**ABSTRACT**

It is widely recognized that the culture and climate of a school have a significant impact on the quality of education provided for students. School culture and climate address shared norms, values, beliefs, and perceptions regarding academics, school safety, and other dimensions (Tichnor-Wagner, Harrison, and Cohen-Vogel, 2016). Many of the levers school leaders utilize to steer schools fall under the umbrella of school culture and climate. As noted by Jones (2009, November), the school leader must monitor the culture and promote positivism in the culture and climate of schools. In this chapter, we discuss the prominence of school culture in professional standards for school leaders and the potential of technology to help school leaders promote and monitor the culture of their schools.

The organizational culture and climate of schools impact every facet of schools; and there are many aspects of school culture and climate that are mentioned in the effective schools' literature (Tichnor-Wagner, Harrison, and Cohen-Vogel, 2016). Instructional leadership and the technology tools to assist school leaders in the role are discussed in Chapter 5, and Jones (2009, November) noted the implications of culture to instructional leadership. We began the chapter with the excerpt from Jones. In 2009, Jones argued that the school leader must monitor the culture and promote positivism in the culture and climate of schools. The article provided below includes culture as a construct of climate. In this chapter, we include the Leadership Standards which are most relevant for culture and climate. The technology tools to assist the leader in assessing/monitoring and promoting positivism in the culture are included.

### Instructional Leadership (Contingency)

The general model of the contingency theory, which was very popular from 1970 into the 1980s, addresses four sets of concepts – traits and skills of leaders, characteristics of situations, the behaviors of leaders and leader effectiveness. There are two hypotheses of the contingency approaches. First, characteristics of situations and traits and skills of leaders combine to impact leadership behavior. Secondly, the effectiveness of the leader is directly impacted by situational factors. Hoy and Miskel (2013) suggested that contingency approaches tend to specify situational variables that moderate the relationship among leader behaviors, traits, and performance criteria. There are five contingency models; they are: instructional leadership, which is specific to educational organizations, distributed or shared that applies to schools, and the least preferred co-worker, substitutes for leadership and path goal theories that apply to a wide range of organizations. Instructional leadership is critical for schools in this era because of its link to performances of students.

As previously alluded to, instructional leadership is gaining more and more attention as linked to accountability and school improvement. Hoy and Miskel (2013) suggested that instructional leadership evolved from "simple heroic conception to rather complex contingency models of leadership." Obviously, the roles of the principal (school leader) become critical in exhibiting dispositions associated with instructional leadership for school improvement in this era of accountability. An article published by e-Lead suggested that instructional leadership roles are those "actions that a principal takes, or delegates to others, to promote growth in student learning." Principals who are instructional leaders become instructional leaders by making instructional quality the number one priority and incorporate this principle in their visions. The school leader must spend time redefining the role of school leadership as the instructional leader becoming the primary learner striving for Excellency. It becomes the responsibility of the school leader to achieve goals, work with teachers, provide authentic professional development and other resources for teachers and staff, and create new learning opportunities for staff members. McEwan (2002) suggested that successful instructional leaders attribute their success to having visions, having the knowledge base, are willing to take risks, are willing to put in long hours, are willing to change and grow constantly, thrive on change and ambiguity, and can empower others. According to Hoy and Miskel (2013), instructional leaders make improvements in schools using their personalities, motivation for success, and administrative skills. In both the 1948 and 1970 perspectives of Stogdill, there are skills and traits that appear to be obviously necessary for effective Instructional Leadership.

McEwan (2002) suggested that Sergiovanni proposed one of the first models of instructional leadership. Sergiovanni identified leadership forces – technical, human, educational, symbolic, and cultural. He suggested that technical forces are aligned with the traditional practices of management. These topics include planning, leadership theory, time management, and organizational developments, which are topics generally, covered in administrative theory courses. The human forces are the interpersonal components of instructional leadership aligned with communicating, motivating, and facilitating roles of the principal. The educational aspects are the instructional roles of the school leader; that is, teaching, learning, and implementing curricula. The symbolic and cultural forces are closely aligned; they combine the leader's ability to become the symbol of what is important (symbolic) while articulating beliefs and values consistently (culture).

The role of culture is indirectly linked to the 1982 perspective of instructional leadership proposed by Bossert, in his inclusion of climate (from the assumption that culture is inclusive of climate). The model makes a link from school climate to teacher behavior, which ultimately impacts student learning. Obviously, there will be a great performance level of teachers in schools when a positive climate is prevalent. The factors that impact climates of schools are the external environmental characteristics; which will influence/shape the behaviors of the leaders. Ultimately, the behavior of the leader initiates change in schools – positive or negative. In 1989, Smith and Andrews suggested that there were ten attributes essential for principals who display strong instructional leadership. The attributes are:

1. Places priority of curriculum and instruction issues;
2. Is dedicated to the goals of the school and school district;
3. Is able to rally and mobilize resources to accomplish the goals of the district and school;
4. Creates a climate of high expectations in the school, characterized by a tone of respect for teachers, students, parents, and the community;
5. Functions as a leader with direct involvement in instructional policy;

6. Continually monitors student progress toward school achievement and teacher effectiveness;
7. Demonstrates commitment to academic goals, shown by the ability to develop and articulate a clear vision or long-term goals for the school;
8. Effectively consults with others by involving the faculty and other groups in the school decision processes;
9. Effectively and efficiently mobilizes resources such as materials, time, and support to enable the school and its personnel to most effectively meet academic goals;
10. Recognize time as a scarce resource and creates order and discipline by minimizing factors that may disrupt the learning process.

Sergiovanni suggested that there are leadership forces for instructional leadership; Bossert et al. (1982) presented the sequence of variable that impact each other leading to instructional leadership; and Smith and Andrews (1989) suggested that there are ten attributes of the leader that impact instructional leadership. In 2002, McEwan provided a different perspective of leadership suggesting that there are seven steps to effective instructional leadership. McEwan's perspectives have some bases in the work of Bennis (1989), Nanus, and Sergiovanni. The following are the seven steps proposed by McEwans (2002):

- Establish clear instructional goals;
- Be there for your staff;
- Create a school culture and climate conducive to learning;
- Communicate the vision and mission of your school;
- Set high expectations;
- Develop teacher leaders; and
- Maintain positive attitudes toward students, staff and parents.

McEwan (2002) also proposed an Instructional Leadership Behavioral Checklist that has thirty indicators; there are several indicators for each of the seven steps (See Appendix A for a copy of the Leadership Behavioral Checklist). The checklist can be used in a variety of ways: (1) to self-assess present instructional leadership levels; (2) to gain information from members of the faculty regarding perceptions of leadership; (3) to help the leader to set goals for improving instructional leadership, and (4) to help the leader evaluate progress toward meeting the goals of becoming a true instructional leader.

Zepeda (2016) viewed instructional leadership as instructional supervision aligned with classroom observations and professional development for teachers; she said that it is not a linear, lockstep process. Zepeda (2016) presented a model in which instructional supervision, staff development, and teacher evaluations are unified. In this cyclic process, clinical supervision (pre-observation conferences, observations, and post- observations) is coupled with a differentiated form of supervision. The principle aligned with differentiated supervision is that teachers are granted autonomy in deciding which additional methods (in addition to the classroom observations) will be used to assess the teacher's performances.

As instructional leaders, school leaders should provide opportunities for teachers to work together on the basis of needs linked to what is observed by school leaders in classroom observations. Study groups, learning clusters, and mentoring are some of the informal mechanisms for teachers to work together. On the basis of observations, school leaders can identify strengths and weaknesses of teachers, which lead to which teachers can serve as mentors and which teachers need mentors. Opportunities should also be provided for formalized professional development (Zepeda, 2016).

The results of the professional development- both formal and informal should be evident in classrooms as school leaders continue the cyclic process of observing classrooms. The additional important principle is that the professional development opportunities that teachers engage in should lead to individual goal setting for teachers which leads to professional development. School leaders should engage in conducting teacher observations and professional development opportunities in a cyclic manner; which aligns with the roles of instructional leadership. In this model, the alignment of professional development with the needs of teachers in the classroom is critical.

## 5 Culture and Its Implications to Instructional Leadership

The leadership traits, skills, and perspectives discussed throughout this paper address competencies and dispositions necessary for leaders to be effective. Effective leadership in schools in this era is linked to the leader's ability to facilitate school improvement. The obvious core of school improvement is the role of the leader as an instructional leader; which is such a complex role. The teachers, staff members, students, and pertinent stakeholders have to buy into the vision of the leader and to assist the leader in the implementation of school improvement. A variable that is directly related to school improvement and to the roles, skills, traits, and perspectives of the leader is the culture of the school.

Hoy and Miskel (2013) present several perspectives of culture. The 1968 Taguiran Typology of Climate embraces culture as an integral part of climate. There are several theoretical perspectives that link culture and climate and/or demonstrate an interrelationship between culture and climate. Taiguri (1968) suggests that ecology (building characteristics, school size); milieu (student and teacher characteristics); social systems (social interactions); and culture (belief systems and values) are the four dimensions of climate. In addition to including belief systems and values of organizations/schools, Hoy and Miskel (2013) suggest that culture includes the norms, shared beliefs, rituals, and assumptions of organization.

An obvious goal for school leaders is for schools to develop and maintain strong cultures. Schools with strong cultures will have effective leadership with exceptional student performance. Deal (1985) identified eight attributes of effective schools with strong cultures:

1. Shared values and a consensus on how we get things done around here.
2. The principal as a hero or heroine who embodies core values.
3. Distinctive rituals that embody widely shared beliefs.
4. Employees as situational heroes or heroines.
5. Rituals of acculturation and cultural renewal.
6. Significant rituals to celebrate and transform core values.
7. Balance between innovation and tradition and between autonomy and control.
8. Widespread participation in cultural rituals.

Selznick (1957) suggested that organizations have distinctive identities; on the basis of practical experiences, Conners (2003) discussed the importance of the leader in monitoring the cultures of schools and responding appropriately. She provides measures that can be used to help promote positivism in cultures of schools. Phillips and Wagner (2003) emphasize that schools have unique cultures; the link is consistently made to demonstrate the impact of culture on the direct influences of both student achievement and job satisfaction of educators. In Phillips and Wagner's 2003 publication, an extensive model is provided to assess culture. Plans of action should also be established to address areas of culture needing improvement.

There are thirteen possible characteristics identified by Phillips and Wagner for cultural improvement in school – collegiality (the way adults treat each other;) efficacy (the feeling of ownership or capacity to influence decisions;) high expectations (excellence is acknowledged; improvement is celebrated;) experimentation and entrepreneurship (new ideas abound and inventions occur;) trust and confidence (participants believe in the leaders and each other;) tangible support (e orts at improvement are substantive with abundant resources made available by all;) appreciation and recognition improvement (people feel special and act special;) humor (caring is expressed through "kidding;") shared decision-making by all participants (anyone affected by a decision is involved in making and implementing the decision;) protect what is important (participants keep the vision and avoid trivial tasks;) traditions (celebrations;) open and honest communication (information flows throughout the organization in formal and informal channels;) and metaphors and stories (evidence of behavior being communicated and influenced by internal imagery.)

Monitoring, assessing, and improving school culture is one of the roles school leaders must assume pertinent to school improvement. As an instructional leader, the leader has to "set high expectations" for teaching and learning which requires the leader to engage in many facilitative roles in the context of the environment of the school. The manner in which the leader facilitates the environment will be dependent on the leader's use of leadership perspectives and skills and traits discussed throughout the paper.

The leadership perspectives presented in the paper emphasize the role of the leader as "key" to school improvement; there is one perspective that challenges the assumption that one individual has to "make the change happen." The distributive leadership model embraces the notion of leadership by teams, groups, and organizational factors as contributing factors to effectiveness in organizations. Therefore, multiple individuals are involved in the completion of leadership tasks. Proponents of distributed leadership suggest that this perspective is essential in schools because schools are so complex, and the tasks are so broad that many individuals must participate in accomplishing tasks (Hoy and Miskel, 2013).

Jones, L. F. (2009, November). The Importance of School Culture for Instructional Leadership, *International Journal of Educational Leadership Preparation*, 4 (4). Retrieved November 4, 2009 from https://files.eric.ed.gov/fulltext/EJ1071384.pdf.

## LEADERSHIP STANDARDS LINKED TO THE TENANTS OF ORGANIZATIONAL CULTURE

The PSEL Standard and standard elements that most align with culture are Standard 5: Community of Care and Support for Students. Effective educational leaders cultivate an inclusive, caring, and supportive school community that promotes the academic success and well-being of each student. Jones (2009, November) suggested that the instructional leader is responsible for the school's environment. Pertinent components for the environment of the school are noted in the Standard Elements a, b, and f below. The implication of instructional leadership is linked to the success of the students – which is promoted through student growth and academic success. These tenants are noted in Standard Elements a, c, d. e, and f.

The following are the Standard Elements of Standard 5:

Effective leaders:

a) Build and maintain a safe, caring, and healthy school environment that meets the academic, social, emotional, and physical needs of each student.

b) Create and sustain a school environment in which each student is known, accepted and valued, trusted and respected, cared for, and encouraged to be an active and responsible member of the school community.

c) Provide coherent systems of academic and social support, services, extracurricular activities, and accommodations to meet the range of learning needs of each student.

d) Promote adult–student, student–peer, and school–community relationships that value and support academic learning and positive social and emotional development.

e) Cultivate and reinforce student engagement in school and positive student conduct.

f) Infuse the school's learning environment with the cultures and languages of the school's community.

(http://www.npbea.org/)

As presented in Chapter 1, NELP Standard 7 aligns with PSEL Standard 5. NELP Standard 7 and its Standard Elements are included below. NELP Standard 7: Building Professional Capacity addresses school culture and climate. The following are the Standard Elements:

Component 7.1: Program completers understand and have the capacity to collaboratively develop the professional capacity of the school through engagement in recruiting, selecting, and hiring staff.

Component 7.2: Program completers understand and have the capacity to develop and engage staff in a collaborative professional culture designed to promote school improvement, teacher retention, and the success and well-being of each student and adult in the school.

Component 7.3: Program completers understand and have the capacity to personally engage in, as well as collaboratively engage school staff in, professional learning designed to promote reflection, cultural responsiveness, distributed leadership, digital literacy, school improvement, and student success.

Component 7.4: Program completers understand and have the capacity to evaluate, develop, and implement systems of supervision, support, and evaluation designed to promote school improvement and student success.

(http://www.npbea.org/)

The ISTE Standard that aligns most with organizational culture and climate is the Empowering Leader Standard. It includes in its descriptor "create a culture." The emphasis of the Empowering Leader Standard is to create a culture where teachers and learners are empowered to use technology in innovative ways to enrich teaching and learning. The competencies are:

a. Empower educators to exercise professional agency, build teacher leadership skills, and pursue personalized professional learning.
b. Build the confidence and competency of educators to put the ISTE Standards for Students and Educators into practice.
c. Inspire a culture of innovation and collaboration that allows the time and space to explore and experiment with digital tools.
d. Support educators in using technology to advance learning that meets the diverse learning, cultural, and social-emotional needs of individual students.
e. Develop learning assessments that provide a personalized, actionable view of student progress in real time.

(http://www.iste.org/standards/for-education-leaders)

As mentioned several times throughout this book, the impetus of the book is to provide technological tools to support school leaders in performing their roles. The technology tools do not serve as a substitute for knowledge, skills, and dispositions needed for leadership. It is essential for school leaders to possess pertinent knowledge of leadership, skills, and dispositions. We limit the remaining discussion of culture in Chapter 6 to academic climate and school safety. These two aspects of climate are used to discuss ways of accessing this information. The use of technology as a tool to monitor and establish the organizational culture and climate of a school is presented in this chapter. Culture is included in this chapter as a subconstruct of climate.

## MONITORING AND ANALYSIS OF THE ACADEMIC CLIMATE OF A SCHOOL

One of the aspects of the culture of a school that has received considerable attention from researchers is the academic climate of a school (Daily et al., 2019). Investigators have found that if the primary focus of a school is on academics, teachers hold high expectations for students, and when rewards are influenced by academic progress; students perform better (Davis and Warner, 2018). As previously mentioned, technological tools to assist school leaders with instructional leadership are included in Chapter 5. Many of the roles of the principal as an instructional leader are linked to the leader monitoring the academic climate of schools through conducting teacher observations and facilitating professional development. Therefore, the principles previously highlighted in Chapter 5 are applicable here along with the technologies mentioned in Chapter 5.

Phillips and Wagner (2003) suggest that schools with positive cultures have academic success. As previously noted, we are referring to culture as an element of climate. Collegiality and efficacy are critical ingredients of schools with positive cultures. Collegiality is evident when ideas are shared among colleagues, observations occur on a regular basis in professional roles, and colleagues teach and coach each other in schools. When professionals feel included, feel appreciated and valued, and feel they can influence their own destiny, efficacy is prevalent in the school. In addition to collegiality and efficacy, schools with positive cultures also have the following attributes (which are included in the article at the beginning):

- High expectations: There are high expectations of self and others,
- Experimentation and entrepreneurship: New ideas are prevalent and inventions occur,
- Trust and confidence: There is belief in the leaders and belief in each other,
- Tangible support: There are substantive efforts for improvement with the availability of resources,
- Appreciation and recognition of improvement: Staff feel and act special,
- Humor: Acts of care are expressed,
- Shared decision-making by everyone: Impacted staff are involved in decision-making,
- Protect what is important - Trivial tasks are avoided with a focus on the vision,
- Traditions: Celebrations occur for important events,

- Open and honest communication: Formal and informative communication channels flow throughout the organization, and
- Metaphors and stories: Internal imagery influences behavior.

Phillips and Wagner (2003) suggest that the best measuring techniques for culture require observations and interviews coupled with surveys in schools. We introduce tools at the end of the section to assess climate (some of the instruments have cultural attributes embedded.) The School Culture Assessment Survey proposed by Phillips and Wagner (2003) is in Appendix B. Hoy and Miskel (2013 characterizes cultures of schools as academies, prisons, clubs, communities, and factories. A school with an academy-type culture has learning as the focus. The school leader is viewed as the master teacher and learner. The prison-type culture has at its core control and discipline. The principal presents his/herself as a warden. In a club-type culture, the school operates as a social club, and the principal is the social director. In the community-type school culture, the environment is a nurturing environment. The school leader is the community leader. The other type of culture proposed by Hoy and Miskel (2013) is the factory-type culture. The principal is in the role of foreman with the school functioning like an assembly line.

In addition to the strategies noted in Chapter 5 pertinent to instructional leadership, school leaders employ a variety of strategies to create a positive academic climate in their schools. Their success is often measured by climate surveys. In contrast to paper surveys used in the past, online surveys are now a practical option; social media posts, blogs, and Twitter are also tools which can provide a window into the academic climate of schools. This is especially true as the number of teachers and students utilizing school-linked social media has increased significantly. For example, the use of sites like Piazza.com, epals.com, Blogger.com, WordPress.org, and others are increasing among teachers and students alike (Hanuscin et al., 2014). Websites and social media platforms are discussed in other chapters that are relative to tasks leaders must perform.

The National Center on Safe Supportive Learning Environments (NCSSLE) includes academic and safety as tenants of school climate along with discipline, the physical environment, and notions aligned with culture previously noted (http://safesupportivelearning.ed.gov/school-climate-improvement). There is a compiled listing of valid and reliable climate surveys on NCSSLE's website with the name of the survey, constructs measure, link to the survey, and the reports generated from previous administrations of the surveys. The purpose of the listing is to assist schools and school districts in the selection of reliable and valid surveys. NCSSLE has a partnership with the U.S. Department of

Education. NCSSLE also suggests that schools should plan, implement, and evaluate school climate improvement efforts. The following are the recommended activities:

- Planning for school climate improvements,
- Engaging stakeholders in school climate improvements,
- Collecting and reporting school climate data,
- Choosing and implementing school climate interventions, and
- Monitoring and evaluating school climate improvements.

The NCSSLE framework for school climate improvement recommends:

> the use of multi-tiered approach to organize interventions, in which the first tier (Tier 1) provides a foundation of universal supports for all students, the second tier (Tier 2) provides extra support for those students in need of extra assistance, and the third tier (Tier 3) provides intensive support for those who most need it. For example, Tier 1 supports could be integrated into classroom instruction, Tier 2 supports could be applied in small group settings, and Tier 3 supports could be used in 1-on-1 sessions between a counselor and a student. It is important to remember that a multi-tiered system of support (MTSS) is not a program or intervention itself; but rather a system of organizing programs or interventions so that they are delivered appropriately to students. Selection of interventions should be aligned to both the potential application and differentiated need in the multi-tiered system
>
> (U. S Department of Education, 2019)

The targeted participants are different for the surveys some surveys target parents, others target students, and others target school staff. In addition, some target a variety of the stakeholder groups previously noted.

The following is a list of weblinks to surveys:

- Academic Optimism of Schools Surveys https://safesupportivelearning.ed.gov/survey/academic-optimism-schools-surveys
- American Institutes for Research Conditions for Learning Survey https://safesupportivelearning.ed.gov/survey/american-institutes-research-conditions-learning-survey
- Arizona YRBS and S3 School Climate Survey https://safesupportivelearning.ed.gov/survey/arizona-yrbs-and-s3-school-climate-survey
- Association of Alaska School Boards School Climate and Connectedness Survey https://safesupportivelearning.ed.gov/survey

/association-alaska-school-boards-school-climate-and-connected-ness-survey

- Authoritative School Climate Survey https://safesupportivelearning.ed.gov/survey/authoritative-school-climate-survey
- California Healthy Kids Survey https://safesupportivelearning.ed.gov/survey/california-healthy-kids-survey
- California School Parent Survey https://safesupportivelearning.ed.gov/survey/california-school-parent-survey
- California School Staff Survey https://safesupportivelearning.ed.gov/survey/california-school-staff-survey
- Center for Research in Educational Policy School Climate Inventory https://safesupportivelearning.ed.gov/survey/center-research-educational-policy-school-climate-inventory
- Classroom Climate Assessment Instrument – Secondary https://safesupportivelearning.ed.gov/survey/classroom-climate-assessment-instrument-secondary
- Communities That Care Youth Survey https://safesupportivelearning.ed.gov/survey/communities-care-youth-survey
- Community and Youth Collaborative Institute (CAYCI) School Experiences Surveys https://safesupportivelearning.ed.gov/survey/communities-care-youth-survey
- Comprehensive School Climate Inventory https://safesupportivelearning.ed.gov/survey/comprehensive-school-climate-inventory
- Consortium on Chicago School Research Survey of Chicago Public Schools https://safesupportivelearning.ed.gov/survey/consortium-chicago-school-research-survey-chicago-public-schools
- Culture of Excellence and Ethics Assessment (CEEA) https://safesupportivelearning.ed.gov/survey/culture-excellence-ethics-assessment-ceea
- Delaware Bullying Victimization Scale https://safesupportivelearning.ed.gov/survey/delaware-bullying-victimization-scale
- Delaware School Climate Survey https://safesupportivelearning.ed.gov/survey/delaware-school-climate-survey
- Effective School Battery https://safesupportivelearning.ed.gov/survey/effective-school-battery
- Flourishing Children Survey Social Competence https://safesupportivelearning.ed.gov/
- Georgia Department of Education School Climate Surveys https://safesupportivelearning.ed.gov/survey/georgia-department-education-school-climate-surveys
- Maryland S3 Climate Survey https://safesupportivelearning.ed.gov/survey/maryland-s3-climate-survey

- Organizational Climate Description for Schools https://safesup portivelearning.ed.gov/survey/organizational-climate-description -schools
- Pride Teaching and Learning Environment Surveys https://safesup portivelearning.ed.gov/survey/pride-teaching-and-learning-environ- ment-surveys
- REACH Survey https://safesupportivelearning.ed.gov/survey/reach -survey
- School Climate Assessment Instrument – Elementary https://safesup portivelearning.ed.gov/survey/school-climate-assessment-instru- ment-elementary
- School Climate Assessment Instrument – Secondary https://safesup portivelearning.ed.gov/survey/school-climate-assessment-instru- ment-secondary
- U.S. Department of Education School Climate Survey (EDSCLS) https://safesupportivelearning.ed.gov/survey/us-department-educa- tion-school-climate-survey-edscls

NCSSLE and the U.S. Department of Education do not promote the use of one survey. As a matter of fact, researchers may recommend surveys to be added by providing the pertinent information (http://safesupport ivelearning.ed.gov/school-climate-improvement).

As early as 1963, Halpin and Croft begin mapping climates of schools; they observed:

- Schools differ markedly in their feel,
- The concept of morale did not provide an index of this feel,
- "Ideal" principals who are assigned to schools where improvement is needed are immobilized by the faculty, and
- The topic of organizational climate is generating interest.

Halpin and Croft (1963) devised an instrument known as the Organizational Climate Description Question (OCDQ; see Appendix C) to identify important aspects of teacher–teacher and teacher–prin- cipal interactions. In addition, six basic school climates are identified ranging from open to closed: open, autonomous, controlled, familiar, paternal, and closed. School climates that are open are characterized by cooperation and respect among school leaders and the faculty, principals provide support to faculty. School leaders give their teach- ers autonomy without scrutiny with a facilitative leadership style. The behaviors of teachers in open climates are complementary to the behaviors of the school leaders. Teachers are committed to their work and work together well. School climates that are closed are opposite to open climates. There appears to be a "going through the motions." School leaders in closed climates stress routine, and teachers demonstrate minimal commitment. Principals also exhibit dispositions that are too rigid; that is, they are unsupportive, hindering, inflexible, and controlling.

The OCDQ also measures six behaviors exhibited by principals or teachers of organizational climate: supportive principal, directive principal, restrictive principal, collegial teacher, intimate teacher, and disengaged teacher. Supportive school leaders demonstrate concern for teachers. The teachers are praised, and constructive feedback is provided. Directive school leaders provide close supervision and maintain control over teachers and school activities. Work is hindered by restrictive principals because the restrictive school leaders focus on paperwork and busy work. Collegial teachers support open interactions among teachers, and they are enthusiastic. Strong cohesive networks are prevalent among teachers who exhibit intimate teacher behaviors. Teachers are friends and know each other well. Teachers who are disengaged have a lack of focus and meaning, and are "simply putting in time." From the list of climate instruments provided above, there are many instruments to measure climate and certain aspects of the school environment. The Organizational Health Inventory uses seven dimensions in order to distinguish healthy schools from unhealthy schools. The seven dimensions include institutional integrity, principal influence, consideration, initiating structure, resource support, morale, and academic emphasis. Like with other technology tools, access to the internet is required for use of the tools. Depending on the survey used, reports can be compiled; etc. It is most important to store data to have access in circumstances when the internet is unavailable.

## MONITORING AND ANALYSIS OF THE SAFETY CLIMATE OF A SCHOOL

In an era in which violence on school campuses seems to be endemic, safety is a major consideration for students, teachers, parents, and stakeholders. Ziegler (2018, June) suggested that school safety is the "most pressing issue." In addition to six other strategies to address school safety, Ziegler notes that school leaders should leverage technology. Reports should readily be generated if students web search, email, or use words on school devices that could be a safety issue. Text messaging should also be used for essential safety alerts. Some school districts are using videos to raise awareness of bullying and other concepts to promote safety and positive climates.

Ziegler (2018, June) argued that safety should be always prioritized through conducting safety drills, assessing campus safety protocols, securing school buildings, and tracking threats. School leaders can promote safety as well by communicating the importance of suspicious behavior. It is important for school leaders to be open and responsive to the concerns of students, staff, and stakeholders. Many schools now have school resource officers which links to the strategy of school leaders advocating for safety. School leaders should advocate for resources, training, and support. Both active shooter and tabletop training are activities that can prove to be advantageous when schools experience related emergencies. Advocacy can also occur at the national level through entities like the National Association of Secondary School Principals' Policy and Advocacy Center. An additional strategy school leaders can implement is to relate to students. School leaders should create cultures where students connect to peers; are cared for by adults in the school; and are valued. Two additional suggested strategies for school leaders are for school leaders to collaborate and expand school safety teams and navigate the "tumultuous" waters of school safety.

Whether violence from individuals external to the school or within the school, a climate punctuated by fear and anxiety is counterproductive to an effective school (Davis and Warner, 2018). As noted by the NCSSLE, school safety is aligned with improved student outcomes. Both physical and emotional safety are linked to improved outcomes. Conversely, students who experience environments which are physically and emotionally unsafe or use/sell illegal substances face the risks of poor attendance, course failure, or dropping out of school. https://safesupportivelearning.ed.gov/topic-research/safety

The NCSSLE defines school safety as "schools and school-related activities where students are safe from violence, bullying, harassment, and substance abuse." It is important to promote character education which helps to promote positivism in the climates of schools. Tools for monitoring the safety climate of a school are greater than ever before. As with academic climate, these include social media, surveys, etc. and these resources can bring insights into many different aspects of the safety climate of a school. In the section **Monitoring and Analysis of the Academic Climate of a School**, several of the surveys are included in a listing of surveys to measure/assess school safety. The National Center for Education Statistics (NCES) also has surveys on crime and safety. NCES administers and reports data from principals/school surveys. Data are collected from principals on the School Survey on Crime and Safety (SSOCS).

The following topics are covered:

- Frequency and types of crimes occurring at school,
- Disciplinary actions allowed and used in schools,

- Policies and practices designed to prevent or reduce crime in schools, and
- Characteristics of school climate related to safety.
                    (https://nces.ed.gov/programs/crime/principals.asp)

In Chapter 3, safe school solutions are introduced pertinent to the capability of providing online national background checks for employees. A volunteer management system is embedded in safe school solutions. The volunteer management system includes arrest alert monitoring, volunteer policy and video training, a national sex offender alert, and a recruiter of volunteers feature. Faculty and staff in schools receive automatic notifications as volunteers or visitors arrive at schools. Geo-fencing, a face recognition technology, provides easy check-in for approved visitors. Virtual or onsite vulnerability assessments, threat assessments, security team development, and active shooter for civilians training are a part of the security consulting services available through Safe School Solutions. https://www.safehiringsolutions.com/safeschool-solutions

As previously alluded to, maintaining effective discipline (internal safety from violent activity) is a critical aspect of climate. According to the National Center for Educational Statistics - https://nces.ed.gov/programs/crime/principals.asp:

> During the 2017–18 school year, 35% of public schools (28,700 schools) took at least one serious disciplinary action—including out-of-school suspensions lasting five or more days, removals with no services for the remainder of the school year, and transfers to specialized schools—for specific offenses. Out of all offenses reported during the 2017–18 school year, physical attacks or fights prompted the largest percentage of schools (25%) to respond with at least one serious disciplinary action.

Fighting and other offenses can negatively impact the climates of schools. In Chapter 2, several of the technology tools presented have features pertinent to discipline and/or climate.

Many features of DeansList (https://deanslistsotware.com) are noted in Chapter 2. It is a way to track behavior across schools. It markets itself as a means to get schools "on the same page" which was also noted in Chapter 2. It is a cultural model which focuses on the values of schools. Social-emotional learning, positive behavioral interventions, and/or multi-tiered systems supports are among the models which can be embedded into DeansList. There is a mechanism included that provides data to school leaders and teachers to reward positive behaviors and address the negative behaviors.

In the event that there are situations on campus in which there is positive culture and climate news to share or when there has been a negative instance, we presented in Chapter 1 ways to communicate with the school community – this is inclusive of students, faculty, and staff and externally to parents and stakeholders. When there are negative situations, it is best to have the school's version reported first as opposed to a perspective by the media. Several social media outlets were presented in Chapter 1 – Facebook, Instagram, Twitter, and LinkedIn. In addition, there is also the schools' website which is discussed in Chapter 7 where information can be posted along with other mass messaging tools discussed in Chapter 7. In addition, many of the Learning Management Systems presented in Chapter 5 have the capability to provide mass messaging to internal and external groups as well as through email, text messaging, and phone calls. We also note automation capabilities throughout the book that are applicable to technology tools.

In Zakrzewski's (2013, August) article *How to Create a Positive School Climate,* she provides research-based suggestions for school leaders – one of the suggestions includes a technology component. In addition, the article embeds concepts of climate that are linked to academics and safety. Zakrzewski noted that disengaged students, teacher burnout, bullying, casual vandalism, and cultural differences are common in schools, and many of these problems can be addressed with a positive school climate. When climates in schools are positive, absenteeism decreases, suspension decreases, achievement improves, and the psychological well-being of students improves. We do not have research-based evidence; however, based on our practical experience, we concur with Zakrewski that it is challenging to create positive school cultures.

In 2007, which was almost, two decades ago, the National School Climate Council identified the criteria for a positive school climate; the tenants are:

- Norms, values, and expectations that support social, emotional, and physical safety.
- People are engaged and respected.
- Students, families, and educators work together to develop and live a shared school vision.
- Educators model and nurture attitudes that emphasize the benefits gained from learning.
- Each person contributes to the operations of the school and the care of the physical environment.

The three research-based suggestions by Zakrewski (2013, August) to begin building a positive climate is to (1) assess the current climate. In this

Chapter, we have provided a list of instruments for assessing the climate. Technology is a useful tool previously noted in assessing climate. (2) Create a shared vision. Zakrewski highlights that a shared vision is one that individuals will work to carry out. When individuals participate in the visioning processes, they own it. We should note that the PSEL and NELP Standards include vision as a Standard (as noted in Chapter 1):

PSEL Standard 1: Mission, Vision, and Core Values. Effective educational leaders develop, advocate, and enact a shared mission, vision, and core values of high-quality education and academic success and well-being of each student.
NELP Standard 1: Mission, Vision, and Improvement
Component 1.1 Program completers understand and demonstrate the capacity to collaboratively evaluate, develop, and communicate a school mission and vision designed to reflect a core set of values and priorities that include data use, technology, equity, diversity, digital citizenship, and community.
Component 1.2 Program completers understand and demonstrate the capacity to lead improvement processes that include data use, design, implementation, and evaluation.

The last suggestion (3) is to work to carry out the shared vision. It should be fun. Highlight the positives in the school. Again, technology can be helpful. A website and social media are ways to complement faculty and staff and share great news.

---

**SCENARIO 1: ADDRESSING NEGATIVITY IN THE CULTURE OF THE SCHOOL**

Pringles Middle School is located in the Midwest of the country. The school is a suburban school with an enrollment of 1,200 students. The district has ten other middle schools, seven high schools, and 15 elementary schools with one magnet-type facility working with universities for early admissions into college. Unlike many districts throughout the country, the district has great retention rates of principals, teachers, and staff. The superintendent has been employed for seven years which exceeds the number of years most superintendents are retained. The district is a high-performing district on all state and national metrics.

In addition to excellence in academics, one of the goals emphasized by the principal is to continue to build and maintain the positivism in the culture and climate of the school. Below are the goals for Pringles Middle School:

## Pringles Middle School Goals

*Student Academic and Behavioral Development*

To improve students' academic performance

To instill students with intrinsic motivation to learn

To assist the school, i.e., administrators, teachers, students, and support staff, to reach their academic and behavioral benchmarks and goals

To instill Positive Action principles into students' cognitive, affective and behavioral learning domains

To contribute to the teaching and achieving of core performance standards and outcomes

To improve students' behavior

To develop students' character

To develop well-rounded students: including physically, intellectually, socially. and emotionally

To develop thinking skills, and the use of the six units as a framework for thinking

To promote good mental health in students

## School-Wide Climate

To assist the school, i.e., administrators, teachers, students, and support staff, to reach their academic and behavioral benchmarks and goals

To achieve a violence and drug-free school

To create a positive learning environment throughout the school

To teach that all activities and curriculum in the school are positive actions, including content area learning (reading, writing, math, etc.)

## Training and Staff Development

To develop teachers who use positive approaches to instruction and classroom management

To develop administrators who use positive approaches to leading and school management

To develop a support staff who use positive approaches to supporting students and school personnel

To understand research-based theories of learning, education, behavior change, and their relationships to Positive Action

## Parents and Community Involvement

To involve parents in their children's education

To involve community members in education by providing support and resources to the school

To involve community members in developing a positive community for children and youth

https://www.positiveaction.net/grant-writing/teaching-goals-and-objectives

Mr. Johns has been principal for five years and has maintained exceptional relationships with pertinent stakeholders as well as students, teachers, and staff members in the school. Furthermore, Pringles Middle Schools is the highest performing middle school in the district. Mr. Johns receives a call from a stakeholder who has been a member of the School Improvement Team for most of his tenure at the school. He is a businessman in the community and a financial supporter of the school.

He shares in his call that there is an unidentified individual or individuals communicating negativity about the School Improvement Planning and this is causing some concern in the community as it is being perceived by some as valid and reliable information. Based on technology tools presented in this chapter, what are techniques that can be employed by the school leader on behalf of Pringles Middle School to determine the current perception of students, faculty, and staff at the school? We also discussed and or referenced in Chapters 1, 2, 5, and 7 tools to communicate with the external public? Should Mr. Johns consider communication with the external public and if so which technological tools are available?

---

**SCENARIO 2: PREPARING FOR A NEW LEADERSHIP ROLE**

Written by Dr. Obie Hill and Dr. Gregg Stal

Karl Jones is still ecstatic over his appointment as the new principal at Jonestown Middle School. There is still a month to go before he will actually begin the job and two and one-half months before the school year starts. This appointment will be Karl's first principal position although he served as an assistant principal at the other middle school in Jonestown.

Bob Smith is the person Karl is replacing. Bob had been principal for the 12 previous years. He inherited a school that had one of the lowest performance ratings in the state. From 1999 until 2009 Jonestown Middle School had experienced steady measurable growth in student performance as determined by increased standardized test scores and reduced student absences. When Bob Smith arrived at Jonestown the school performance score was 36; the percentage of students successfully passing their state assessment tests was 31%; and on average, only 41% of the students enrolled attended school each day. By 2009; the school performance score was 84%, with 77% of students passing state assessment tests, and average daily attendance at 91%. However, after ten years of consistent gains, percentages on all three metrics had declined over two consecutive years.

Karl Jones' charge upon appointment was simple: Reverse the trend! He already had some ideas he was prepared to implement. However, as he prepared plans and strategies to implement his ideas an incident occurred at his former school that awakened him to another reality. Simply put, that reality is: school leaders charged with school reform and turnaround have to be prepared to deal with unexpected problem issues, especially in the absence of policies that cover those issues.

Although he did not have all of the details, Karl Jones had these facts about the incident that took place at his former school. An eighth-grade student there had used his smartphone to download and forward pornographic material to ten of his friends. Several of those friends in turn forwarded the material to their friends and before anyone knew what was happening, 89% of the sixth-, seventh-, and eighth-grade students at the school had received and saved the porn material on their personal electronic devices including smartphones and personal computers. As soon as the principal of Karl's former school became aware of the incident, he enlisted the help of Jonestown City Police and confiscated the smartphones and personal devices of all the students who had them at school. Karl had no other information. The only policy in place at the school forbade students to use school computers to view or download any illicit material. What surprised Karl Jones the most; however, and as reported on the local television station, was not the fact that middle school students were viewing porn material; the biggest surprise was the large number of parents objecting to the confiscation of their children's electronic devices.

Karl Jones was preparing to implement reform and turnaround measures at his new school. However, he could not help reflecting on how he would approach such an incident at his new school if there was no school or district policy to address it. He reasoned "My reform initiative now must be forward thinking to the extent of developing school policies that, driven by rapid changes in technology, are general and comprehensive enough to encompass such unexpected incidents."

## SUMMARY

In the beginning of the chapter, culture and climate are conceptualized. An excerpt is cited connecting instructional leadership to culture and climate. The multi-dimensions of culture and climate are also noted. We discuss culture as a construct of climate. The Leadership and Technology Standards that are most aligned with culture and climate are addressed. The focus of this chapter is on the academic climate and safety climate of schools. Technological tools to assist school leaders in maintaining academic climates are cited. A listing of online surveys provided by the partnership between NCSSLE and the U.S. Department of Education are also referenced. Two scenarios are also included at the end of Chapter 6 to apply concepts noted throughout the chapter.

## TECHNOLOGY TOOLS

DeansList software: https://www.deanslistsoftware.com/features

Climate Surveys

- Academic Optimism of Schools Surveys https://safesupportivel earning.ed.gov/survey/academic-optimism-schools-surveys
- American Institutes for Research Conditions for Learning Survey https://safesupportivelearning.ed.gov/survey/american -institutes-research-conditions-learning-survey
- Arizona YRBS and S3 School Climate Survey https://safesup portivelearning.ed.gov/survey/arizona-yrbs-and-s3-school-cli mate-survey

- Association of Alaska School Boards School Climate and Connectedness Survey https://safesupportivelearning.ed.gov/survey/association-alaska-school-boards-school-climate-and-connectedness-survey
- Authoritative School Climate Survey https://safesupportivelearning.ed.gov/survey/authoritative-school-climate-survey
- California Healthy Kids Survey https://safesupportivelearning.ed.gov/survey/california-healthy-kids-survey
- California School Parent Survey https://safesupportivelearning.ed.gov/survey/california-school-parent-survey
- California School Staff Survey https://safesupportivelearning.ed.gov/survey/california-school-staff-survey
- Center for Research in Educational Policy School Climate Inventory https://safesupportivelearning.ed.gov/survey/center-research-educational-policy-school-climate-inventory
- Classroom Climate Assessment Instrument – Secondary https://safesupportivelearning.ed.gov/survey/classroom-climate-assessment-instrument-secondary
- Communities That Care Youth Survey https://safesupportivelearning.ed.gov/survey/communities-care-youth-survey
- Community and Youth Collaborative Institute (CAYCI) School Experiences Surveys https://safesupportivelearning.ed.gov/survey/communities-care-youth-survey
- Comprehensive School Climate Inventory https://safesupportivelearning.ed.gov/survey/comprehensive-school-climate-inventory
- Consortium on Chicago School Research Survey of Chicago Public Schools https://safesupportivelearning.ed.gov/survey/consortium-chicago-school-research-survey-chicago-public-schools
- Culture of Excellence and Ethics Assessment (CEEA) https://safesupportivelearning.ed.gov/survey/culture-excellence-ethics-assessment-ceea
- Delaware Bullying Victimization Scale https://safesupportivelearning.ed.gov/survey/delaware-bullying-victimization-scale
- Delaware School Climate Survey https://safesupportivelearning.ed.gov/survey/delaware-school-climate-survey
- Effective School Battery https://safesupportivelearning.ed.gov/survey/effective-school-battery
- Flourishing Children Survey Social Competence https://safesupportivelearning.ed.gov/

- Georgia Department of Education School Climate Surveys https://safesupportivelearning.ed.gov/survey/georgia-department-education-school-climate-surveys
- Maryland S3 Climate Survey https://safesupportivelearning.ed.gov/survey/maryland-s3-climate-survey
- Organizational Climate Description for Schools https://safesupportivelearning.ed.gov/survey/organizational-climate-description-schools
- Pride Teaching and Learning Environment Surveys https://safesupportivelearning.ed.gov/survey/pride-teaching-and-learning-environment-surveys
- REACH Survey https://safesupportivelearning.ed.gov/survey/reach-survey
- School Climate Assessment Instrument – Elementary https://safesupportivelearning.ed.gov/survey/school-climate-assessment-instrument-elementary
- School Climate Assessment Instrument – Secondary https://safesupportivelearning.ed.gov/survey/school-climate-assessment-instrument-secondary
- U.S. Department of Education School Climate Survey (EDSCLS) https://safesupportivelearning.ed.gov/survey/us-department-education-school-climate-survey-edscls

## APPENDIX A: INSTRUCTIONAL LEADERSHIP BEHAVIORAL CHECKLIST
### STEP ONE:

1. Involves teachers in developing and implementing school instructional goals and objectives.
2. Incorporates the designated state and/or system curricula in the development of instructional programs.
3. Ensures that school and classroom activities are consistent with school instructional goals and objectives.
4. Evaluates progress toward instructional goals and objectives.
5. Works with teachers to improve the instructional program in their classrooms consistent with student needs.
6. Bases instructional program development on sound research and practice.
7. Applies appropriate formative procedures in evaluating the instructional Programs.

**STEP TWO:**
1. Establishing inclusive classrooms that send the message that all students learn.
2. Providing extended learning opportunities for students who need them.
3. Observing and reinforcing positive teacher behaviors in the classroom that ensure an academically demanding climate and an orderly, well-managed classroom.
4. Sending messages to students in a variety of ways that they can succeed.
5. The establishment of policies on students' progress relative to homework, grading, monitoring progress, remediation, reporting progress, and retention/promotion.

**STEP THREE:**
1. Establishing high expectations for student achievement that are directly communicated to students, teachers, and parents.
2. Establishes clear rules and expectations for the use of time allocated to instruction and monitors the effective use of classroom time.
3. Establishes, implements, and evaluates with teachers and students (as appropriate) procedures and codes for handling and correcting discipline problems.

**STEP FOUR:**
1. Provides for systematic two-way communication with staff regarding the ongoing objectives and goals of the school.
2. Establishes, supports, and implements activities that communicate to students the value and meaning of learning.
3. Develops and utilizes communication channels with parents for the purpose of setting school objectives.

**STEP FIVE:**
1. Assists teachers in setting and reaching personal and professional goals related to the improvement of school instruction and monitors the successful completion of these goals.
2. Makes regular classroom observations in all classrooms, both informal and formal.
3. Engages in preplanning of classroom observations.
4. Engages in post-observation conferences that focus on the improvement of instruction.
5. Provides thorough, defensible, and insightful evaluations, making recommendations for personal and professional growth goals according to individual needs.
6. Engages in direct teaching in the classroom of his or her school.

**STEP SIX:**
1. Schedules, plans, or facilitates regular meetings of all types (planning, problem solving, decision-making, or in-service training) among teachers to address instructional issues.
2. Provides opportunities for and training in collaboration, shared decision-making, coaching, mentoring, curriculum development, and making presentations.
3. Provides motivation and resources for faculty members to engage in professional growth activities.

**STEP SEVEN:**
1. Serves as an advocate for students and communicates with them regarding aspects of their school life.
2. Encourages open communication among staff members and maintains respect for differences of opinion.
3. Demonstrates concern and openness in the consideration of students, teacher, and/or parent problems and participates in the resolution of such problems where appropriate.
4. Models appropriate human relations skills.
5. Develops and maintains high morale.
6. Systematically collects and responds to staff, student, and parent concerns.
7. Acknowledges appropriately the earned achievements of others.

**APPENDIX B: SCHOOL CULTURE ASSESSMENT SURVEY**
Items are Ranked Twice – presence in the school; importance to be present.

1 – Not present; Not important    10 – Always present; Extremely Important

1. Democratic decision-making
2. Strong Leadership from administration, teachers, or teams of both
3. Staff-stability – low turnover from year to year
4. A planned, coordinated curriculum supported by research and faculty
5. School-wide staff development
6. Parental involvement and support
7. School-wide recognition of success for students and staff
8. An effort to maximize active learning in academic areas
9. District support for school improvement efforts
10. Collaborative planning and collegial relationship
11. Sense of community, family, and team
12. Clear goals and high expectations commonly shared
13. Order and discipline established through consensus

(Phillips and Wagner, 2003)

## APPENDIX C: THE ORGANIZATIONAL CLIMATE (HTTPS://WWW.WAYNEKHOY.COM/OCDQ-RE/)

1. The teachers accomplish their work with vim, vigor, and pleasure.
2. Teachers' closest friends are other faculty members at this school.
3. Faculty meetings are useless.
4. The principal goes out of his/her way to help teachers.
5. The principal rules with an iron fist.
6. Teachers leave school immediately after school is over.
7. Teachers invite faculty members to visit them at home.
8. There is a minority group of teachers who always oppose the majority.
9. The principal uses constructive criticism.
10. The principal checks the sign-in sheet every morning.
11. Routine duties interfere with the job of teaching.
12. Most of the teachers here accept the faults of their colleagues.
13. Teachers know the family background of other faculty members.
14. Teachers exert group pressure on non-conforming faculty members.
15. The principal explains his/her reasons for criticism to teachers.
16. The principal listens to and accepts teachers' suggestions.
17. The principal schedules the work for the teachers.
18. Teachers have too many committee requirements.
19. Teachers help and support each other.
20. Teachers have fun socializing together during school time.
21. Teachers ramble when they talk at faculty meetings.
22. The principal looks out for the personal welfare of teachers.
23. The principal treats teachers as equals.
24. The principal corrects teachers' mistakes.
25. Administrative paperwork is burdensome at this school.
26. Teachers are proud of their school.
27. Teachers have parties for each other.
28. The principal compliments teachers.
29. The principal is easy to understand.
30. The principal closely checks classroom (teacher) activities.
31. Clerical support reduces teachers' paperwork.
32. New teachers are readily accepted by colleagues.
33. Teachers socialize with each other on a regular basis.
34. The principal supervises teachers closely.
35. The principal checks lesson plans.
36. Teachers are burdened with busy work.

## REFERENCES

Bennis, W. G. (1989). *On becoming a leader.* Addison-Wesley.

Bossert, S. T. (1982). The instructional management role of the principal. *Educational Administration Quarterly, 18,* 34–64.

Connors, N. A. (2003). *If you don't feed the teachers, they will eat the students.* Incentive Publications.

Daily, S. M., Mann, M. J., Kristjansson, A. L., Smith, M. L., & Zullig, K. J. (2019). School climate and academic achievement in middle and high school students. *Journal of School Health, 89*(3), 173–180. https://doi-org.libezp.lib.lsu.edu/10.1111/josh.12726.

Davis, J. R., & Warner, N. (2018). Schools matter: The positive relationship between New York City high schools' student academic progress and school climate. *Urban Education, 53*(8), 959–980. https://journals.sagepub.com/doi/abs/10.1177/0042085915613544

Deal, T. E. (1985). The symbolism of effective schools. *Elementary School Journal, 85*, 601–620.

Hanuscin, D. L., Cheng, Y.-W., Rebello, C., Sinha, S., & Muslu, N. (2014). The affordances of blogging as a practice to support ninth-grade science teachers' identity development as leaders. *Journal of Teacher Education, 65*(3), 207–222. https://doi-org.libezp.lib.lsu.edu/10.1177/0022487113519475.

Halpin, A., & Croft, D. (1963). *The organizational climate of schools.* University of Chicago Press.

Hoy, W., & Miskel, C. (2013). *Educational administration: Theory, research, and practice.* McGrawhill.

International Society of Technology of Education. https://www.iste.org/standards/for-education-leaders.

Jones, L. F. (2009, November). The importance of school culture for instructional leadership. *International Journal of Educational Leadership Preparation, 4*(4). Retrieved November 4, 2009, from https://files.eric.ed.gov/fulltext/EJ1071384.pdf.

Jones, L., & Kennedy, E. (2012). *Passing the leadership test* (2nd ed.). Rowman and Littlefield Publishing.

McEwan, E. (2002). *Seven steps to effective instructional leadership.* Corwin Press, Inc.

National Center for Educational Statistics (NCES). Crime and safety surveys (CSS). https://nces.ed.gov/programs/crime/principals.asp.

National Center on Safe Supportive Learning Environments (NCSSLE). Engagement, safety, & environment. http://safesupportivelearning.ed.gov/school-climate-improvement.

National Educational Leadership Preparation (NELP) Standards. https://www.naesp.org/communicator-november-2018/nelp-standards-approved-how-affects-you

National Policy Board for Educational Administration (2015). Professional Standards for Educational Leaders 2015. Reston, VA: Author.

Phillips, G., & Wagner, C. (2003). *School culture assessment: A manual for assessing and transforming school-classroom culture.* Mitchel Press.

Positive Actions. https://www.positiveaction.net/grant-writing/teaching-goals-and-objectives.

Safe School Solutions. https://www.safehiringsolutions.com/safeschool-solutions.

Selznick, P. (1957). *Leadership in administration.* Harper & Row.

Smith, W. F., & Andrews, R. L. (1989). *Instructional leadership: How principals make a difference.* Association for Supervision and Curriculum Development.

Taguiri, R. (1968). The concept of organizational climate. In R. Taguri & G. H. Litwin (Eds.), *Organizational climate: Exploration of a concept* (pp. 11–32). Division of Research, Graduate School of Business Administration, Boston: Harvard University.

Tichnor-Wagner, A., Harrison, C., & Cohen-Vogel, L. (2016). Cultures of learning in effective high schools. *Educational Administration Quarterly*, *52*(4), 602–642. https://journals.sagepub.com/doi/abs/10.1177/0013161X16644957?journalCode =eaqa.

U. S. Department of Education. (2019). Parent and educator guide to school climate resources. https://www2.ed.gov/policy/elsec/leg/essa/essaguidetoschoolclimat e041019.pdf.

Zakrzewski, V. (2013, August). How to create a positive school climate. Greater Goods Magazine. https://greatergood.berkeley.edu/article/item/how_to_create_a _positive_school_climate.

Zepeda, S. J. (2016). *Instructional supervision: Applying tools and concepts* (4th ed.). Routledge.

Ziegler, B. (2018, June). 7 strategies to enhance school safety. National Association of Secondary School Principals. https://www.nassp.org/2018/06/27/7-strategies -to-enhance-school-safety/.

# CHAPTER 7

## Leadership for External Relationships

**ABSTRACT**

The importance of strong relationships between schools, families, and community partners has been well established in the research literature (e.g., Byrk, 2010; Bryan and Henry, 2008). Families and community groups can provide the out-of-school support students need and help bridge the cultural gap that may exist between schools and the communities in which their students live. School leaders play a key role in establishing and maintaining relationships with external stakeholders in the communities in which their schools are located. In Chapter 7, we discuss the external relationships of school leaders linked to the leadership and technology standards and the role of technology in helping school leaders build external relationships with a specific look at the types of parental involvement defined by Epstein et al., (2002), Action teams are purposed as a way to develop, nurture, and sustain the parental involvement types discussed in Chapter 7. We also discuss mass messaging, mobile apps, school websites, and social media platforms as tools that school leaders may use to build and support external relations. Several social media platforms have been discussed in depth in Chapter 1; therefore, we refer to the section **Technology and the Work of the School Principal** when discussing social media platforms. We also include additional social media platforms in Chapter 7 that were not discussed in Chapter 1. Learning Management Systems were discussed in Chapter 5 as well; we refer to those as a means of mass messaging.

DOI: 10.4324/9781003269472-7

## EXTERNAL RELATIONSHIP OF SCHOOL LEADERS LINKED TO THE LEADERSHIP STANDARDS

The constituencies school leaders interact with, which may include parents, community organizations, businesses, religious organizations, etc., can be critical when dealing with issues such as financial support for the school, finding volunteers to support school initiatives and priorities, to name a few. The importance of this role of the school leader is reflected in the prominence this area holds in various leadership standards. The most relevant Leadership Standards (NELP 5, PSEL 8, and ISTE 3) and the competencies are listed below:

NELP 5
Standard 5: Community and External Leadership.

Program completers who successfully complete a building-level educational leadership preparation program understand and demonstrate the capability to promote the success and well-being of each student, teacher, and leader by applying the knowledge, skills, and commitments necessary for 1) effective communication, 2) engagement, 3) partnerships, and 4) advocacy.

The standard competencies of Standard 5 are:
Component 5.1
Program completers understand and demonstrate the capacity to collaboratively engage diverse families in strengthening student learning in and out of school.
Component 5.2
Program completers understand and demonstrate the capacity to collaboratively engage and cultivate relationships with diverse community members, partners, and other constituencies for the benefit of school improvement and student development.
Component 5.3
Program completers understand and demonstrate the capacity to communicate through oral, written, and digital means within the larger organizational, community, and political contexts when advocating for the needs of their school and community.

PSEL 8
Standard 8: Meaningful Engagement of Families and Community.

Effective educational leaders engage families and the community in meaningful, reciprocal, and mutually beneficial ways to promote each student's academic success and well-being.

The competencies of Standard 8 are effective leaders:

a) Are approachable, accessible, and welcoming to families and members of the community.
b) Create and sustain positive, collaborative, and productive relationships with families and the community for the benefit of students.
c) Engage in regular and open two-way communication with families and the community about the school, students, needs, problems, and accomplishments.
d) Maintain a presence in the community to understand its strengths and needs, develop productive relationships, and engage its resources for the school.
e) Create means for the school community to partner with families to support student learning in and out of school.
f) Understand, value, and employ the community's cultural, social, intellectual, and political resources to promote student learning and school improvement.
g) Develop and provide the school as a resource for families and the community.
h) Advocate for the school and district, and for the importance of education and student needs and priorities to families and the community.
i) Advocate publicly for the needs and priorities of students, families, and the community.
j) Build and sustain productive partnerships with public and private sectors to promote school improvement and student learning.

(http://www.npbea.org/)

ISTE Standard 3:
3.2
Establish partnerships that support the strategic vision, achieve learning priorities, and improve operations (of ISTE Systems Designer Standard) aligns with school leaders building external relationships.

(https://www.iste.org/standards/for-education-leaders)

## EXTERNAL RELATIONSHIPS AND THE ROLE OF TECHNOLOGY

Because of the importance of external relationships, effective school leaders actively work to build and nurture positive relationships with external constituencies (Epstein et al., 2002). Babin and Gallagher (2001) suggested over 20 years ago, the importance of school–community relations was growing rapidly. Epstein has focused on the importance of parental involvement. According to Dr. Epstein, Director of School and Community Partnerships (1997, 1999, 2000), student achievement improves when parents are involved in their children's education. Epstein et al. (2002) also noted that involving parents in school partnerships helps improve school programs, improves school climates, improves collegiality among parents; helps teachers with their work, provides services and support, and increases leadership skills of parents. Research findings also suggest:

- Most, or all, families care about their children and desire for them to succeed,
- Most, or all, teachers and administrators would like families involved, and
- Most, or all, students at all levels desire for their parents to be knowledgeable partners in schools.

We traditionally think of parental involvement as having parents volunteer at schools; however, Dr. Epstein et al. (2002), identify six types of involvement for school–family–community partnerships – parenting, communicating, volunteering, learning at home, decision-making/participation and leadership, and collaborating with the community. Each of the parental involvement types has definitions, redefinitions, and challenges. As the types of parental involvement are implemented, there are also results for students and results for schools. To implement parenting, school leaders should assist families with parenting and child-rearing skills. Sponsoring workshops, parental education training, and family resource rooms are among the ways school leaders can facilitate parenting.

School leaders should facilitate school-to-home and home-to-school communication with families about school programs and student success. The technological tools available in this era enhance the accessibility to facilitate communication. Learning Management Systems (LMS) were presented in Chapter 5. The LMS allows for conferences to be scheduled and grades to be shared. The sending home of papers in folders is rather obsolete. We will discuss communication more in-depth in the remainder of this chapter; however, there are technological tools throughout the book applicable that assist in facilitating communication (Epstein et al., 2002).

Parent volunteering is one of the more prevalent kinds of parental involvement and the oldest. It is important to have parents involved on campus to support students. Many of the activities have been suspended due to COVID 19. As conditions are improving, parent or family rooms on school sites are good resources to facilitate parental volunteering. "Learning at home" involves families with their children in learning activities at home including homework and other curriculum-related activities and decisions. School leaders should require that teachers provide pertinent information to families on all subjects and information on homework policies (Epstein et al., 2002).

The fifth type of parental involvement is decision-making. School leaders should involve families as participants in school decisions, advocacy, and governance. Decision-making is facilitated in schools through active PTA/PTO or other parental organizations, action teams for partnership, and networks. Epstein et al. (2002), address the community through the last of the six kinds of parental involvement – collaborating with the community. Providing services to the community, "one-stop" shopping for family services, and school-business partnership are manners in which school leaders facilitate collaboration with the community.

To nurture and build parental involvement, Epstein et al. (2002), propose the development of Action Teams. There are five steps – create an Action Team, obtain funding and support, identify starting points, develop a plan, and continue planning and working. Step 1 is Create an Action Team, a team approach is an appropriate way to build partnerships. The Action Team can be the "action arm" of a school. The team should include:

- Three teachers from different grade levels,
- Three parents with children in different grade levels,
- At least one administration, and
- A member of the community at large.

A leader should be selected. Any member with the respect of other members who has good communication skills may serve as the leader.

Step 2 is Obtaining Funds and Other Support. A "modest" budget is needed for guiding and supporting the work and expenses of each school's action team. State-level and district-level coordinators may be involved in helping to facilitate processes of action teams. The following are the possible funding sources:

- Title I,
- Title II,
- Title VII,
- School Improvement Resources,
- Separate fund raisers (not over-burdening), and
- Business support.

School leaders should include individuals on action teams who will invest time to accomplish school goals.

Step 3 is to Identify Starting Points. The action team members should identify which parental involvement types are in place. It is necessary to collect information about the school's present practices of partnerships along with the views, experiences, and wishes of teachers, parents, administrators, and students. Questionnaires, telephone interviews, and panel discussions are possible assessment starting points. In addition, the following questions to be addressed include:

- Present strengths: Which practices are working? At which grade levels?
- Needed changes: Which practices should be continued?
- Expectations: What do teachers expect of families? What do families expect of teachers and other school personnel?
- Sense of Community: Which families are we presently reaching? Which are we not reaching?
- Links to Goals: How are students faring in such measures of academic achievement? How might family and community connections assist the school in helping more students reach higher goals?

Step 4 is to Develop a Three-Year Plan. From the information collected, the team can develop a three-year outline of the specific steps that will help the school progress. The members of the team should include a plan that outlines how each subcommittee will work to make important advances. The following are components which should be addressed by the Action Team:

- Details: What will be done each year to implement the program with each of the six types of parental involvement?
- Responsibilities: Who will be responsible for developing and implementing practices of partnership for each type of involvement? Will staff development be needed?
- Costs: What costs are associated with the improvement and maintenance of the planned activities? What sources will provide the funds?
- Evaluation: How will we know how well the practices have been implemented and what their effects are on students, teachers, and families?

Step 5 is to Continue Planning and Working. The action team members should work with the school leader to schedule an annual presentation and celebration of progress at the school so that all teachers, families, and students will know about the work accomplished. A report of the accomplishments should be presented. Technology tools can be used to help to facilitate this work at each step.

Lasater (2016) also noted the importance of external relationships for schools. We discussed the importance of parents as a stakeholder group and alluded to the need for community partnerships. However, one source of challenge is the diversity of the stakeholder groups. The groups include parents, businesses, civic and social organizations, political leaders and government agencies and departments, and the ubiquitous general public. The interests, priorities, and communication channels of these groups may differ significantly and may often be in conflict. Prior to modern technologies, developing and delivering customized messages and communications with these various groups often taxed human and financial resources. With modern technologies; however, developing materials and communicating with constituencies is easier than ever. Mass messaging through email, texts, and posting to social media allow administrators to reach large numbers of persons with minimal commitment of human and financial resources. Additionally, personalized communications through mobile apps and social media allow administrators and teachers to connect with parents and other constituencies in ways that are personal and thus address psychological barriers to engagement such as fear or alienation from the school. Below we briefly describe selected tools and describe how they might be used by school administrators.

## MASS MESSAGING

Mass messaging services are applications that allow users to distribute messages to a large number of contacts via phone, email, text, and social media accounts. These can include emergency alerts and notifications, recorded video, audio, text files, etc. Messages can be distributed instantly or at a preset time. In some instances, they can be customized or personalized for specific audiences. For example, Blackboard Collaborate (Blackboard Connect, https://www.blackboard.com) and similar service providers offer an efficient tool for school leaders to communicate with stakeholders. School officials call a toll-free number, record a message for the pertinent group(s), and select the time at which the desired message should be sent. Messages can be sent via email, text, Facebook post, Twitter, and/or RSS feed. An important feature of Blackboard Collaborate is the ability to track the unsuccessful delivery of messages. In Chapter 5, we discussed several Learning Management Systems. Varied forms of mass messaging are available through these systems.

In Chapter 2, there is a section **Technological Tools Applicable to Many Administrative Tasks**. Several technologies noted in this section are applicable for mass messaging as well as other applications. DeansList (https://

www.deanslistsoftware.com/features) and ParentLocker (http://www
.parentlocker.com) are two of the applications featured in Chapter 2 that
have capabilities to mass message. The social media outlets discussed in
Chapter 1 facilitate mass messaging as well. In Chapter 1, we discussed
Facebook, Twitter, Instagram, Tumblr, and LinkedIn. Several other social
media outlets will follow in this chapter. It is important to note in Chapter 1,
we noted which audiences cater to the type of social media. We previously
mentioned the diverse nature of stakeholder groups. Different social media
outlets garner the attention of different stakeholders. We should also note
that the Learning Management Systems discussed in Chapter 5 and mentioned in other chapters have the capabilities to mass message users of the
particular groups which are advantageous for all internal stakeholders –
teachers, staff, and students. School leaders can provide instant notifications through these systems.

The ability of mass messaging services to distribute communications
through a variety of mediums is a significant advantage over more traditional techniques. For example, messages sent home to parents may not be
delivered by students, newsletters and other documents sent via mail are
costly, or phone calls may arrive at a time when they cannot be answered.
In contrast, emails are cost-effective, reach parents when notes do not,
can be less formal than letters, increase responsiveness, promote positive
public relations, and help transform parents into advocates for technology
(Bernstein, 1998). Similarly, text messages tend to be brief in comparison
to emails and thus increase the likelihood that they will be reviewed by the
recipient. Finally, as noted below, interactions with social media such as
Instagram are nearly constant with some segments of the population checking their accounts several times an hour throughout the day. Thus, messages
distributed via social media stand an increased chance of being noticed by
recipients.

In summary, mass messages have much to offer schools. They can
be used to notify constituencies of school events or emergencies, share
positive stories, and, in general, build support for the school. There are
a variety of mass messaging services available to school administrators.
The task of an administrator is to select a service and determine how it
will be used in an overall communication strategy. We provided an index
in Chapter 1 for school leaders to review products and their capabilities.
In addition, several organizations and entities have proposed guidelines
for selecting mass messaging providers as well as offered annual reviews
of existing products. The following is a brief list of online articles in
which different services are described.

- The Balance Small Business https://www.thebalancesmb.com/best
  -bulk-text-message-services-5074431

- Educational Technology and Mobile Learning https://www.educatorstechnology.com/2012/04/9-awsome-group-text-messaging-tools-for.html
- Business News Daily https://www.businessnewsdaily.com/15044-best-text-message-marketing-solutions.html
- 360 News Quadrant https://www.360quadrants.com/software/mass-notification-systems-solutions
- Quick Sprout https://www.quicksprout.com/best-email-marketing-services/

Features to note in selecting a service provider include the following: (1) the costs of the service should be competitive, (2) the service interface should be easy to use, (3) the service should be customizable for the particular needs of the local school, (4) the service should offer monitoring capabilities and other controls for two-way communications, and (5) the service should offer analytics and reports on performance. In addition to functionality, it is important to include compliance as part of the planning process. For example, the CAN-SPAM Act (2003) should inform mass messaging practices.

## MOBILE APPS AND SCHOOL COMMUNICATIONS

The use of mobile devices for communication purposes has increased dramatically in the past few decades. Teachers, parents, students, and most individuals involved in education own and use mobile phones, tablets, or other devices on a daily basis. Mobile app developers have created numerous school-related applications. Some of the more popular apps are described by Winans (2019):

> *Remind* provides communication in the classroom, at home, and anywhere in between. The main purpose of Remind is to *help* manage parent communication and encourage further community engagement. Part of what makes this app so effective is the ability to easily send messages and reminders to specific individuals, groups, or the entire class.
>
> *ClassDojo* is designed to keep parents informed about what's happening in their student's school and build a classroom community. Being used in 90% of K-8 schools, it's no wonder teachers enjoy this app. Students can collaborate on projects more easily and teachers can reach parents right through the app, making ClassDojo a great classroom tool.
>
> *School Messenger* helps to simplify parent and community engagement by combining school notifications, mobile apps, and website content in one easy place. It saves parents and districts time and energy with School Messenger. It's also a preferred PowerSchool partner!

*Bloomz* is the parent-teacher communication app that helps keep everyone informed. With two-way messaging, calendar integrations, class updates and more! All these features have helped Bloomz be recognized as one of the best parent-teacher school communication apps.

*Appletree* helps connect parents with their school community and keep them up-to-date with what's going on in the classroom. Updates about the classroom, homework, events and more can easily be sent right where they need to be.

*Edmodo* is the social learning platform that helps connect students with their peers and increases parent-teacher communication. Providing students with access to everything they need to know and learn helps make your classroom centralized.

*Campus Suite* provides engagement like never before. Offering website design and a single dashboard to manage all digital communication, it combines all of the channels needed to help connect and engage parents in the school community.

*GroupMe* is primarily a messaging app that allows teachers to keep parents informed of what's going on in the classroom. GroupMe works on every device to make communication easy and staying in touch simple.

*SchoolCircle* was designed to save time and increase family engagement in one, easy-to-use app. Organizing parent-teacher communication and providing reminders for what's going on in the classroom has been simplified.

*TalkingPoints* allows districts to reach all of their student's families to build stronger relationships. Used in over 2,000 schools, TalkingPoints helps connect schools, teachers, and their students through multilingual messages in one centralized platform.

It is also important to note that frequently new applications are readily available and are user-friendly. These tools have the potential to help increase school engagement, build community, and inform key constituencies. Because of the widespread use of mobile devices, school-based mobile apps help alleviate the impact of inequities in access to technology that may exist in a student population (Shkurina, 2018).

## School Website

A school website is often one of the first points of contact of an individual with a school. Beasley (2015) discusses what is provided by a website. School principals can include general information regarding the school and district, contact information, news, current events, and other information. In order to increase the efficiency of websites, Beasley

(2015) stressed the importance of websites including a means for two-way communication. Lunts (2003) suggests that the following are the components of a family-friendly website:

- Welcome message for parents – a warm greeting with an invitation to journey through the school webpages,
- School's mission statement,
- "What's new?" section – inform parents about upcoming and past events,
- School history section – consists of highlights of school history,
- Frequently asked questions section – including school hours, rules for school visitors, school handbooks, etc.,
- How to contact section – contains information about the school location (can include a map) and school telephone directory and email contacts,
- Faculty and staff showcase section – include images of administration and teachers,
- Extra-curricular activities section – displays students' artwork and include a calendar of sports event,
- Media center link – include educational resources available for students and parents,
- Only for parents (PTA) section – information about events organized for parents or entire families, including links to other organizations that support families, and
- Community information section – links about the community, local businesses, the school system, and the weather.

Charette (2022) cites Forbes noting that the lifespan of a website is two years and seven months because design trends emerge very quickly. Many of the first impressions of stakeholders are formulated through website design. The credibility of a school can also be influenced by the design of the website. There are six top school website design trends for 2022 for school leaders to consider. They are:

- The Goal-Driven Approach,
- The Mobile-First Philosophy,
- The Bolder Layouts with Color Schemes,
- The Creativity with Character,
- The Storytelling beyond the Homepage, and
- The Purposeful and Engaging Content.

As implied in the name, goal-driven websites have aims and objectives, audiences which are targeted, value propositions, and voice and brand.

The goal influences the design and other features on the site including content, navigation, calls-to-action, media, testimonials, and layout. Because people are spending more time on mobile devices, the Mobile-First Philosophy is gaining popularity. Charette (2022) notes that websites which simultaneously value both desktop and mobile experiences will have increased website traffic. The designs should be succinct including large type and vibrant colors, larger buttons for interactions, and strategic use of white space.

School leaders should keep in mind that the branding of schools "come to life" with color schemes. This makes the bolder layouts and color schemes viable. People tend to value images and color on websites. Layouts with stronger, brighter visuals are welcome. Creativity is also welcomed. Schools can "come to life" in new ways using expressive gradients, typography, textures, graphic details, and photo treatments. Opportunities are often missed by schools as the storytelling is not included. As users select "high trafficked" pages, this is an opportunity for schools to tell the stories of their schools. It is also critical for content to be purposeful and accessible in 2022. Attention spans are short in every sector of society; including websites. Users look for personalization.

Martin discusses personalization in the blog, *What is Content Personalization and Why does it Matter to Schools?* (https://www.final-site.com/blog/p/~board/b/post/why-content-personalization-matters-to-schools). Personalization is described as a process in which experiences are customized and tailored for specific visitors to websites. Visitors can be of a specific language, state/province, country, or continent. This matters for schools because users have become accustomed to personalization. Obviously, meeting people where they are is important for schools. School leaders must keep in mind how to maximize each technology tool to the best of his or her advantage.

The advantage of webpages is that stakeholders generally have access 24 hours per day and that they can include a wide range of content, including text, video, and images. Well-designed webpages attract and inform visitors and provide the owner of the page with diagnostics about traffic on the site. Webpage development software differ in their capabilities, the sophistication required of users, the types of diagnostics they offer, and costs.

It is noted on this weblink – https://mycodelesswebsite.com/school-website-design – examples of good websites. Webpages should have a "contact us" section. When this tab is selected, individuals may submit online inquiries. The two-way communication is facilitated through this inquiry. When we discussed Epstein's parental involvement types, we cited communication as one of the types of parental involvement. One of the points Epstein makes is that the communication should be "school-to-home" and "home-to-school. The "contact us" feature is a way to facilitate Epstein's recommendation about two-way communication.

The following sources provide rankings and reviews of providers of webpage development software:

- MorWeb https://morweb.org/post/school-website-builders
- Colorlib https://colorlib.com/wp/education-website-builders/

The selection of a webpage provider is only one part of the process of establishing a school website. School leaders must clearly specify the goals and purposes of the website, and provide the human and other resources needed to establish and maintain the site. Typically, a school-based technology staffer will be responsible for developing and maintaining the site and a broader external communications group of administrators and staff will govern content.

## SOCIAL MEDIA

We discussed social media in Chapter 1, in the context of facilitating effective communication, and social media is also mentioned in other chapters. We cite Delack (2022, January) in Chapter 1. Delack notes that Facebook, Twitter, Instagram, and LinkedIn should be used by school districts in 2022. In this chapter, we discuss social media platforms from the communication perspective and include social media as a specific way to improve external relationships. Having a social media presence is a must for the modern school. Social media is a collection of internet-based applications and platforms that permit users to build networks in which they share information, ideas, etc. According to Dean (2021, October 10th), there were 4.8 billion people in the world using social media in 2021, roughly 56% of the world's population aged 13+ years. In North America, this goes up to 82%. In the United States, 72% of the population uses social media. It is also true that the percentage is higher among young adults and school-aged children.

Whether the goal is advertising, developing a network of supporters and followers, or simply branding your school, having a social media presence is necessary in the modern era (Garces, 2019). Facebook, Twitter, LinkedIn, Instagram, and Tumblr were noted in Chapter 1. Please refer to the discussion on **Technology and the Work of the School Principal** in Chapter 1 for specifics of Facebook, Twitter, LinkedIn, Instagram, and Tumblr. In addition to Facebook, Twitter, LinkedIn and Instagram, and school websites, the following are other platforms:

*YouTube* is a social media platform that permits users to upload videos and comments or stream live videos and make them available to others. Users can subscribe to a user's channel.

*Blogs* are web-based sites that permit users to post essays and other artifacts that are made available to a broad audience. Typically, they permit readers to post comments or responses to the posted material. A blog post from February 24, 2022 has a listing of the Top 15 Educational Leadership Blogs and Websites – https://blog.feedspot.com/educational _leadership_blogs/. At the time of print of the publication, there were 11 listed, they are listed below:

- A Principal's Reflections: reflections on teaching, learning, and leadership – is a blog about digital leadership, pedagogy, and transformative change in education.
- Emerging Education Technologies Blog: includes tools to assist educators in improving learner outcomes, engaging students, and engaging administrative productivity.
- The @DavidGeurin Blog: provides insight and ideas to "busy educators committed to growth and learning."
- The Compelled Educator Blog: focuses on innovation, professional learning, social media, leadership, and education.
- Lisa Nielsen: The Innovative Educator: features Lisa Nielsen who speaks with educators globally. In the blog, she shares ideas about relevant learning and innovation.
- Dangerously Irrelevant Blog: has a focus on the leadership side of technology.
- Principal Principles – Blog for Educational Leaders: is a blog facilitated for educational leaders to share ideas.
- Connected Principals – Sharing. Learning. Leading: is also a sharing blog for principals to share best practices in education.
- Michael Fullan Blog: this blog is facilitated by Michael Fullan who is a global authority on reform.
- The Ed Tech Roundup Blog: provides regular updates on educational technology and reviews.
- Thomas C. Murray Blog: is facilitated by Thomas C. Murray who discusses K-12 digital leadership.

*Podcasts* are internet-based productions similar to television shows, but without the production and distribution costs. Podcasts can be weekly, monthly, etc. but are produced on a regular basis for users. They can be prerecorded or live. The following site provides an overview of podcasts – https://kinsta.com/blog/what-is-a-podcast/. Like the information provided on blogs, there is also a listing of the best podcasts for educational leaders – According to the web link: https:// blog.feedspot.com/educational_leadership_podcasts/, the following are the top ten podcasts. Many of the leaders have experienced success in their schools:

- The Better Leaders Better Schools Podcast With Daniel Bauer: is a podcast for educational leaders motivating leaders to challenge the status quo.
- Principal Center Radio: focuses on professional practice for school leaders.
- Principal Matters – The School Leader's Podcast with William D. Parker: is a weekly podcast featuring William D. Parker, an author and speaker, who addresses school leadership, culture, and communication.
- Aspire – The Leadership Development Podcast: is a podcast focused on building leadership capacity.
- School Leadership Reimagined: features Robyn Jackson who shares information for principals, assistant principals, and instructional coaches on strategies to improve instruction.
- The School Leadership Show: is a podcast focused on helping school leaders thrive and reach their full potential.
- Leader Of Learning: is a podcast which emphasizes effective leadership as a means to transform education.
- Education Leadership and Beyond: features Andrew Marota who shares practical experiences to impact school leaders and their schools.
- School Leadership Series With Daniel Bauer: is a daily five-minute podcast featuring Daniel Bauer who gives quick inspiration and encouragement to educators.
- The Principal's Office Podcast: is facilitated by Dr. Tom Miller; he provides insight on innovation for school leaders.

*TikTok* is a popular application that allows users to create and share videos for upto 15 seconds on any topic (https://www.influencerm arketinghub.com/what-is-tiktok/). This application has drawn some controversy.

There are opposing positions on using this application. Schaffer (2022a, January) suggests five reasons why TikTok is the hottest marketing tool. They are (1) TikTok is newer and has a greater opportunity for personalization. (2) The ads are dominated by this application. While TikTok ads are more expensive, they are dominating. In-Feed Ads, Brand Takeovers, and TopViews are the most popular. The benefit of In-Feeds is they allow for a great deal of creativity. Only one Brand Takeover ad appears per day; however, users see these ads as soon as TikTok is opened, and the advantage of TopViews is these ads show at the top of the page. In Chapter 1, we cited that school leaders should consider the use of advertising for branding purposes.

(3) TikTok has a focus on diverse content; most of the posting on TikTok has a focus on music and/or comedy. It is the most informal platform. (4) There is a greater potential to get the most views with TikTok. (5) Tiktok is "ripe" for innovation due to the newness of the platform. We alluded to controversy centered on TikTok; it was banned by one president in 2020 and restored by another in 2021 due to content exchanged through TikTok. Herman (2021, June) argues that lifting the ban on TikTok is a mistake. He noted that a great deal of confidential information is shared on TikTok, and a great deal of data can be gathered with the use of the platform.

*Pinterest* is another social media platform; it has a specific intent to "pin" recipes and inspiration. It is not necessarily a popular platform for schools. However, we included Pinterest because schools often sponsor events in which this platform may be most appropriate (https://www.pinterest.com/).

Several of the following strategies were shared in Chapter 1 for increasing engagement through social media content. However, Schaffer (March, 2022b) has 15 suggestions. We offer these as techniques for school leaders to consider. Schaffer says (1) post daily, weekly, or monthly. This strategy was introduced when discussing Facebook. The concept of "series of posting" is an add-on by Schaffer. Regular engagement of followers can occur by starting a series. A consistent plan makes the community aware of the agenda of content for the week. (2) Hold giveaways or competitions. The followers increase when the word "free" is included, and contests are as effective in increasing engagement and following.

Schaffer (March, 2022b) notes that a third-party system is not required for content. It is only necessary to have: something to hand out, terms and conditions, a contact point, and a unique method of entry. (3) Host "asks me anything" sessions. These sessions (Host: "asks me anything" sessions) allow hosts to increase brand awareness with a non-aggressive approach and to obtain a deeper knowledge of the concerns and knowledge of the audience. Schaffer's fourth, fifth, and sixth suggestions were referenced in Chapter 1 in the section *Technology and the Work of the School Principal.* (4) Engage in social media takeover, this provides an opportunity for someone else to run the social media accounts. (5) Regram, retweet, and share. It is important to share content from others. (6) Make video segments that are "bite-sized." In making videos, school leaders or designees should prioritize information, avoid information overload, structure the content, manage the video duration, and make the most of review features.

(7) Consider using content in new ways. Repurpose as much as possible to get the most out of each piece of content. At the beginning of the chapter, we noted information from Dr. Joyce Epstein and colleagues about the importance of school leaders acquiring partnerships with businesses and other entities for the school. (8) Attempt to partner with companies. Coordination with companies can be facilitated with ease. (9) Create tutorials, social media accounts provide excellent opportunities for school leaders to explain and provide step-by-step instructions. (10) Go live when there are opportunities. Real-time interactions with people establish personal connections with users/followers. Some of the material captured in real-time may also be repurposed.

In Chapter 1, we cited the strategy from Major (2019, October) that school leaders or the designated social media managers should interact with followers. Schaffer (March, 2022b) makes the same recommendation. It is important to respond to followers promptly as time is invaluable. (12) Take a look behind the scenes. Users should see the mascots and "snapshots" of schools. (13) Encourage followers to tag your posts. Simply, this will increase the social feed. (14) Take advantage of trending subjects. Trends attract users; this is a way to capitalize on trends. (15) Share successes. It is a critical part of branding to share successes and triumphs.

---

**SCENARIO 1: USING TECHNOLOGY TO BUILD RELATIONSHIPS WITH COMMUNITY PARTNERS**

Kaiden Elementary School is located in Jones School District and houses grades Pre-K to 4th grade. It is a very rural area north of a major city. The majority of residents in Jones School District are residents of the area and rarely do any newcomers gravitate to the area. It is a quiet area with few distractions. Most individuals who live in Jones School District work in the district or drive to neighboring towns. There is no major industry in the area; however, there are several car dealerships, tire shops, art and clothing stores, convenient stores, and Dollar Generals.

Jones School District has four schools — two elementary schools, a middle school, and a high school. Seventy percent of the students in the district are African American or students of color, and the district is performing at or above average on all state accountability metrics. Of the two elementary schools, Kaiden is the higher performing. Kaiden has about 350 students with 40 teachers, an assistant principal, and a school leader. Ironically, most of the teachers drive into Kaiden Elementary School from neighboring areas outside of the district because of its stellar reputation for discipline. The DeansList report for 2019 indicated that there were only three infractions per grading period for the entire academic year.

The principal of Kaiden is a native of Jones School District, Paula Sudden. Paula matriculated through Jones School District graduating from the only high school and is revered by the Jones School District. She has nearly 25 years of experience with five years of leadership experience. In addition to improving test scores, Paula has a goal to improve the partnerships for Kaiden Elementary School. Paula's main reasoning for improving the partnerships is to "tap into the benefits" cited in the literature regarding the presence of others on the campus along with the support that partnership brings.

Partnerships are an essential resource for schools (Epstein, 2002). Partners can be organizations, businesses, or other entities that collaborate with a school toward the end of meeting the needs of both organizations. Among other factors, effective partnerships consist of the following:

- Clearly specified and agreed upon purpose, goals, and objectives,
- Clear expectations with regard to the contributions and activities of partners,
- Well-defined plans for review, accountability, etc., and
- Well-developed organizational structure and procedures.

A partnership can be as simple as a car dealership providing uniforms for the school football team and using the expense as a charitable donation. They can also be extensive, impacting multiple aspects of the operation of a school and span multiple years. Finding and nurturing partnerships is an important role of the school leader. Technology can greatly facilitate this process. Either through direct recruitment activities and requests or by offering more *passive* opportunities. The former is addressed below in marketing and public relations. The latter involves ensuring that the opportunity to partner with a school is included in all school electronic communications. These can be as simple as dropdown menus or hot links with headings such as *Become a Supporter or Partner*.

In the general faculty meeting at the beginning of the school year, Paula shared her goals with the entire faculty. All appeared supported. She informed the faculty that she would work with the

School Improvement Planning Committee to facilitate ideas for improving partnerships. The current partnership that Kaiden has is with Jones Bank. There is a Bank-at-School Program with the 4th graders. The Bank-at-School Program started in 2017 at Kaiden Elementary School. According to the article Empowering Kids to Learn About Money (https://www.pnc.com/en/about-pnc/topics/pnc-pov/community/school-bank-kids-learn-money.html), Bank at School is a way to empower students to learn about money early. Working with banks, schools open a branch which gives students access to savings accounts. Schools set up "bank days" which provide days for students to deposit into their accounts. The program builds financial literacy skills for students very early. It may be more appropriate in a high school setting, but students can serve as tellers – providing an authentic experience for the students. The Louisiana Bankers Association recommends the following guidelines:

1. Banker and school officials meet to review the Bank-at-School concept and the opportunity for opening a branch in the school.
2. School official assigns faculty member to work with a banker.
3. Bankers and school officials select the opening date and subsequent schedule for bank days.
4. Bankers decide on a minimum and maximum deposit amount to be deposited on school bank days. Most banks do not allow withdrawals to be made at the school.
5. The banker decides on the interest rate of savings accounts in the program and how statements will be rendered and delivered to the students.
6. The school sends a notice to the parent/guardian explaining the specifics of the program and asking for information to open a savings account, which includes the student's name, address, social security number, and parent/guardian name, address, phone, social security number. The parent/guardian signs the notice to allow the student to open a savings account through the Bank-at-School program.
7. The banker prepares signature cards with the above information then sends the signature card back to the parent for signature. The bank sends rules governing the account to the parent/guardian with the signature card.
8. The banker contacts Louisiana Bankers Association to obtain a teacher's manual for the Bank-at-School lesson to be taught in the classroom.

9. Bankers may work with students who act as tellers and bank officers during bank days.
10. Banker and school contact decide on a "Grand Opening" of the Bank-at-School and invite school officials, bank officials, Louisiana Treasurer, and Louisiana Young Bankers to the "ribbon cutting" ceremony.
11. The school contact may invite bankers into the classroom during lessons as guest speakers.

Kaiden Elementary School has experienced success with the Bank-at-School program. Paula uses the school's website and Facebook pages to publicize and market the program. Parents are also sent reminders of the banking days through mass messaging. The School Improvement Team has been slow at generating ideas for partnerships for Kaiden Elementary. Are there technology tools presented in this chapter that can be used to garner partnerships?

## SCENARIO 2: THE NEW PRINCIPAL AT FROST

Frost Elementary School, with a population of 1,100 students from pre-K to 6th grade, is located in the inner city of a larger southern metropolitan area. The ethnic/socioeconomic makeup of the school is African American and poor. The make up of the faculty is 45% Caucasian and 55% African American. Although the school district has been desegregated for a number of years, Frost's enrollment remains totally African American.

Scores on achievement tests, which are used to measure student progress and serve as a means of comparison with students in other parts of the city and state, are at an all-time low. They have been some of the lowest scores in the district for a number of years. Mr. Shaw, who served as principal of the school for 15 years, was considered by most faculty members to be an individual who loved children and had their best interests at heart. He was always in the community conveying to parents his interest in the children, the school, and the community. Mr. Shaw was quite knowledgeable and worked diligently with the faculty to enhance the school's instructional program. However, in spite of his efforts, achievement scores remained low and incidents of discipline high. During the last five years of his tenure, the average daily attendance of students fluctuated between 84% and 86%. Nevertheless, his traditional instructional program was highly supported by faculty, students, and staff. In addition, the school was several thousand dollars in debt, and fundraising was virtually nonexistent.

With the appointment of the new superintendent and a push for educational reform and restructuring, Mr. Shaw retired, and Dr. Sterling was appointed principal. Upon her appointment, she received directions to improve student achievement at Frost, using some form of site-based management. During the first week of her assignment, she sent the following memorandum to the staff:

> *Memorandum to Faculty and Staff*
> *August 21, 2007*
> *I would like to request volunteers to serve on a task force to develop a plan of action to bring about improvements in the instructional program here at Frost. One of the responsibilities of the task force will be to survey the entire faculty and staff for the purpose of ascertaining their ideas, suggestions, and recommendations for program improvements. The work of the task force will be very time consuming; however, the results should propel us into the 21st century and beyond.*
>
> *Please notify my secretary by September 1, 2007, if you are available to serve. Thank you for your cooperation in this matter.*

On September 1, Principal Sterling asked her secretary for the list of volunteers; there were no responses. The word of the grapevine was, "The new principal has considerable work in mind for the faculty, and the faculty is already totally consumed with maintaining discipline."

## Selecting the Task Force

Having received no volunteers, the principal invited (selected) one teacher from each grade level to serve on the task force. The individuals selected were not thrilled about being drafted; however, they accepted the principal's invitation and attended the first meeting on September 5, 2007. All subsequent meetings were held once a week (between Principal Sterling and the task force) until the plan was ready for partial implementation on October 2, 2007.

*Developing the Plan*

The task force met for approximately 40 hours to develop the plan. Having read Leo Bradley's *Total Quality Management for Schools* (Technomic Publishing Company, 1994), the principal introduced the task force to the Affinity, Fishbone, and Pareto designs. The reader will find it beneficial to read Bradley's *Total Quality Management for Schools* to fully understand the technique, which are excellent approaches to assessing the prevailing conditions for a school.

The faculty at Frost used the Affinity Diagram to brainstorm and define the issues that needed to be addressed. The Affinity Diagram allowed her to organize output from the brainstorming session of the task force. Using this design, all of the information could be consolidated. The Fishbone Diagram (cause and effect) was used to get an overall picture of how to move from current reality to the established goals. Using this design, elements that may have been contributing to the problem and their cause-and-effect relationships could be identified. The Pareto Diagram (a simple bar chart) was utilized to identify the pros and cons of various challenging school issues (separating major problems from trivial ones) and to ensure that the programs selected for implementation would be effective. Reports were provided to the faculty and staff, who, in turn, provided feedback to the task force on their work. Of the issues identified, the most pressing was student discipline. Thus, the task force made the recommendations to the principal that improving school-wide discipline should be the first issue addressed. Principal Sterling accepted the recommendation, and improving student behavior school-wide became the order of the day.

*Implementing the Plan*

Realizing that faculty would need professional development to effectively implement new programs in the area of discipline, Principal Sterling again turned to the task force for an assessment of the professional development program needs of the faculty. By a large majority, the faculty voted to be trained in various methods of assertive discipline, discipline with dignity, and discipline techniques for today's children. In addition, the faculty requested that Principal Sterling formally develop a school-wide discipline plan and schedule workshops during faculty meetings so teachers could begin to implement various techniques in their classrooms. They also requested that Principal Sterling actively recruit male teachers to provide students with male role models. In concluding their work, the task force clearly stated, "For the new programs to be successful, it will be necessary for all faculty and staff to be involved. There can be no exceptions."

In subsequent meetings with the task force, a decision was reached to open the lines of communication between the home and school so that parents would not feel isolated from the process. Principal Sterling announced an open-door policy and instituted school conferences to inform parents about appropriate and inappropriate behaviors. Communication to homes included phone calls, notes from teachers, and monthly informational calendars. An automated phone system was installed and a website was created to keep parents informed of all school activities and events.

### Results of the Plan

During the first year, discipline was hard and fast; 80 out-of-school suspensions were issued to students. Parents were extremely upset and they never had this problem with the previous principal. However, the administration, faculty, and staff held firm. Parent workshops were conducted on parenting skills and the fair, firm, and consistent policies used by the administration, faculty, and staff. The faculty was able to focus on the instructional program.

After an improvement in discipline began to occur, Principal Sterling turned to the second item on the list generated by the faculty: "curriculum, instruction, and evaluation." Again, she asked for individuals to serve on a committee, and this time the responses were quite different; 16 individuals volunteered to serve. In her business-like manner, Principal Sterling accepted all 16, and the committee went to work. After three weeks of discussion, the committee determined that the school had to change and change drastically. Student regression (failure to retain information from the previous year) over the summer nullified any achievement gains the students had made the previous year. Year-round education was determined to be the educational course for the school to pursue.

### Remaining on the Fast Track

To continue to make improvements at Frost, subcommittees were formed for various initiatives, frequent fundraising events were held, teachers were in the community visiting with parents, and instructional planning meetings were continuous. With the planning and implementation of year-round education, Frost became the talk of the educational community. Professors from the local university took an interest in the school and often asked to be allowed to help implement programs. Visitors from other schools in the city, state, and other states in the nation frequently visited the school, and Principal Sterling received and accepted invitations to participate in a variety of local, state, and national conferences. At the end of Principal Sterling's fourth year, discipline had improved. The year-round school concept had been implemented, and most of the faculty members were supporting the site-based management concept. However, teacher turnover was about 10%. Some of the turnover appeared to be initiated by the principal, and some was teacher-initiated.

What technology tools can Principal Sterling use to continue to communicate with the internal and external public? Are any of Epstein's recommendations feasible to implement for sustainability of the growth?

## SUMMARY

In Chapter 7, we focused on the use of technology for the purposes of establishing and maintaining external relationships between schools and various constituencies. We noted the important role of external relationships for school leaders and include the leadership and technology standards that address the knowledge, skills, and dispositions school leaders need aligned to building external relationships. School leaders must establish relationships with a diverse group of stakeholders including parents. Dr. Joyce Epstein is a leading parental involvement advocate, and she and her colleagues identified six kinds of parental involvement. We include Epstein's definitions and ways to build and nurture the types of parental involvement.

We discuss mass messaging to facilitate the task of communicating with a large number of persons in a cost-effective and efficient way. In particular, we note that mass messaging via phone, email, text, and social media can be used for emergency notifications; marketing, branding, and public relations; and routine communications. We also note that school websites and other social media platforms are powerful tools for building networks of support and followers. We referred to social media platforms discussed in Chapter 1. We introduce and discuss others in this chapter. Because of the sheer number of services, providers, and apps available, we examine annual rankings and descriptions/reviews provided by various organizations and publications. We also include two case studies for the application of content in this chapter as well as other chapters as deemed appropriate.

---

**TECHNOLOGY TOOLS**

Blackboard: https://www.blackboard.com
DeansList: https://www.deanslistsoftware.com
Facebook: https://www.facebook.com
Instagram. https://www.instagram.com
LinkedIn: https://www.linkedin.com
Mobile Apps
   *Remind*
   *ClassDojo*
   *School Messenger*
   *Boomz*
   *Appletree*
   *Edmodo*
   *Campus Suite*
   *GroupMe*
   *SchoolCircle*
   *TalkingPoints*
ParentLocker: https://www.parentlocker..com
Principal Bloggers
Pinterest: https://www.pinterest.com
TikTok: https://www.tiktok.com
Twitter: https://www.twitter.com
Youtube: https://www.youtube.com

---

**REFERENCES**

Babin, D., & Gallagher, D. (2001). *The school and community relations.* Pearson.

Beasley, A. (2015). *Administrators using technology to increase family engagement.* Kennesaw University Library.

Bernstein, A. (1998). Using electronic mail to improve school-based communications. *The Journal, 25*(10). http://thejournal.com/articles/14087.

Blackboard Collaborate. https://www.blackboard.com.

Bradley, L. (1994). *Total qualtiy management for schools.* Routledge.

Bryan, J., & Henry, L. (2008). Strengths-based partnerships: A school–family–community partnership approach to empowering students. *Professional School Counseling, 12,* 149–156.

Bryk, A. S. (2010). Organizing schools for improvement. *Phi Delta Kappan, 91,* 23–30. https://nieer.org/wp-content/uploads/2015/07/Organizing-schools-for-improvemnt-Bryk.pdf.

Charette, M. (2022, January). Top school web design trends for 2022. https://www
.finalsite.com/blog/p/~board/b/post/school-web-design-trends-2022.

Dean, B. (2021, October 10). Social network usage & growth statistics: How many
people use social media in 2021? Retrieved December 22, 2021, from https://
backlinko.com/social-media-users.

Delack, M. (2022, January). 4 social media platforms your district should be
using in 2022. https://www.finalsite.com/blog/p/~board/b/post/top-social-media
-platforms-for-districts.

Epstein, J.,Sanders, M., Simon, B., Salinas, K., Jansorn, N., & Voorhis, F. L.
(2002). *School, family, and community partnerships: Your handbooks for action.*
Corwin Press.

Garces, K. (2019). 10  school branding ideas that will make you stand out. Retrieved
December 20, 2021, from https://penji.co/school-branding-ideas/.

Herman, A. (2021, June). Lifting the TikTok ban is a mistake. *Forbes.* https://www
.forbes.com/sites/arthurherman/2021/06/10/lifting-the-tiktok-ban-is-a-mistake/
?sh=88b3f4729531.

Jones, L. (2012). *Passing the leadership test* (2nd ed.). Rowman & Littlefield
Publishing.

Lasater, K. (2016). School leader relationships: The need for explicit training on
rapport, trust, and communication. *Journal of School Administration Research
and Development*, 1(2), 19–26.

Lousiana's Bankers Association. Financial Literacy: Bank at School. https://www
.lba.org/LBA/Financial_Literacy/Louisiana_Bankers_Education_Council/Bank
-At-School_Program/LBA/Financial_Literacy/Bank_at_School_Program.aspx
?hkey=8a4eb5f6-b96d-46a4-8721-32ccc55d823d.

Lunts, E. (2003). Parental involvement in children's education: Connecting family
and school by using telecommunication technologies. *Meridian: A Middle School
Computer Technologies Journal*, 6(1), 1–8.

Major, M. (2019, October). How to use facebook groups to connect your school
community.    https://www.finalsite.com/blog/p/~board/b/post/facebook-group
-strategies-for-schools.

National Educational Leadership Preparation (NELP) Standards. https://www.naesp
.org/communicator-november-2018/nelp-standards-approved-how-affects-you.

National Policy Board for Educational Administration (2015). Professional
Standards for Educational Leaders 2015. Reston, VA: Author.

ParentLocker. https://www.parentlocker.com.

Pinterest. https://www.pinterest.com.

Point of View. Empowering kids to learn about money. https://www.pnc.com/en/
about-pnc/topics/pnc-pov/community/school-bank-kids-learn-money.html.

Schaffer, N. (2022a, January). 5 reasons why TikTok marketing is the hottest
social media trend for businesses today. https://www.nealschaffer.com/tiktock
-marketing/.

Schaffer, N. (2022b, March). 15 social media ideas to increase engagement. https://
nealschaffer.com/social-media-content-ideas/.

Shkurina, E. (2018, November). List of 10 best school management software solutions.
https://blog.youragora.com/list-of-8-best-school-management-software.

Top 15 Educational Leadership Blogs & Websites. (2022, February). https://blog
.feedspot.com/educational_leadership_blogs/.

Winans, N. (2019, March). 10 awesome apps schools are using to communicate
with    parents.    https://blog.heartlandschoolsolutions.com/10-awesome-apps
-schools-are-using-to-communicate-with-parents.

# CHAPTER 8

# Technology and Its Uses for Action Research and Traditional Research

**ABSTRACT**

In the previous chapters, we discussed the range of technology used in contemporary schools as school leaders execute their various roles. Specifically, we addressed the types of technology used by school principals as they function as instructional leaders, managers, and leaders of school climate, culture, and external relationships. In this chapter, we focus on the role of school leaders with respect to research, specifically action research. Action research is research focused on addressing practical issues. It can entail formulating and testing action plans, collecting and analyzing data, reporting results, formulating plans based on data, and monitoring results. Action research is linked to the school improvement process and data-driven leadership. Sagor (2000) notes that action research promotes experimentation, inquiry, and dialogue, which are all essential in schools. In this chapter, we review the basic concepts and techniques of action research and discuss the role technology can play in action research projects. Toward the end of the chapter, we provide a list of action research resources as well as several examples of school-based action research projects.

## WHAT IS ACTION RESEARCH?

Stringer and Aragon (2021) describes action research as a systematic approach to investigation and inquiry leading to an increased understanding of issues and problems investigated. As early as 1940, Kurt Lewin, an educator and social psychologist, used research in his "natural" setting to change the manner in which researchers interact with settings. That is, he explored a challenge in his work environment, and he is "credited with coining "action research." Stephen Corey at Teachers College in Columbia was among the first to use action research. Corey believed that the value of action research is the change that occurs in daily practice. In the 1950s, action research was characterized as unscientific; however, it rebounded in the 1970s and has been very visible since. There have been shifts in the meaning of action research, and it has increasingly become centered as a tool for professional engagement and school reform (Ferrance, 2000).

Dana (n.d.) identifies five reasons principals conduct action research: action research enables best practices to flourish at a school, action research focuses and strengthens school improvement efforts, action research helps principals slow down and take control, action research enables principals to become role models for the teachers and students in the building, and action research brings principals out of isolation. At its core, action research differs from traditional academic research in its purpose. It can be conducted by an individual teacher, a group of teachers as you might have in a professional learning community, and/or led by the school leader. In all cases, its purpose is to understand and address specific issues experienced at the school. For example, a classroom teacher might be interested in identifying the most effective strategy for teaching fractions to third graders. Action research offers a systematic and structured approach to addressing this issue. At the department level, a collaboration of teachers might want to develop a plan for improving student performance on standardized tests. In this instance, action research would entail a systematic review of previous student performance, reflection on possible causes of the observed pattern, and experimentation with alternative approaches. Finally, at the school level, an administrator might be interested in improving rates of disciplinary referrals by classroom teachers. Again, action research offers a structured way to explore possible cause/effect relationships and evaluate alternative solutions.

As early as 1985, Watts noted that teachers and school leaders are participants in their own practice, and there are four based on the following four assumptions:

- School leaders and teachers work best on problems they have identified,
- School leaders and teachers are more effective when assessing and examining their own work,
- School leaders and teachers assist each other as they work collaboratively, and

- School leaders and teachers are assisted in professional development when they work together.

Whether conducted by an individual teacher or for the entire school, the school leader plays a central role in action research. First, the school leader is best positioned to promote a climate in which school personnel view research, whether individual or collaborative, as a systematic and valued process. The school leader can provide the professional development needed to ensure that building-level staff not only understand the action research process but value the potential benefits from engaging in the process. Second, action research requires resources. These may include material resources (e.g., assessments, software for analysis, etc.), staff support, and time needed to design and execute action research projects. School leaders are encouraged to develop plans as to how they will develop and sustain a plan for data use at their schools and action research is an intricate part of the process. Several associations and organizations offer guidance to school leaders with regard to the action process:

- The Collaborative Action Research Network (https://www.carn.org.uk/?from=carnnew/).
- Action Research Network of America (https://arnawebsite.org/).
- Center for Collaborative Action Research (https://www.actionresearchtutorials.org/).

## ACTION RESEARCH DESIGNS

The steps involved in conducting action research are similar to those of traditional academic research, but the motivations for the study and how the results are used differ. In academically oriented research the goal is to understand some phenomenon for the purposes of contributing to the body of literature. One of the enduring issues of academic research is its relevance to practitioners. In contrast to academic research, the primary goal of action research is to address issues and challenges experienced by practitioners. Below we describe nine steps in the action research process that was developed for this publication.

### Nine-Step Model

*Step 1. Determine the Focus or Problem Area*

The first step in any action research project is to decide on the problem area. For the individual teacher, the scope of the problem is likely to be narrower than for an academic department or the entire school.

Nevertheless, it should be a priority. One technique frequently used in management is to develop a list of issues (phenomena that need change/improvement) and then rank them with regard to characteristics: high impact/low impact, major resource investment/minor resource investment, etc. These lists can help lead the action researcher to identify a problem that if successfully addressed will have a meaningful impact. For other strategies for setting priorities, see the blog post *Effective Priorities Management Methods and* Techniques (https://everhour.com/blog/priorities-management/). Action research in schools is often placed into the following categories: academic issues, behavioral issues, administrative issues, and engagement issues. A typical problem statement is the following: what can be done to improve the performance of students on the district's benchmark examination in mathematics?

### Step 2. Determine the Purpose of the Action Research Project

Once a general problem area has been identified, it is then necessary for the action research to narrow the problem down to a specific focus. As is often the case, the greater the specificity, the better. For example, "...improve performance in math" is much less specific and useful than "...improve performance on the arithmetic section of the district's benchmark examination." The latter has a degrée of specificity that is measurable and can thus be evaluated. Further, the specificity allows for greater precision in targeting and focusing the project. Action research projects can be classified with respect to the purposes for which they are undertaken:

- Research for purposes of identifying trends and for prediction,
- Research for purposes of classifying and categorizing, and
- Research for purposes of understanding process and testing hypotheses.

### Step 3. Conduct a Review of Existing Literature

As a third step in the action research process, it is important for the researcher to undertake a discovery process in which the goal is to obtain information on what is known about solutions to the identified problem. This can take the form of a review of research literature, recommendations from experts, etc. The more extensive and comprehensive the literature review, the more likely the researcher is to identify potentially impactful strategies and approaches for addressing his/her problem. Technology can play a key role in the process of reviewing existing literature. Prior to modern technologies, a review of existing literature required a visit to a local library. Further, often the resources available were limited and often required the use of interlibrary loan programs. In contrast, in the modern era, literature reviews can primarily be conducted electronically.

The following are online databases for educational-related literature reviews (https://alliant.libguides.com/c.php?g=692753&p=4908081):

- PsycINFO,
- ERIC (Educational Resources Information Center),
- Academic Search Premier,
- Google Scholar,
- SpringerLink,
- JSTOR,
- Nexis Uni, and
- ProQuest Criminal Justice.

Searching electronic databases can be done from any location and with a minimal investment of time. Further, many products are available online in the form of PDF files and can be downloaded directly by researchers. The following resources provide guidance on the process of developing and conducting a review of the existing literature:

Literature Search Strategy: https://libguides.csu.edu.au/review/Search_Strategies

Literature Search Tips: https://rauterberg.employee.id.tue.nl/lecturenotes/literatur-search-tips-2004.pdf

Synthesize Main Ideas: https://libguides.cmich.edu/lit_review/LR_synthesize

*Step 4. Develop a Conceptual Model That*
*Will Be Used to Guide the Project*
An important part of an action research project entails reflection. The researcher must reflect on the problem and the possible factors that act to increase or decrease the problem in its severity. From this, it is possible to start to formulate possible solutions. A tool for formalizing this process is the theory of change. A theory of change is a summary of the processes operating for a given phenomenon. In practice, a theory of action guiding an action research project would be more complex than this simple depiction, but either way, they would serve the same purpose. Resources for constructing diagrams are plentiful and include the following:

How to Build a theory of Change: https://knowhow.ncvo.org.uk/how-to/how-to-build-a-theory-of-change

Theory of Change: A Practical Tool for Action, Results and Learning: https://www.aecf.org/resources/theory-of-change

Other tools for depicting the causal processes operating in some phenomena include the fishbone diagram, as well as others.

*Step 5. Research Designs*

Once a conceptual model has been developed for the project, the next step is to decide upon a research design. There are several different types of research designs commonly used in action research. We discuss the designs below:

1. The Experimental Design. This type of design entails the random assignment of subjects to different treatments. For example, a teacher might decide on strategies for having students do homework. Half of the class might be assigned to one strategy and the other assigned to a second strategy. The performance of students in the two groups could then be compared. This design has the advantage that it is easier for the researcher to draw inferences about the causal effects of the treatments studied.

2. The Correlational Design. This design involves establishing whether or not variables in a study are correlated with each other. There are no claims about causal effects, just interest in knowing whether or not variables are correlated. An example would be comparing the number of questions students ask during a unit to their performance on the unit test. Again, the objective of this approach to research is to determine whether or not the two variables are correlated.

3. Qualitative Designs. The two previous designs are often referred to as quantitative designs in that they focus on numbers and so-called objective criteria. Qualitative designs offer an alternative approach. The objective of qualitative designs is often to obtain information about the experiences of subjects. What happened and how did they respond? The techniques of this approach to research often include interviews, observations, and similar. Their goal is often to understand how something happened and what dynamics were involved.

4. Mixed Methods Designs. These designs are a mixture of both quantitative and qualitative research techniques. For example, the quantitative approach may answer the question as to whether or not test scores improved and the qualitative approach may help the researcher understand why they improved.

There is considerable variation in the designs mentioned here. Many resources are freely available to help guide the action researcher. These include the following:

Research Designs https://www.scribbr.com/methodology/research-design/
Research Designs https://libguides.usc.edu/writingguide/researchdesigns#:~:text=The%20research%20design%20refers%20to,measurement%2C%20and%20analysis%20of%20data

*Step 6. Identify Measures and Collecting Data*

With well-designed studies, the next step is to identify the variables used and collect the data. Variables are the characteristics of your subjects that will be considered in the analysis. In *A Guide to Data-Driven Leadership in Modern School* (Information Age Publishing, 2015), Jones and Kennedy present Blankstein's (2010) categorizations of data which are prevalent in schools. The required data come in a wide variety of forms and types (Blankstein, 2010):

- Assessment data: includes grades, GPA, and state assessment;
- Perceptive data: includes parent data, student fata, teacher surveys, news articles, media coverage, school websites, and discipline incident;
- Demographic data: includes attendance, enrollment, ethnicity, gender, disability, economic status, grade level, and work habit; and
- Program data: includes institution and culture placement.

Data can be collected in action research through experiencing (observing), enquiring (asking), or examining (using records). An important attribute of measures is that they are both valid and reliable. A valid measure reflects the standing of subjects on the intended attribute. A reliable measure generates scores that are not overly influenced by errors of measurement. Researchers can either use existing measures or create their own. The following resources are helpful for both activities:

Creating Tests https://teaching.washington.edu/topics/preparing-to -teach/constructing-tests/
Choosing a Standardized Test https://heav.org/virginia-homeschool -laws/testing/resources/choosing-standardized-tests/

Technology can significantly enhance the data collection process. Online or web-based surveys, handheld devices such as clickers and PDAs, text messages, and social networking sites like Twitter, MySpace, and Facebook can be used to collect data that were traditionally captured by paper. Su and Liang (2017) present a detailed discussion of ways to collect data through social media. Once these data have been obtained, they can then be converted to electronic files for analysis. Two of the more popular online survey applications are SurveyMonkey (http:// www.surveymonkey.com/) and Qualtrics (http://www.qualtrics.com).

*Step 7. Data Analysis*

Data obtained from an action research project are in need of processing. This can be thought of as a process in which data are summarized to facilitate communication and analyzed for purposes of drawing conclusions about the significance of results. The former is called descriptive analysis and the second is referred to as inferential analysis. Techniques for describing data include summary statistics such as measures of central tendency (e.g., means, medians), variability (e.g., variances, standard deviation), and location (e.g., quartiles, percentiles). Additionally, graphic techniques are commonly used to communicate data. These include bar charts, scatter plots, and other visualizations. In addition to describing data, researchers typically report measures of association. These include commonly used techniques such as Pearson correlation coefficients and the like. Finally, for purposes of determining if a treatment made a meaningful difference, tests of significance are commonly reported. Details on these techniques are beyond the scope of the present chapter but are widely available in other sources:

Introduction to Statistics https://www.analyticssteps.com/blogs/introduction-statistical-data-analysis
Understanding Statistics https://writing.colostate.edu/guides/guide.cfm ?guideid=67

Technology has significantly enhanced data analysis. Software programs such as Excel and Statistical Package for the Social Sciences (https://www.ibm.com/us-en?ar=1) offer researchers statistical tools and graphic tools for data analysis purposes. Like many current resources, contemporary products often require little to no programming by the user, frequently consisting of a variety of drop-down menus. Researchers can simply point and click to both analyze and graphically display their data.

For interviews, observations, and other types of qualitative data, the analysis process differs. These data are often in the form of text. Textual data can be characterized with respect to the frequency with which words occur. For example, word clouds are useful for identifying terms that are dominant in a response to a prompt. If a group of third graders were asked to select three of ten words that describe their school, a word cloud could be used to graphically depict the terms that occur with the greatest frequency. Word cloud functions are available in many word processing programs, such as Microsoft Word.

While word clouds can be used to gain insights into terms, which occur frequently in written or spoken text, data from interviews, and written responses must be interpreted to gain insights into the views and perspectives of research subjects. The process entails analyzing the data for purposes of identifying themes and concepts that are dominant in the responses. The process typically entails transcribing interview data, reading the transcribed responses, summarizing the main idea in the form of codes, comparing codes across respondents, and developing themes, or major ideas, which occur in the data. It is these themes that provide insights into the process experienced by subjects. While there are many variations on these basic ideas, technology can play an important role in the process of analyzing qualitative data. The following are two software programs for the analysis of qualitative and mixed methods data:

MAXQDA https://www.maxqda.com/
Altas.ti. https://atlasti.com/

*Step 8. Reporting Results*
A research report presents the results of the study in a structured and organized format. The scope of the report varies depending on the intended audience. For example, a report for an individual teacher will be much less extensive than a report prepared for a school board. Producing reports for research has been simplified by processing programs. Many incorporate graphic and statistical techniques. Additionally, many allow for the production of interactive reports, including dashboards. The following sections should be included in reports:

- Abstract: brief summary of the study and its conclusions;
- Introduction: description of the goals and scope of the study;
- Background/Context: literature review, theory, conceptual basis of the study;
- Methods: procedures used to select subjects, measure variables, analyze data;
- Results: data analysis for various research questions; and
- Conclusions: conclusions and action plan.

See the following resources for guidance on producing research reports:

- Writing a Research Report https://www.adelaide.edu.au/writing-centre/sites/default/files/docs/learningguide-writingaresearchreport.pdf
- 'The Mayfield Handbook of Technical & Scientific Writing'-https://web.mit.edu/course/21/21.guide/rep-resc.htm

Producing reports from research is easier than ever, given modern word processing programs. Many incorporate graphics and even statistical techniques. Additionally, many allow for the production of interactive reports, including dashboards, etc. Software for producing research reports includes familiar word processing packages (e.g., Microsoft Word) and more specialized visualization applications:

Tableau https://www.tableau.com/products/trial
Microsoft Power BI https://powerbi.microsoft.com/en-us/

*Step 9. Implementation and Monitoring*
The ultimate outcome of an action research project is the implementation of a solution to a problem. This process entails the development of a carefully designed rollout plan for the program, the allocation of needed resources, and the development of a process to monitor the impact and effectiveness of the program.

*Allocation of Resources.* The allocation of resources needed to implement a program requires a careful analysis of the human and material resources needed to perform the various tasks associated with implementation.

*Program Rollout.* Following the development of a plan for the allocation of resources, the next phase is to develop a timeline. This process starts with an analysis of the steps needed to implement the program. During this phase, questions such as what needs to be done, by whom, and when are asked and answered. This is followed by stages such as preparing program participants for their roles and the goals of the change.

*Monitoring Implementation.* The final stage of this process is to monitor implementation. This involves identifying key performance metrics associated with the program. A common way of organizing these indicators is as inputs, processes, and outputs. Inputs address the services provided and the participants' levels of engagement with the program's services. The processes entail metrics on what is actually done. Finally, outputs are measures of key outcomes of the project. These might include performance on standardized tests, attendance rates, or behavior reports.

The following resources provide guidance on program implementation:

Detailed Guide to Program Implementation – Guide on the Implementation of Evidence Based Programs: What Do We Know So Far? https://www.publicsafety.gc.ca/cnt/rsrcs/pblctns/gd-mplmnttn -vdnc-prgrms/gd-mplmnttn-vdnc-prgrms-en.pdf
Learning Environments and Program Implementation https://safesup-portivelearning- .ed.gov/topic-research/program-implementation

## Sagor's Model
The steps involved in conducting action research are similar to those of traditional academic research, but, again, the motivations for the study and how the results are used differ. Sagor (2000) describes a seven-step model for action research (1) selecting a focus, (2) clarifying theories, (3)

identifying research questions, (4) collecting data, (5) analyzing data, (6) reporting results, and (7) taking action. According to Sagor (2000), action research begins with serious reflection to identify a topic that can be studied. Activities should be considered as topics that can add to the central part of the work. In Step 2, the researcher identifies values, beliefs, and theoretical perspectives that researchers hold relative to their focus. Clarification occurs in Step 2. In Step 3, the research question should be identified from the focus. In Step 4, data collection occurs. Reliability and validity of data are essential. To ensure a reasonable level of validity and reliability, researchers should use multiple sources of data. In data analysis, Step 5, answering the following two questions is advantageous: what story is told by these data; and why did the story play itself out this way. Step 6 requires the reporting of the results by the researcher; and in Step 7, the action developed in the process should be implemented.

Sagor (2000) notes that there are three purposes for action research:

- Building the reflective practitioner,
- Making progress on schoolwide priorities, and
- Building professional cultures.

## Ferrance's Model

Ferrance (2000) presents a cyclic model of action research which can be district-, school-, or classroom-based. Ferrance's model begins with identifying the problem. The problem addressed must involve a higher-order question; not a simple yes/no. The problem should also be concise and meaningful. After the problem is identified, it is necessary to collect data. The role of the data is to help understand what is occurring in the district, school, or classroom (depending on if the problem is school-based or classroom-based). In the nine-step approach presented in this chapter, we note the role of technology in data collection. Technology tools can be applied in this model as well. Ferrance notes many vehicles for collecting data. It is important to use the data that fits the area being researched.

After the data is collected, it must be analyzed. The data analysis used will depend on the nature of the data. Creswell and Poth (2018) propose a model for analyzing qualitative data. Techniques for analyzing quantitative data are included in the nine-step approach included in this chapter. After the data is interpreted, the facilitators of the research must act on the evidence. A plan of action must be developed which is to be evaluated Each action item must be evaluated. The next steps to be taken include identifying additional questions raised and an assessment of the plan for improvement.

## Stringer's Model

Stringer (2014) is cited at the beginning of Chapter 8 and proposes a three-part model of action research. Tenants of the model require facilitators of action research to *Look*, *Think*, and *Act*. In the *Look* stage – similarly to Ferrance's model – problem identification is key. It is difficult to state problems clearly because a "web" of relationships, interactions, and activities permeate work environments. The following are questions to get to the core of the problems:

- What are the "actual" challenges?
- Who are the key stakeholders?
- How are the stakeholders perceiving the problem?
- Are there links to other challenges within the problem?

Information is also gathered in the *Look* phase. Qualitative and quantitative data can be gathered. In the *Think* stage, the data gathered in the *Look* phase must be analyzed. The analyses employed depend on the kind of data. We discussed above in Step 7 of the nine-step model processes and technologies for analyzing quantitative and qualitative data. In the *Act* phase, a solution is implemented on the bases of data analyses. It is critical for the facilitators of the research to involve critical stakeholders throughout the process particularly in data gathering in the *Act* stage, data analyses in the *Think* stage, and action planning in the *Act* stage. Stringer suggests multiple iterations of the phases. In the second iteration, the action plan becomes the basis of looking, thinking, and acting.

## TECHNOLOGY AND ACADEMICALLY ORIENTED RESEARCH FOR LEADERS

Using technology to enhance the roles of educational leaders in managerial and instructional leadership roles is discussed throughout the book as it relates to the instructional and managerial roles of leaders. Some of these uses of technology can be used for "academically oriented" research particularly as it relates to improving student achievement.

The importance of professional development has been discussed several times throughout the book pertinent to school principals aligning professional development for teachers as a part of the classroom observation cycles. We discussed the use of technology as a tool in conducting observations – mobile apps to schedule and record data from observations. This may also be tied/linked to journaling (there are apps available for teachers and principals to engage in electronic journaling – https://zapier.com/blog /best-journaling-apps/). Technology can also be used as a tool to enhance professional development for school principals and to prepare school principals. There are many preparation programs that are totally online.

The U.S. Department of Education reports that online courses are offered through a learning or course management system. Some of the Learning Management Systems including Blackboard and Moodle were discussed in other chapters. Knewton and DreamBox Learning are examples of learning platforms. According to Ed Leadership SIMS, the findings of the research show that computer-based simulations are one of the best ways for practical and effective delivery of experiences across organizations (https://www.edleadershipsim.com/computer-based-sims).

The current listing of simulations from Educational Leadership SIMS (ELS) includes:

- Difficult conversations: dress code,
- Academic goal setting: common core,
- Disruptive teacher: the faculty bully,
- Difficult conversations: race,
- Girls basketball coach,
- New teacher evaluation,
- Board relations,
- Playground mishap,
- Middle school budget challenge,
- Student in crisis,
- Small school district budget challenge,
- Administrator: first week on the job, and
- Community partnerships: digital readiness.

The goal of ELS is to capture and deploy key experiences for leaders that provide opportunities to exercise judgment, engage in meaningful peer-driven conversation, and deal with real life situations as they occur.

## DATA MINING AND LEARNING ANALYTICS

Principals, teachers, and other educational researchers often deal with large amounts of data. Educational data mining and learning analytics are pertinent to the collection and analysis of large amounts of data. According to Tetsuya (2019, January), educational data mining uses tools and techniques needed to analyze large amounts of data as is found in educational records, online logs, examinations, etc., to analyze and formulate conclusions. The International Educational Data Mining Society (2012) Tetsuya suggests that educational data mining is concerned with developing methods for exploring large-scale data from educational settings using methods to understand the settings of student learning.

Tetsuya (2019, January) notes that educational data mining is closely aligned with learning analytics. In a Report by the U.S. Department of Education, *Enhancing Teaching and Learning Through Educational*

*Data Mining and Learning Analytics* (2012), learning analytics is the measurement, collection, analysis, and reporting of data about learners and their contexts, for understanding learning and the environments in which it occurs. It is suggested that educators should increase the use of educational data mining and learning analytics to improve student learning. In Chapter 1, the critical role of the principal is presented; and in Chapter 5, the critical role of the principal as an instructional leader is presented – both aligned to improving student learning.

The following are additional suggestions provided by the U.S. Department of Education for educators pertinent to educational data mining and learning analytics:

- Develop a culture for using data in making instructional decisions,
- Include technology departments in efforts to improve instruction,
- Understanding details of learning software and learning management systems,
- Begin small and leverage the work of others,
- Communicate to students and parents the sources and usefulness of learning data, and
- Advocate for state policy to support online learning.

## EXAMPLES OF ACTION RESEARCH FROM THE FIELD
## Example 1: 3rd Grade Math Teacher – Nine-Step Model

*Step 1. Determine the Focus or Problem Area*
    *Problem*: Provide a clear statement of the problem.
    Students are performing poorly on the mathematics subtest of the district benchmark exam. The scores from the October administration are considerably below that of previous classes.
    *Focusing the Problem*: Review existing score reports and identify specific areas (e.g., standards, content, etc.) where students appear to be having problems.
    Score reports from the students are examined and it is determined that they are doing poorly with respect to the standard focused on the equivalence of fractions.

*Step 2. Determine the Purpose of the Action Research Project*
    *Importance/Significance*: Clearly identify the importance/ significance of the problem.
    If this is not addressed, these students, based on analyses done at the district office, can be expected to perform poorly on the statewide accountability assessments administered at the end

**TABLE 8.1** https://tech.ed.gov/wp-content/uploads/2014/03/edm-la-brief.pdf.

| Application Area | Questions | Types of Data Needed for Analysis |
|---|---|---|
| User knowledge modeling | What content does a student know | Student's responses (correct, incorrect, partially correct), time spent before responding to a prompt or question, hints requested, repetitions of wrong answers, and errors made |
| | | The skills that a student practiced and total opportunities for practice |
| | | Student's performance levels inferred from system work or collected from other sources such as standardized tests |
| Use behavior modeling | What do patterns of student behavior mean for their learning? Are students motivated | Student's response (correct, incorrect, partially correct), time spent before responding to a prompt or questions, hints requested, repetitions of wrong Answers, and errors made Any changes in the classroom/ school context during the investigation period of time |
| User experience modeling | Are users satisfied with their experience? | Response to surveys or questionnaires Choices, behaviors, or performance in subsequent learning units or courses |
| User profiling | What groups do users cluster into? | Student's responses (correct, incorrect, partially correct), time spent before responding to a prompt or question, hints requested repetitions or wrong answers, and errors made |
| Domain modeling | What is the correct level at which to divide topics into modules and how should these modules be sequenced | Student's responses (correct, incorrect, partially correct) and performance on modules at different grain sizes compared to an external measured |

*(Continued)*

**TABLE 8.1** Continued

| Application Area | Questions | Types of Data Needed for Analysis |
|---|---|---|
| | | A domain model taxonomy |
| | | Associations among problems and between skills and problems |
| Learning component analysis and instructional principle analysis | What components are effective at promoting learning? What learning principles work well? How effective are the whole curricula? | Student's responses (correct, incorrect, partially correct) and performance on modules at different levels of detail compared to an external measure |
| | | A domain model taxonomy |
| | | Association structure among problems and between Skills and problems |
| Trend analysis | What changes over time and how? | Varies depending on what information is of interest, typically, would need at least three data points longitudinally to be able to discern a trend |
| | | Data collected include enrollment records, degrees, completion, student source, and high school data in consecutive years |

of the school year. This would carry negative consequences for student promotion to the next grade as well as negative consequences for teacher evaluation.

*Purpose of the Project*: Provide a clear statement of the goals of the project.

The project should identify, based on data, approaches which can be used to improve students understanding in regards to fractions. As a result of greater understanding, students are expected to perform better on benchmark and statewide standardized tests.

*Step 3. Conduct a Review of Existing Literature*

*Literature Review*: Review relevant literature and identify potentially promising solutions.

Databases maintained by the district (e.g., academic search complete), resources provided by professional associations (e.g., National Council of Teachers of Mathematics), etc. are examined. Search terms include improving phrases such as "student understanding of fractions," etc.

*Step 4. Develop a Conceptual Model That Will Be Used to Guide the Project*

*Theory of Action*: Develop a theory of action, which will guide the project.

Based on a careful review of existing literature, discussions with colleagues, and self-reflection, it is determined that the current instructional model does not incorporate key components of the learning process for fractions: Breaking wholes into parts, representations of fractions with manipulations, and understanding numerators and denominators. The teacher also determines that an active learning approach is needed. Toward this, she determines to incorporate manipulatives into class discussions, group projects related to fractions, and integrate an app which assesses and tailors activities for students related to fractions. The essential logic is that these components will improve engagement, connections to other concepts, and deep understanding of key ideas related to fractions.

*Step 5. Research Designs*

*Research Design*: Develop a design, which can be used to answer the key research question.

After reflection, the teacher decided that she wanted evidence that the interventions she selected actually do make a difference in student achievement. To determine this, she selected an experimental design. Half of the students in her class were assigned the "complete package" of the intervention and the other half were assigned to work on a drill and practice program for fractions. She planned to run the study for a period of one week.

*Step 6. Identify Measures and Collecting Data*

*Measures*: Develop measures that are both valid and reliable. Develop plans to collect needed data.

The teacher developed an assessment focused on the content of the lessons taught during the week in which the study was run. She followed guidelines for test construction to ensure that the assessment was both valid and reliable (see references above). She planned to enter the results of the assessment into an Excel spreadsheet for processing.

*Step 7. Data Analysis*

*Data Analysis*: Develop plans to process and analyze the data.

Once the data were entered into the spreadsheet, the teacher planned to generate graphs based on how the two groups performed on the assessment. She would also generate other descriptive statistics (e.g., means, variances, etc.). Following this, she would conduct a test to compare the performance of the two groups. If the group that received the "complete package" of interventions performed better than the comparison group, she would take this as evidence that the treatment did improve performance.

*Step 8. Reporting Results*

*Reports*: Determine the audience for the results of the study and produce a report.

The teacher, in this instance, is the primary consumer of the report. Given this, she determines to create a relatively informal document using word processing software.

*Step 9. Implementation and Monitoring*

*Implementation*: Develop a plan to implement and monitor the program.

Based on the conclusions of the study, the teacher decides to implement the "complete package" for the entire class. This is done by first introducing it to those students that did not receive it during the week of the study. From there, this material is integrated into the remaining lessons.

*Monitoring*: Develop a plan to monitor the outcome of the program.

To monitor the program, the teacher develops a plan to compare the performance of the present class against the performance of previous classes. These comparisons are largely descriptive in that she simply compares the average performance on weekly tests for the current class against the average of previous classes. The performance is compared using trend lines available in the Microsoft Word software graphs/charts menu. The data show that while the present groups started below the weekly average, following the intervention their performance rose above the average and stayed there.

## SCHOOL EXAMPLE 1: DISCIPLINE REFERRALS BY TEACHERS – NINE-STEP MODEL

*Step 1. Determine the Focus or Problem Area*

*Problem*: Provide a clear statement of the problem.

Discipline referrals by classroom teachers have increased dramatically over the past three years.

*Focusing the Problem*: Review existing score reports and identify specific areas where there may be problems.

Discipline referrals are posted in the school records management system. The school management team noted a sharp increase in referrals, a trend which started three years ago. Using the system's dashboard, the data were disaggregated by grade level, the reason for the referral, and student demographics. Based on these analyses, it appears that the increase in referrals at this K-12 school is concentrated in grades six through eight. Further, the students receiving the referrals are largely from three neighborhoods in the school's attendance zone. Finally, further analysis reveals that students receiving the referrals are largely from a school that was closed three years ago. This led to a refinement of the problem to focus on this segment of the student population. Further, it was found that the most frequently cited reason for the referral was "disrespect for authority."

*Step 2. Determine the Purpose of the Action Research Project*

*Importance/Significance*: Clearly identify the importance/significance of the problem.

The referral rate is an indication of disruption to the educational process at the school. The increasing rates suggest that the problem is not improving on its own, but needs purposeful intervention. Should the problem not be addressed, it is determined that the entirety of the school's educational processes could be adversely impacted.

*Purpose of the Project*: Provide a clear statement of the goals of the project.

The project should identify reasons for the referrals and data-based solutions or strategies.

*Step 3. Conduct a Review of Existing Literature*

*Literature Review*: Review relevant literature and identify potentially promising solutions.

Databases maintained by the district (e.g., academic search complete), resources provided by professional associations (e.g., National Center for School Safety), etc. are examined. Search terms include improving phrases such as "disrespect for authority," etc.

*Step 4. Develop a Conceptual Model That Will Be Used to Guide the Project*

*Theory of Action*: Develop a theory of action, which will guide the project.

Based on a careful review of existing literature, discussions with colleagues, and self-reflection, the school management team determined that incidents of disrespect for authority were most often associated with a lack of engagement with the culture of the school, personal stressors, and ambiguity regarding the enforcement of disciplinary policies. As a result of this, the team identified six potential evidence-based programs which appeared to have the potential to effectively address the problem at the school. The program selected involved professional development and support for teachers, counseling for students, parent engagement, etc. The essential logic is that these components will improve knowledge of rules and policies, student engagement, teacher preparedness, etc., and thus lead to a reduction in disciplinary referrals.

*Step 5. Research Designs*
*Research Design*: Develop a design which can be used to answer the key research question.

After a period of reflection and planning, the team selected a design in which the selected program would be implemented, schoolwide, starting in the spring semester. The focus of the analysis would be to compare the referral rates before the introduction of the program to the referral rate after the introduction of the program.

*Step 6. Identify Measures and Collecting Data*
*Measures*: Develop measures that are both valid and reliable. Develop plans to collect needed data.

The key performance indicator for the success of the program was the referral rate. Additionally, the vendor provided school safety surveys which could be administered to teachers and students to gauge the nature of changes that were occurring. These data were deemed to be both valid and reliable.

*Step 7. Data Analysis*
*Data Analysis*: Develop plans to process and analyze the data.

Data on referral rates were collected and analyzed using a statistical analysis program. The vendor was contracted to assist with the analysis. These analyses not only addressed the issue of whether or not there was a meaningful drop but provided data on teacher and student perceptions of the safety climate at the school.

*Step 8. Reporting Results*
*Reports*: Determine the audience for the results of the study and produce a report.

Because of the costs associated with the program, it was determined that a formal report would be produced and a presentation would be made to the district administrators and possibly the school board.

*Step 9. Implementation and Monitoring*
*Implementation*: Develop a plan to implement and monitor the program.
The program and its implementation would entail significant costs for the school. It was determined that the best course of action would be to have selected staff spearhead the project and, as needed, utilize external expertise. The team developed an implementation plan, including professional development for teachers, awareness training for students and parents, etc.

*Monitoring*: Develop a plan to monitor the outcome of the program.
To monitor the program, performance metrics were identified. The key performance metric was the count of referrals, but additional metrics were also identified as being of value to the school management team.

## SCHOOL EXAMPLE 2: STRINGER'S MODEL
Written by Dr. Jeremye Brooks

The purpose of this study is to explore strategies to induct new academy principals into XY Charter Management Organization that will better meet the needs of the new academy principals as they assume their new roles. This study explored the current practice of inducting new school leaders into the role of the principalship at XY Charter Management Organization. A phenomenological approach was used to gain insight and to understand the experiences of new school leaders in the charter network. XY Charter Management Organization is a network that comprises eight schools. There are five elementary and three high schools in the network. The organization serves more than 5,500 of the 45,000 students who reside in City B, and who Common School District is responsible for serving

XY Charter Management Organization is organized in the following manner: there is one chief executive officer, one chief officer of academics, one chief officer of finance, and one deputy chief of strategy and advancement. Executive directors, directors, senior managers, specialists, and secretaries report to the various chiefs. The organizational structure of the schools is organized with a head of schools, two academy principals, and teachers. The academy principals supervise specific grade levels in both elementary and high schools. In the elementary schools, there is an academy principal who is responsible for grades pre-K–4 and an academy principal who is responsible for grades 5–8. There is an academy principal for grades 9 and 10, and an academy principal for grades 11 and 12 in the high schools. The research facilitator invited six academy principal participants and four Action Planning Committee members to participate in the study. These two groups played pivotal roles in implementing the study.

### Action Research Framework

The research facilitator utilized Stringer and Aragon (2021) Action Research Model. This model has three stages, *Look*, *Think*, and *Act*. The model is an iterative process. The researcher conducted two iterations from early Summer 2021 through to late Summer 2021. The research facilitator will now discuss each stage and iteration.

### Iteration I

**Look stage.** The first stage of action research is the *Look* stage. In the *Look* stage, the research facilitator gathered information to understand the experiences of the academy principal participants through semi-structured interviews. The facilitator conducted a series of 45-minute interviews with each participant. He interviewed each participant three times.

The first interview was conducted to develop a relationship of trust and to allow participants to respond to the interview questions. The second interview allowed the research facilitator to ask clarifying questions identified during the initial analysis of the first interview to ensure that a complete depiction of the experiences of each participant as new principals in the organization is evident. For the third interview, each participant summarized the responses to ensure that the research facilitator had a coherent understanding of their lived experiences.

In addition to the interviews, the research facilitator gathered quantitative data. These data consisted of the current policies, procedures, and artifacts from the current principal induction process. The artifacts include, but are not limited to, leadership agendas from the "Leadership Week" and the leadership performance evaluation rubrics. The purpose of collecting these artifacts is to see if there is a connection between the documents the organization has to induct and evaluate leaders and the themes identified from the interviews. The research facilitator reviewed and organized the information to share with the Action Planning Committee members.

**Think stage.** The second stage of action research is the *Think* stage. The research facilitator met with the Action Planning Committee members to share the themes identified in the *Look* phase. In this stage, the Action Planning Committee and research facilitator reviewed and make sense of the information using the first two steps of the Stanford Design Thinking Model, *empathize and define*. The research facilitator developed an empathetic understanding of the data with the committee by discussing the themes identified from the interviews. Together, the facilitator and the Action Planning Committee analyzed the additional qualitative data to identify and define the problem that persists with the current induction process of XY Charter Management Organization.

**Act stage.** In the *Act* stage, the Action Planning Committee and the research facilitator developed a plan using steps three and four of the Stanford Design Thinking Model, *ideate* and *prototype*. These steps assisted the Action Planning Committee with improving the current induction process of XY Charter Management Organization. During this phase, the Action Planning Committee and the research facilitator started to *ideate* or brainstorm possible solutions to mitigate the problem identified in the *Think* phase. Once the committee members decide on the solution, then the committee created the *prototype* to *test*. The final step of the Stanford Design Thinking Model is a test. *Testing* took place in the second iteration. The second iteration follows the same three stages, *Look*, *Think*, and *Act*.

## SUMMARY

In this chapter, we discussed the use of technology for the purposes of school-based research, particularly action research. Action research is characterized along with a brief history. The steps and/or research designs and the way data is collected in action research are also presented. We note that technology has significantly enhanced the research process, including reviewing existing literature, collecting data, and data analysis. Although the focus of this chapter is on action research, information included about research processes is applicable to both action and traditional research. Social media in particular can be used to enhance data collection processes. There is a section for **Technology and Academically Oriented Research for Leaders** and we also discuss educational data mining and learning analytics. In the conclusion of the chapter, we include **Stories from the Field ("School Example" sections)**, action research projects that have been implemented.

## REFERENCES

Bienkowski, M., Feng, M., Menas, B. (2012). Enhancing Teaching and Learning Through Educational Data Mining and Learning Analytics. An Issue and Brief. *U. S. Department of Education: Office of Technology*. Retrieved from https://tech.ed.gov/wp-content/uploads/2014/03/edm-la-brief.pdf.

Blankstein, A. (2010). *Failure is not an option: 6 principles for making student success the only option*. Corwin.

Creswell, J. W., & Poth, C. N. (2018). *Qualitative inquiry & research design: Choosing among five approaches* (4th ed.). SAGE Publications, Inc., Thousand Oaks.

Dana, N. (n.d.) Top 5 reasons for principals to engage in action research. American Association of School Superintedents. https://www.aasa.org/content.aspx?id =12826.

Ferrance, E. (2000). *Action research.* Northeast and Islands Regional Educational Laboratory at Brown University.

Jones, L., & Kennnedy, E. (2015). *A guide to data driven leadership in modern schools.* Information Age Publishing.

Kulakov, M. (2018, December 18). Effective prorities management methods and techniques. https://everhour.com/blog/priorities-management/.

Sagor, R. (2000). *Guiding school improvement with action research.* ASCD.

Stringer, E. T., & Aragon, A. (2021). *Action research* (5th ed.). Thousand Oaks Publications.

Su, S. C., & Liang, E. (2017). Action research of the multiple intelligence (MI), cooperative learning, and game-based teaching into summer intensive English classes for mixed-level and mixed-age students. *Universal Journal of Educational Research, 5*(11), 1977–1985. Retrieved July 20, 2022, from https://www .learntechlib.org/p/190185/.

Tetsuya, J. (2019, January). Why is educational data mining important in the research? The value of conducting educational data mining for the research in the pedagogical domain. Towards Data Science. https://towardsdatascience.com/why -is-educational-data-mining-important-in-the research-378ed1a17908.

Watts, H. (1985). When teachers are researchers, teaching improves. *Journal of Staff Development, 6*(2), 118–127.

# INDEX

Made in United States
North Haven, CT
03 July 2024

54369407R00133